WATCHES I HAVE KNOWN

Barry Marcus

BARRY J. MARCUS, WATCHMAKER
MILFORD, MASSACHUSETTS

The following pages are a compilation of stories and American drama that my dad captured during his incredible career at his watchmaker's bench. What began as a way to preserve "Papa Barry stories" for his five grandchildren became an emotional glimpse of Americana. My dad is very respectful of his customers' privacy, so I have changed names and an occasional town to honor his request.

~ Julie Campisi

ISBN: 1496155068
ISBN 13: 9781496155061
Library of Congress Control Number: 2014904454
CreateSpace Independent Publishing Platform
North Charleston, South Carolina

Dedicated to the United States servicemen and women whose lives protect the freedoms most take for granted.

with love for
Alex
Adam
Melanie
Katie
Sarah Beth

in memory of
Dad
Uncle Abe
the Polish watchmaker whose name I never could pronounce
and others along the way

I n 1945, a young boy of ten, whose hands had grown large enough to hold basic watchmaking tools, was presented with a 16S Waltham pocket watch movement. Fifteen minutes later, the young boy, me, knew that for the rest of his life he would be repairing watches. Now, over sixty-five years later, he still regards the repair of watches as "fun."

I still arise in the morning looking forward to another day at the bench, another day of continuing the life and utility of tiny machines, impossible in their complexity, improbable in their longevity, and ridiculous in their tiny size. It is the task of the watchmaker to work on and repair mechanical devices he can barely see.

In 1908, my grandfather, Hyman Marcus, left Lithuania for the United States. He was a watchmaker and jeweler who, having seen the anti-Semitic trouble and pogroms in Eastern Europe, knew he must join the tide of people fleeing to America. He left behind his wife, Hinda, and his children, and eventually settled in Worcester, Massachusetts. After approximately three years of running his store on Millbury Street in Worcester, Hyman was able to send for Hinda and their six children. The family made its way across Europe and eventually resided on Fox Street in Worcester.

Hyman Marcus, as was common at the time, spoke several European languages in order to communicate with his customers, virtually all European immigrants. Also common was passing your trade to your sons. Son Abraham was taught the watchmaker's trade, but Jacob did not take to the tiny, close work. My father, Israel, the youngest of the six children, was to be *the* Marcus to attend college. He attended Classical High in Worcester, and with the assistance of the entire family, he graduated from Boston University in 1929, having majored in journalism. When the Great Depression prevented a life as a journalist, my father sold insurance in Lawrence until the second half of World War II.

Cousin Martin Comen, son of the oldest Marcus girl, Rose, had apprenticed to Uncle Abe as a child. Martin was the oldest of the third generation of the Marcus family and the first of that generation to follow the watch repair trade. In 1942, Marty was drafted and, as a watchmaker, was sent to England to care for the timepieces of a photo-recon squadron.

Uncle Abe, now alone, asked his youngest brother, Israel, to come to Worcester to learn the "family trade." In 1943, Israel's family packed up and left Lawrence for the "new world" of Worcester. My father entered his apprenticeship in the store on Trumbull Street.

By the end of 1944, it was obvious the United States would win the war, and Marty thankfully returned to his position in Uncle Abe's store. Israel, my father, now trained and comfortable at the bench, was approached about a jewelry store in faraway Milford.

In 1944, the twenty-one miles between home in Worcester and Milford was quite a distance.

The war ended, and the Marcus family of watchmakers grew apace. Marty returned to the bench. Cousins and sons-in-law were apprenticed. Marty's sister Harriet married Harold, who came to Milford to study watch repair. The younger sister, Hinda, met and married Morty, who went to work for Uncle Abe, replacing Marty, who had opened his own store. Jacob's daughter, Phyllis, married Udell, and he too joined the "Marcus Watchmaker Club."

Israel's oldest son, Barry (me), at the tender of ten years, had been introduced to the thrill of seeing a newly serviced timepiece restored to accurate performance. As I said, it took just about fifteen minutes for a young lad to *know* that he had found his life's work. Born in 1934 and shown my first watch movement in 1945, I write this in 2008, still enjoying every minute at the bench.

The bench in Uncle Abe's Front Street store was just inside the front door. Then there were three showcases that butted up to "my" bench, which was at a ninety-degree angle. Customers could walk right up to my bench and watch me work, which many did, as they seemed to be quite interested in the "little boy" who, it seemed, could actually repair watches. Often in the store watching me were two of my uncle's friends. The three of them would frequently speak while looking back and forth at me. I often wondered what I'd done wrong. After several months of such conferences between the three men, I finally asked my uncle what the problem was.

"No problem, Barry. My friends are both surgeons, and they are amazed at what they see you do. They both say that your hands belong beside an operating table. One insists you have *magic hands*. He says he's watched you repair things so tiny he can't see them even if you are using a loupe."

"Listen carefully now. We've begun to think you were born actually knowing how to do watch repair. You've been doing things long before you could possible know how. You watched me re-staff a Hamilton last year and then quietly started staffing balances without me knowing. Last month I took in a gent's Elgin that the customer had poked at. He bent the hairspring and broke the staff, and I gave you the watch to strip and clean then I'd do the rest. When I picked up the watch, I found it had a new staff and the hairspring was perfectly flat and trued. You just sat and staffed the watch and repaired the hairspring like new, but never told me."

"It's not possible for you to do what you're doing. We are amazed and proud of your progress. The biggest problem you've had was trying to memorize the names of the parts. I've seen you stare at the pictures as you tried to remember the names, and you've had a tough time. Once you have them firmly in your mind, you never seem to forget anything, but actually studying is not that easy, it seems. I told my friends only that your hands truly belong at the bench, not in an operating room."

Uncle Abe was right in a way, but not as he thought. My weakness was in studying something I didn't care about…because I just didn't care. Anything I was interested in came to me with complete ease. My father was bitterly disappointed when I dropped out of Worcester Classical High to transfer to Commerce High. I was not willing to study Latin, biology, physics, or any classical subject. My transfer brought me to a school that taught subjects that would be of direct use in a repair business. I could never have gotten into a medical school, let alone graduate. My world was and would always be centered on and around a watchmaker's bench.

Since this will be read by my grandchildren, Papa Barry will be honest. I still enjoy 98.5 percent of each minute at the bench. As with any profession or trade, now and then I must deal with a watch that truly needs a LARGE hammer. Never have I considered the idea of doing something else.

To most people, a watch is a device that tells the time. Actually a watch tells its owner it is time to go to work, time to eat, time to go home, and time to turn on our favorite show. Today the watch tells us our TV program is almost on. Years ago, it informed us when to tune into "Mr. Keen, Tracer of Lost Persons." At the end of the day, it tells the wearer that it is bedtime. Some watches also tell the wearer the day and the date, still others inform as to the phase of the moon or even the month. Other watches, of infinite complexity, can record and indicate short periods of time, indicating down to one-tenth of a second within a twelve-hour period.

In the mid-1940s, when I first sat at the bench, the watch was of critical importance. In Worcester, Massachusetts, as in most cities, there was an extensive trolley and bus system that provided basic transport to thousands of people. Being on time to work was more than necessary, and catching the trolley or bus on time was the key to being on time. Just as Big Ben and Baby Ben alarm clocks got people up on time to start the day, the watch, fastened to the wrist, told its owner, "time to catch the trolley." It was of such importance that one of the first things I was taught was to ensure that the timing error, present in all watches, was such that the watch was ahead of time. If the watch gained time, the owner was a little early for the bus, or the radio was turned on a couple of minutes before the program started, all leading to a happy customer. Heaven forbid the watch was losing time and the trolley was missed. The watchmaker, working in his tiny world, kept the world synchronized and running.

Mechanical watches, considered obsolete by today's technology, continue to perform as if new many, many years after electronic devices have been long discarded. In fact, a perfectly functioning watch of 150 years of age is *not* a rarity. Thousands of "mid-level" American watches of the latter 1800s still function as designed to this day. I believe the makers of those watches, if informed of the long service of their products, would have expressed no surprise, but would have replied that the watches were intended to last and last, period. Clean and oil them when needed and they will keep running, and they do.

Many thousands of watches are not cherished merely as "timekeepers." Watches—both men's and ladies'—are beloved mementoes of persons no longer alive. Watches that were received as gifts marking life's special events are dear to the hearts of their owners. Some are kept as reminders of events best forgotten

Often the repair of an expensive watch is refused as "not worth it" because the owner thinks it is "time for something new," and just as often a lower-priced or mid-priced watch "must be restored NO MATTER THE COST."

Last month (December 2008) I repaired a very typical, seventeen-jewel watch of a 1941 vintage, American made by Hamilton Watch Company and once again running as the company intended. Inside the case were date marks indicating repair dates, the earliest in the fall of 1945, when the watch was cleaned and oiled by my father. I recognized every repair mark in the case. It seemed that only my father and I had ever fixed this watch. When I handed the watch to the owner, I remarked that I looked forward to the next repair when needed.

With a sad negative head shake, I was told, "No, it belongs to my father. It is the only watch he has ever owned. He landed, wearing this watch, on D-Day plus one on Omaha Beach and carried it across France and Germany. Later, it went with him to Korea and came home with him. He is dying and asked that the watch be cleaned and oiled and then buried with him. We now all live in Connecticut, but he insisted the watch be brought back here for service."

He paused, sighed, and continued, "My dad said when he first brought the watch to your father, he was still in uniform and visibly bandaged from some minor wounds. When he went to pick up the repaired watch, by then in civilian clothes, your father refused to charge him for the cost of the repair. I guess you and your dad are the only people ever to work on this watch."

Needless to say, I too refused the repair money. I told the soldier's middle-aged son, "It is my honor. No, it was *our* honor."

After he left, I sat with a cup of coffee, (black, no sugar) thinking of other watches and their owners, so many with different stories. From tragedies to triumphs…a watch was an integral part of the story. I thought, why not write them down? Why not, indeed?

(A personal note: After a reread, I realized that this has not been written in true chronological order. Some musings are of a distant past, remembered after typing out a recent event. Some watches may have following stories years later. My relationship with my father, Israel Marcus, and my uncle, Abe Marcus, lasted naturally over most of my life. And beyond. Sometime I specify a year or an age; only those are from a specific time.)

I remembered something Uncle Abe said, oh so many years ago. In his store in Worcester I'd chuckled at an elderly man who insisted that a "nothing" watch be repaired. "What a waste of good money," I said.

Uncle Abe rose from his bench and walked down behind the counters, and this gentle man scowled at me, pointed at my bench chair, and ordered, "SIT!"

He began, "Barry, that watch was the wedding gift from his bride. In fact, my father, your grandfather, sold the bride that watch in 1919. They were married shortly after he came home from the trenches late in 1918. He is only elderly to a fifteen-year-old like you. Last month his wife died, and that watch is a constant reminder of her. Each time he looks at the watch he thinks of her, and each time he looks for the time, she is with him. You must learn that we deal with people...their watches are merely what brings us together." I repaired that watch with an understanding that, proud to say, I've never lost. Some watches have stories, and that is enough reason to love what I do.

After losing a "discussion" with Dad in the early 1950s, I unhappily prepared to do an overhaul on an 1857 Waltham 18S pocket watch. This was an early-model American pocket watch, of such size and weight that personally I believed they were the reason so many people years ago walked hunched over. Typical thought for a seventeen-year-old. This watch, though, was quite unique, in that there was a *hole* clear through the watch. When I held it to my eye, I could see completely through the watch, despite the gears and levers in the middle of the movement. The crystal (the glass in the front of the case) had a hole between the center post and the "8" on the dial, a hole that had been very carefully plugged with what looked to be a circular piece of beautifully transparent clear quartz. The dial too had a hole, but it had not been repaired or plugged. The back of the case had, like the crystal, been plugged, but the hole was larger in diameter.

This was the strangest damage I'd seen yet, and even at seventeen I'd seen many badly broken and abused watches. The plates were likewise holed, and I discovered narrow brass strips carefully brazed into place bridging the gaps in the plates, and this was strange, both strips had jewel setting pressed in place. Just as I finished taking the watch apart, I realized that this was a watch that had been *shot*, and the hole was a bullet hole.

When I asked my dad, he did not have the slightest idea, except that the thought of a bullet hole was quite logical to him. When the customer came for the watch, I could not resist asking about the origin of the watch's "wound." It turned out I was quite correct.

This watch, old, out of date, obsolete, too heavy, ugly by my standards, had been "wounded" at the Battle of Gettysburg during the Civil War. The then owner of the watch, a resident of Maine, had stood at *the* stone wall that was the goal of Pickett's Charge. The fighting was fierce, and soon, I was told, all semblance of military organization was lost, and organized combat became a bloody free-for-all. Suddenly the Maine soldier was "punched in the gut, felt severe pain" but was able to shoot the foe who'd shot him.

After a "lifetime," the Southerners retreated, the battle was done, and the Confederacy had reached its high point. Only then was it found that the watch had indeed been shot but had saved the life of its owner. The gun was close enough for the bullet to pierce the entire watch case and movement, but the watch and movement were solid enough to slow and stop the bullet, only part of which entered the soldier's body. Eventually the Maine man returned home, fully recovered, grateful to be alive, and with a watch that was "wounded worse than him."

The watch was carried to the Waltham factory, and the service department was informed that *it must find a way to repair this watch.* Moving parts were easy to replace as they were merely taken from parts boxes, but I had to admire the man who, in 1866, had the idea of bridging the bullet hole to replace the jewel setting that had been shot away. New plates or solid plugs would have hidden the damage, and that would never do. The remnant of the bullet was punched out and the hole filled with a crystal piece so one could peer through the watch. Unique, to say the least.

So, in the middle of the 1900s, this watch had become a highly cherished family talisman, handed from father to son for generations. In 1951 or so, I asked the owner if the watch was still being carried; after all, it was so old and heavy. I was told the watch had been to Cuba when we fought Spain, then to Europe and the Argonne. The watch "toured the Pacific" in World War II and would be going to Korea in a couple of months.

In the late 1950s, the customer returned with a watch to be repaired, but this time it was a Bulova "23" automatic. Remembering, I asked about the "wounded watch." In a very quiet voice, the customer informed me that "the watch is *still* somewhere in North Korea." I am ashamed to admit that I did not, for a few minutes, understand what that meant.

Over these many, many years at the watchmaker's bench, I have repaired many such watches, held as precious possessions that could not be set aside. People hold things close to the heart as reminders of many events. Confirmation, Bar Mitzvah, graduation, engagement, wedding, retirement, business success, and one man who cherished a watch given on his release from prison. All different kinds of people, men and women, attach special memories to their watches as well as to jewelry or other articles.

I've been surprised, though, at the number of men over the years who have hung on to a watch that went through the hell of war with them. Beginning with the Waltham watch that was shot at Gettysburg, the years have seen a parade of timepieces, most of average make and quality, most without prestige, but each beyond the value of money.

In late 1948, it was one of my "take the bus to Milford after school" days and I was at my bench practicing watch repair. My father, a gentle man who treated each and every customer with great respect, rudely told a young man to "get that damn watch the hell out of my store!" I could not believe my ears and quickly went to "help" my dad, whatever the problem was. The customer looked quite embarrassed as Dad stalked back to his bench. I looked down at the watch and my temper flared. There on the counter was a sort of large, stainless steel, rugged-looking watch, complete with what was at the time a *real* radium dial and a pair of easily visible *real* radium hands—and a *large black swastika*. No wonder the reaction.

Dad sat at his bench, head down as he repaired the watch of the hour. I sensed he would not listen but could still hear.

"Mr. Marcus," said the customer, "please. I understand your reaction to this watch. I know you and your son are Jewish, and I don't blame you, but hear me out. In March 1945, my outfit fought our way into what was left of a German town…kind of like the size of Milford. We'd heard the Russians had made it into Berlin, and soon the whole thing would be over and done with. At this point we were being extra careful, and our sarge found some kind of a loudspeaker and gave it to the captain. Several German soldiers had given up, but they said there was an SS major in the town hall demanding a fight to the last bullet.

"Our captain said things had gotten real quiet and he was going to give talking a try. Despite our worries for his safety, he said he was sick to death of the killing and would do anything to make it end. The captain crossed the town square toward the town hall, speaking to the enemy of an honorable surrender in the light of what was now obvious."

"The captain's name was German and he called out in German. We knew he had enlisted but came to us after getting a battlefield commission. How he got it we never knew, but the ribbons on his uniform told a hell of a story. We were, what you could say, driven by duty, but he was obviously driven by a deep, deep hatred. His eyes could scare you. Several times he had told us the distance to the next town and the name of that town. But he did not have a local map. We wondered about that."

From the corner of my eye I could see my father's head was up. Now he was listening to the story.

"As we took this town, some of our guys were wounded. Our medic treated them and even treated some wounded Germans and was running short of field dressings and stuff. He went to the captain.

"The captain said, 'Around the corner is Schmidt's Drug Store. Take a couple of the guys, break in, and take whatever you think you'll need. Take whatever the hell you want, in fact.'"

Our customer continued, "Now it all made sense. This American captain must have been born and raised near here. A while later the medic came back with more than a full supply of what he needed. A couple more minutes this German civilian comes around the corner yelling bloody murder. Said he was the pharmacist.

"The Kraut ran up to the captain, still yelling and waving, took one look at this American barbarian who'd ordered his store looted, and... stopped dead in his tracks.

"The captain stood straight and said, 'Guten tag, Heinrich.'

"The German turned white as a ghost, backed up two steps and, honest, peed his pants right there in the middle of the street, then turned and set a record for the hundred-yard dash.

"Mr. Marcus, what I haven't told you was we knew the captain was Jewish."

I looked, and sure enough, Dad was standing beside his bench.

"After a few minutes a German officer came out the front door of the town hall, and as he got closer I could see the SS insignia on his collar. This was the major the prisoner had warned us about. All of a sudden the major stopped and his jaw dropped. He yelled something in German, raised his Luger, and shot our captain. Believe me; I put a full clip from my M1 into that Nazi bastard before he hit the ground. Actually I think that six or seven other guys did the same thing. Our captain was helped up, holding his shoulder, as I wasted time checking the Kraut. I saw this watch on his wrist and without thinking I took the damn thing. A corporal got the Luger."

Now Dad was halfway down front.

"As I stood there, the captain approached and knelt beside the dead German. Kneeling close over the dead Nazi, he sighed and shook his head. Only a couple of us, standing close, could hear the captain softly say, almost to himself 'Rest in hell, Rudi.'

"Suddenly there was a terrible scream. Heads and rifle barrels swung around, and we saw a German woman running toward us as she kept repeating, '*Rudi, Rudi!*'

"She threw herself down beside the dead Nazi, weeping and screaming as she cradled him in her arms. She looked up at the captain and gasped, 'You—How—Why?'

"The reply came softly, but he spoke in German to her, and she fell back as though struck across the face.

"He said to us, 'I said, Hanni, Rudi had his chance. This was his choice.'

11

"He turned to our sergeant. 'They were our next door neighbors...
once.'

"The captain was taken away for medical treatment and the war
ended. We never saw him again, I guess because the war ended.

"I will never, ever wear it. I will never wind it to keep it going. I want
it cleaned so I can put it away. If things get rough, I will open the box
and look at it and remember something I really should forget. My family brings all their watches here, so I came here."

My father came down front, but with his arms folded. "The watch
will be cleaned and oiled here, but I will *not* touch it. I know he is
young, but my son is capable, and I'll supervise the job. However, there
will be *no money* involved...I will not quote a price and you will not ask
how much it is. Agreed?"

There was agreement, and as the customer left, my father said,
"Oh, bless you for your quick action and thank you." The watch was
cleaned and oiled, then picked up, all without a word. We never saw
the watch again. Nor did we miss it.

It was a nice day in 1950, down on Front Street in Worcester at Uncle
Abe's store after a day at Commerce High School. A man walked
in and put a pocket watch on the counter. I could see what appeared
to be a 12S "something" American. The dial was too dirty to see the
brand and the hands appeared to be very badly rusted. Rust in a watch
is akin to a lighted match in a gas tank...disaster results.

My uncle asked if it would be okay for his nephew to examine the
watch. He (me) was learning the family trade and this would help his
training. I opened the watch to discover that at least I had the size
right, it was a 12S, so badly rusted I couldn't read the name on the
movement, but by the shape of the plates it was, of course, a Hamilton,
seventeen jewels in a twenty-five-year case. A twenty-five-year case was
next best to solid gold. This thing, anyhow, was beyond any hope of
repair. I didn't think there was a single part that could be saved. What

could I possibly do to try and fix a watch that was beyond repair? Anything I could think of.

With a slight smile the man began, "In late 1944, a lucky gunner on a Jap cruiser put a shell into the engine of my Corsair. Luckily nothing blew or burnt, but that engine was positively not going to get me back to the carrier. The engine and I stuck it out together until I was about thirty miles from the Jap ships. Then, like it or not, I had to ditch. Rough splash, and I managed to get the raft out, as well as a canteen I'd always carried. So there we were, the raft, me, and this watch in my pocket, keeping company in the middle of the Pacific. For two days we floated around, me keeping the watch wound so I knew what time it was. On the third night, a storm came up and the raft flipped, and into the water we went, both the watch and I. Anyway, three more days and a US tin can still looking for missing pilots found me and got me back to the carrier. A week in sick bay and then back to duty. Anyway, with all the gauges, and clocks and watches needed to run the ship and all those planes, we had a real watch and clock repair shop on the ship. Those were the US Navy Instrumentmen guys." (In 1954, when I joined the US Navy, I too ended up as an IM...small world).

"All that time in salt water killed the poor watch, I was told. Couldn't even get the thing apart. Now, frankly, things have been good, and I want this repaired and running, and I don't care what it costs. Neither do I want a new movement put into the case...could have had that done years ago...that was what the Hamilton factory suggested."

Uncle Abe thought for several moments then said, "This watch is indeed dead. No one could save it. But I'm going to have young Barry study it. Truthfully, his grandfather, his own father, and his uncles are watchmakers. So are three of his cousins. Let's see what he can think of."

Name and address were taken, and the watch was put into my hands. Now, if Uncle Abe, the one who other watchmakers in Worcester came to for help pronouncing a watch dead, said it was dead, then it was dead. I felt nervous. I was only fifteen with a mere five years of training, and I was to bring life to a watch long declared dead. I propped up the watch, minus the case back, where I could see it every time I raised my eyes from whatever I was working on. Gradually an idea grew, and

I called the customer in for a conference. A conference with a kid! I remember wondering if I knew what I was doing.

I'd found that the dial (face) of the watch was merely filthy dirty. Being porcelain, the dial cleaned off with a wetted finger. Just enough to let me know it could be done. The hands were a rusted mess, but that was part of my brainstorm. The owner and I went next door for a Coke (my treat), and I started with questions. "Is it true you want the watch to run, no matter how it looks?"

"Yes."

"Do you care what the movement looks like, so long as it runs as a Hamilton should?"

"No."

"Good," I replied, "it can be done."

Back to the store, where the man put the question to Uncle Abe: "Do you really think this kid can do what the factory said couldn't be done?"

Then came one of the best compliments I'd ever received. Uncle Abe smiled and said, "I've told you the family history. You've heard of musical or artistic families in the past. His father and I think he was born knowing how to repair watches. He had to wait until his hands got big enough, and then we had to teach him the names of the parts. The rest he did himself."

To work I went. I still found the details fascinating and so simple. With some difficulty I got the hands off the watch and with a strong plier twisted the crown until the heavy pocket watch stem actually broke. I broke the heads off the two case screws and was able to remove the block of Pacific rust from the case. Then, shielding the watch from Uncle Abe, I dunked it into a baby food jar filled with Coca-Cola. I'd heard that men in the service used Coke as a rust loosener, and what was there to lose?

For a month I dunked...Coke...oil...Coke...oil, and a couple of times...naphtha. After a month, I was able to get enough screws out to get the plates off the watch, not caring what I had to do to any moving parts...they were gone anyway. Soon I'd either removed or broken out every moving part from the watch, leaving nothing but the rusted remnants of the five plates: pillar plate, the balance, train, and barrel bridges, and the pallet bridge.

I went to my uncle with an outline of my plan. Under the rust were brass bridges and plates, precision cast and not required for the actual running of the watch. I scraped, filed, chiseled, poked, and ended up with five of the worst-looking watch plates in history. However, mechanically they were perfect. Even the jewels were still in place. I scraped the badly rusted hands until they were in perfect shape but terrible appearance. I felt my uncle's presence behind me and I turned to see a big smile. He had caught on to my plan, which was to take the former pilot at his word. I was going to produce a disgracefully messed up timepiece that ran perfectly.

Quietly I had ordered from Hamilton the least expensive pocket watch that utilized that same 12S movement. A cheap case, what was called Silveroid, along with a good-looking but cheap inked dial were set aside for future need. I totally disassembled the entire new movement and then rebuilt it using the battered brass plates of the original. I used every screw, spring, and other moving part from the new watch movement to create the worst-looking watch I'd ever worked on, and of course it ran beautifully, as a Hamilton should. The original porcelain dial, only slightly stained, together with the awful-looking hands, were re-installed in the carefully cleaned but not polished case.

The customer was called, and it seemed he walked into the store even before I'd hung up the phone. Proudly but a little nervously, I handed over my project. When I think back, I can understand how, at fifteen, I could be astonished to see tears in the eyes of a veteran Corsair pilot over nothing more than a watch...a watch.

Still, I was proud of what I had done. (Three years later, I was out of high school, into the navy, and then went to work in my dad's store in Milford.) Twice over the years, the watch was brought to my uncle's store for cleaning and oiling, provided he was able to hand over the watch to "the kid who saved it." Now that I'm seventy-four, I doubt the pilot still lives, but somewhere, I'm sure, that Hamilton 12S pocket watch, the most beat- up movement in history, is still running as new.

Time is jumping around. (No pun intended.) This very day, March 23, during a family history discussion with a cousin, a long-forgotten period of my life jumped back into my mind. During my junior year at Commerce High School in Worcester, the last two periods of the day on my schedule were study periods. These periods, spent sitting in the back of ongoing classes, were to be used for actual study and/or the finishing of homework. I had nothing to do as I always did homework "at home."

Because of this idle time, it was suggested that I visit the Worcester School Department to apply for an "early dismissal" as I was apprenticed into a recognized trade. If I could obtain an early release from school, I could spend more time learning that trade. There wasn't an actual printed form for this kind of appeal, so I filled out a blank sheet of paper describing what I was asking for and the reason for it. I also had a copy of my to-date high school transcript as evidence that my scholastics were well near the top.

I was ushered into the office of the superintendent, a tall man who looked strangely familiar. I stood before his desk as he scanned the paperwork. Once he looked up and asked, "Do we know each other, young man?" We didn't, I thought.

"I would like to know just what trade you're learning, Barry," he said "You forgot to write that down."

"I'm learning the family trade. For six years now, under my father and under my uncle, I've been learning to be a watchmaker," I replied.

Mr. I-Just-Can't-Remember-His-Name jumped to his feet. "I thought it was you! You worked on my watch about three weeks ago at Marcus Jeweler down on Front Street. A man's Longines that had been repaired and needed a little adjustment. It took you about half a minute...it's been running wonderfully since. I'll be proud to sign this for you. You'll need a 'leave school pass' and another one for any policeman that asks why someone your age is not in school during these hours."

Occasionally the man came in to Uncle Abe's store and always stopped by my bench to ask how I was doing. After we spoke, he went to the front of the store and spoke quietly with my uncle. As he left, I remember Uncle Abe smiling at me.

My story must jump ahead about sixty years as history sort of repeats. The next watch "adventure" is, but for the sizes of the watches involved, truly an echo of the distant long ago.

Three days ago, I received, by FedEx, a man's Patek Philippe. This is a watch for which I really *should* put on a good suit, shirt, and tie before sitting down to work. I carefully opened the 18K gold case to behold... A SOLID BLOCK OF RUST. This watch was not rusty; this was a solid block of rust. I wondered why this block of rust was important enough to send to me. I closed the case and picked up the envelope that came with the "dead and gone" Patek. The envelope had something inside. I opened it and pulled out—to my astonishment—another Patek movement that...was *not* a Patek movement. Yes, it was...no, it wasn't...what the hell?

Time for a cup of coffee (black, no sugar) to figure this out. I knew that sometimes even the most prestigious of companies sold their movements to companies of equal fame. The good movement was, in fact, a genuine Patek, but the train and mainspring bridges had no Patek markings.

I e-mailed my customer and got the full list of facts. The Patek had been sold to a *big, big* shot from out west. For three whole weeks he'd worn the watch on a surfing trip...salt water converts any watch to a solid block of rust regardless of its prestige. The job for me was to overhaul the substitute movement and mount it into the 18K Patek case. With the sole exception of the removal of the dial, this was actually a basic overhaul and no big deal, except for the extreme quality and prestige of the watches involved.

I was able to remove the real Patek from its case and movement ring and pried the dial off...a lucky break. The surface of the dial was perfect, but I'd had to punch out *both* dial legs. I put the watches aside until the morning and went home. I spent the evening at the computer, typing additions to this "story." During a reread to look for typos and misspellings, I suddenly came to the tale of the totally rusted Hamilton pocket watch from World War II and the Pacific. I was excited because, but for the differences of war and peace, both watches had the same problem. I had what I thought was a truly inspired idea. Wait till morning.

Tuesday, March 8, saw me coming to the shop early. Much earlier than usual. I was excited about my brainstorm regarding the Patek. For a moment I laughed at myself. Here I was, seventy-four years old with sixty-four years at the bench and I was all excited about a single watch repair. I was like a little kid with a new toy.

I made coffee (black, no sugar), put on a classical music CD, and grabbed the corpus patheticus and went to work. I dropped it into a baby food jar filled with a liquid I'd had great success with and let it soak for a half hour. I then put the wet movement on a piece of glass and put a flame to the watch. As the flames burnt out, I put the movement back into the liquid to soak some more. One more burning and I put the movement quickly onto the ice in the back room freezer compartment. The heat of the burning slightly expanded the metal of the dead watch, and the sudden freezing shrunk it. This had the effect of loosening the hold of the rust on the pieces of the watch.

Very carefully, I soaked the watch once more, in a special oil, which seeped down into each microscopic space in the watch. I thought and hoped that a week would be long enough and chose the day to begin the restoration. I worked on a couple of watches and had a cup of coffee (black, no sugar) and then, with my fingers momentarily crossed, went where brave men feared to tread. With extreme care and extreme pressure I was able to safely remove twelve tiny screws from the rusted hulk, without the slightest trace of damage to the two plates I needed. I gently pried up the opposing sides of the plates, and slowly they rose up and out of the main plate. Success to the brave, or maybe the foolhardy.

It was worth it though, as I now had two *genuine* Patek bridges, the train and mainspring bridges, but best of all, and most critical, these plates were embossed with all the special Patek Philippe marking, logos, serial numbers, and model number. With a sharpened piece of watchmakers' pegwood, I managed to rub off 95 percent of the rust coating from both bridges. This I had to report in.

I e-mailed my customer, a collector and international rare watch dealer, to let him know of my plans. "I am going to rub off the remaining rust and then use jewelry polish to restore the original Patek bridges. When everything is cleaned, oiled, assembled, and timed, I will (or the customer will) have a perfect watch that is completely genuine Patek Philippe." It would have the right lettering, logos, numbers, and model indicators. I pushed the button to send out the e-mail and went back to the bench.

First thing Wednesday morning my phone rang. A voice that could only be described as joyous to the point of hysteria was shouting over the phone, so loud that if I hung up the phone and opened the window, I could still hear him, "How can you do that? What gave you the idea? Will it work? What a genius! Do you understand you will add greatly to the value of that watch?"

"Whoa...wait one second. What the heck is this watch worth anyway?" I asked.

"Don't you know what you have there?" he asked, laughing. No, I didn't, I really didn't. As I've said before, I repair watches...I pay no attention to any stated value of anything. I was surely aware that a Patek was a Patek, but that kind of money stunned me.

Then I realized that my price for this repair had risen quite a bit. I told him to relax, and I would make a special point to keep him up-to-date on progress. Time for more coffee (black, no sugar).

I returned to earth as I sipped hot coffee. Here was a watch of impossible (to me) value, and so what? All it meant to my customer and his future buyer was as an extremely expensive device that happened to indicate the time of day. No memories of people long gone...no recollection of an event fading into an old man's memory...no smiling memory of a favorite aunt...nothing of a past. For me, years and decades have passed and still I hear the voice of Uncle Abe and my father: "Barry, while we repair whatever timepiece is brought to us, never forget that we are dealing with *people*."

It's been a long sixty years, but that advice...that quiet lecture I'd received as a little kid...was as true today as it was in the 1940s.

Back to work, especially on the original bridges. It had been my intent to polish both bridges to improve their looks as much as possible. At the last second I realized that the polishing wheel would probably strip off the plating. Bad idea. With all the actual rust removed, I laid a jewelry polishing cloth on the desk and just rubbed the bridges back and forth for several minutes each. This turned out to be a very good idea as the bridges now looked excellent...obviously worked on, but excellent in appearance.

As this is being typed, the watch, now fully assembled, is running under a glass cover, but still out of the case. So far, everything is perfect. Another forty-eight hours of perfect running and I will re-case the movement.

Eventually I learned to examine the owners as well as their watches. I also learned to listen to them. Therein lay the problem with many watches. While I was away in the navy, the Bulova Watch Company introduced a new line of self-winding, twenty-three-jewel men's watches. Most watches had legitimate places for seventeen jewels, but Bulova had jeweled the pivots on the automatic unit. A great movement, rugged, dependable, and, from my point of view, a pleasure to work on and a lesson to learn about people.

In early 1957, a woman brought in a gent's Bulova 23, crystal broken and the sweep second hand missing and really needing a good cleaning. Two weeks later, the newly repaired watch was reclaimed and I reminded her that the watch was guaranteed to run; any problems, just bring it back. Three days later, she did just that... the watch was not running properly and kept stopping.

Apologizing, I kept the watch, taking it apart to check everything and running it on a crude "automatic watch winder" I'd made. This was a windmill-looking thing that I could attach a self-wind watch to in order to ensure the proper function of the automatic unit. Everything was fine, so I again called for the watch to be picked up.

Just two days later, an angry woman brought the watch back, still stopping and starting. Again I double and triple checked the watch, and there was nothing wrong. The watch was picked up, along with my promise that everything was okay, and she left the store muttering about that "(censored) accident."

That evening as I watched TV, a now forgotten comedian complained about a brother-in-law who was *so* lazy he could not keep his self-winding watch running. I sat up straight...my customer's wife had said the word "accident." The very next morning, as soon as I opened the store, I called the customer's number and asked if her husband was somehow laid up and very inactive. The answer was (as I suspected), "Yes, since the accident he has nothing to do but watch TV, and he's missing the start of his programs 'cause the darn watch keeps stopping even after you've had it so much."

Quietly I explained that her husband's watch required an active lifestyle in order to self-wind and run properly. I invited her to come to the store and accept a loan, without responsibility, of a manual wind watch that would see her husband through his confinement. Five weeks later, he slowly walked into the store to return the loaner watch. In later years, I repaired the watch when needed, and as he picked up the Bulova, he never missed the opportunity to point out how active he remained. We smiled.

I don't do clocks. Period. I seem to have a mental block that prevents me from working on large timepieces. No wall clocks. No mantle clocks. No shelf clocks. I've never repaired a clock that belonged to me. Out it goes and I find a new one. While in the navy, I went to Instrumentman Class A School at the Great Lakes in Illinois. The "students" were taught the repair of typewriters, mimeograph machines, pressure gauges, and precision instruments. I learned that higher-ranking sailors were sent to the "C" school for either precision office machines or actual watch and clock repair. Most of our time was spent on typewriters, which of course are larger than clocks. They didn't count, as typewriters, while large, did not tell time. It was at school at the Great Lakes that I was introduced to coffee (black, no sugar).

The first time I was on duty standing the mid watch at the school (12:00 a.m. till 4:00 a.m.), I had a difficult time staying awake. Maybe coffee would help, but how to get it. I had a brainstorm and stole a coffee cup the next day at supper (I hope the statute of limitations has run out) along with a spoon. I bought a small jar of instant coffee to try, and the next duty night, I poured a cup of nearly boiling water from a sink at the school. A spoonful of instant powder and—voila!—a cup of coffee (black, no sugar). Thus it has ever been.

If I am to be truthful, I must confess to the repair of *one* particular clock. During the summer of 1958, my grandfather walked into my dad's store with a familiar mantle clock under his arm. I recognized the clock as a Seth Thomas key-wind, Westminster chime high-quality mantle clock. Understand that in 1958, a drive from Lawrence down to Milford meant driving fifty-five or so miles down a two-lane "highway" laid out by colonial-era cows. Today, it is a simple trip down Route 495.

Anyway, I was told, "Your grandmothers' clock has stopped and she hasn't slept for three days. When your grandmother doesn't sleep, neither does your grandfather. Fix it while I visit with your father."

Grandpa gently put the sick clock on my bench and sat down to visit with his son-in-law. I knew that my grandmother had become so used to the every-fifteen-minute chiming that the silence intruded on her sleep. Like a person from New York being unable to sleep in the silence of the country.

"Grandpa, I don't fix clocks. Sorry, but I can't help you. We can bring it to one of the guys in Worcester," I suggested.

"Fix the clock." Grandpa was a man of few words, as noted.

"Gee, Grandpa, I really don't do *any* clocks. I just don't."

"Fix the clock."

"But Grandpa—"

"Fix the clock."

"But—"

"FIX THE CLOCK!"

My father jumped to my defense. "Pa, Barry really doesn't do any clock repair. He's never been willing to work on things that big. We'll get it taken care of in Worcester. Be about a week."

Grandpa's answer was either in Polish, Russian, Yiddish, Hebrew, or German, but definitely *not* English.

Grandpa looked from Dad to me, then reached for the phone. I knew who he was calling, and sure enough, I heard Grandpa say, "Grace, Barry says he doesn't fix any clocks and there is nothing he can do. What should I do?" He listened a moment and then handed me the phone, "Your grandmother wants to speak to you."

A little nervously I answered, "Hi, Nana, how are you?"

A loving voice answered, "I am heartbroken to learn that my oldest grandson no longer wants his nana to make him a personal pot of lentil soup and dessert for his visits to Lawrence. That makes me sad."

Cheerfully I replied, "Okay, Nana, I'll get right on it so Grandpa will be back in Lawrence before dark. Love you. Bye. Here's Grandpa again."

Grandpa was home just before dark.

After a phone call from Lawrence, I drove up the following week to regulate the clock. As I crossed the town line from Methuen to Lawrence, I could smell lentil soup cooking. Nana's broken heart was fixed, just like her clock.

I always wondered if the courts would have found Nana guilty of extortion, or blackmail, or culinary assault, but I never pursued the issue. Smart.

There was a large group of watchmakers always in and out of my uncle's store, and they took a sincere interest in the "boy watchmaker." Once, when I was only thirteen, I went along with one of the Worcester watch and clock men, R. C., to repair a clock. I was already "anti-clock," but I was asked to go with him to provide some "helping muscle." At thirteen, I was well over six feet.

Anyway, it was explained that the clock in trouble was an eight-day grandfather clock that he'd repaired twice, but it still would not run more than five days. In his shop the clock ran the full eight days, but when it was installed back in its case, the run was only about five days, and it was driving him frantic. Even if I couldn't help with the repair of the clock, I could help carry it if need be.

On the way I received a lecture from R. C. "Where we are going is an old mansion that once belonged to a big Worcester gangster many years ago. For a number of years the house was empty until it was bought by a big shot Worcester manufacturer. He says the clock was just sitting in the living room; it was beautiful and he wants it to run. I've had it in the shop twice, but there is still something wrong. You can help carry it if it must go back downtown." No wonder I was needed.

I sat back and enjoyed the ride, paying no attention to where we were going. I was still too young to drive, so what did I care about streets and directions?

The house was large and beautiful and the clock was large and beautiful. The clock stood about eight feet tall, was rich cherry wood with a very ornate "Tempus Fugit" dial and hands. Of course there were multiple weights hanging from chains that powered the clockworks. Three weights for time, Westminster four-note set, and the last for the chime count. The pendulum slowly swung back and forth as I walked around the room playing tourist while R. C. examined his patient. I passed behind the clock a couple of times, just idling while the real pro did his thing. At that stage of my training I already had the habit of trying to think "outside the box" to solve puzzles. I noticed something strange, but it was a something that had nothing whatsoever to do with the clock mechanism.

"Hey," I said, "this is weird, I think. The back of this clock is as nicely finished as the front and sides. I don't think this was made to go against a wall. I've seen these all nicely done from the sides and the front, but not the back, like this one. But look, there's a square piece cut out of the back and another piece of wood is stuck in there."

I was told that we were not worried about the back of the clock and to *sight-see* inside the case. I looked inside, and asked, "Why is this shelf here? The other tall clocks I've seen, the weights dropped way down below the door. In fact, I think that without this shelf the weights would really take a full eight days to near the bottom. Wouldn't the weights come down onto the shelf and make the clock stop?"

R. C. was curious. "How did you come up with that brainstorm?"

"Look," I came back, "if you repaired this clock, and twice, it's repaired. Maybe the problem is not the clock at all."

With that I began to run my hand around the outer edges of the mystery shelf. Hidden on either side, behind the trim for the front edges, I felt metal projections, like buttons. Awkwardly I pushed on both buttons at the same time, and the front edge of the "shelf" popped up about an inch. I heard a sharp intake of breath over my shoulder as I carefully lifted the rear-hinged shelf.

"Oh my dear God," I heard behind me as my eyes beheld at least a dozen handguns, both revolvers and automatics. What was it about the prior owner? A hand reached around me, the shelf was pushed back into place, the front carefully closed, and I was hustled through the living room to the foyer and out the front door.

"But-but," I started and was cut off instantly.

"Barry, listen very carefully to me. You never saw this house in your life. You were never in this house in your life. You have no idea where this house even stands! Do you hear me? And you never, never helped me with a tall clock in this house you've never even seen. Do you understand?"

I did *not* understand, but I really had no idea where the house was located. I wasn't even sure if it was actually inside Worcester. I was sure, though, of one thing—the man I was with, watchmaker and master clock man, was as white as a sheet and his hands trembled on the steering wheel. As he dropped me off at my uncle's store, he cautioned me, "Barry, forget that you ever lived this day. For your own sake." That day, a thirteen-year-old student watchmaker did not know what had happened, but some instinct kept me from telling even my uncle, let alone anyone else.

Four years later, when I was at his store helping my clock-making friend, something came over me and I quietly asked, "Whatever happened with that troublemaking clock from *that* day?"

R. C. leaned very close to my ear and replied, "That clock you *never* laid eyes on, in that house you've never been in, on that day you didn't go with me, has been running perfectly for over three years now."

I was smart enough to never mention that day again. Now, addition says I am the only one still alive, and I still don't know where that clock was located.

In the spring of 1952, shortly before high school graduation, I walked from school to Uncle Abe's store. As I entered the store, I saw my uncle speaking to a very well-dressed man. "Ah, here is my nephew now. Barry is the one to help you," Uncle Abe said.

I was introduced to Attorney Petersen, a name even a high school kid was familiar with (not professionally, of course). His hand went into the paper bag on the counter and came out with a smallish black clock with a hole in the outer edge! I said to myself, "You don't do clocks."

Uncle Abe knew what I was thinking and quickly said, "Barry, that is *not* a clock. It is merely an oversized watch. Listen to Attorney Petersen."

"In 1945, I was flying CAP (combat air patrol) over the fleet at Okinawa. My group was trying to protect the destroyers on the outer radar picket line from Japanese suicide attacks. We did our best, but—well—we did our best. Sometimes the suicide planes had their own protection and we'd dogfight.

"Just as I blew up a kamikaze, a Zero got me with a burst from the side. The bullet came in behind me to the right, went between two ribs and out again, then through the front of the clock. The plane was, very luckily, okay, and I stuffed a hanky into my wound and flew back to the carrier. Anyway, I made a safe landing and was taken to the sick bay for treatment while the plane was brought below for repairs. A couple of days later, an enlisted sailor came to me in sick bay with this clock in his hand."

In those days, I believe the Instrumentman rating was called "Machinist's Mate." (By the time I got there, we were called Instrumentmen.)

"Sir," the machinist said," I'm from the watch and clock shop. We're going to install a new clock in the panel of your plane and not bother with this one. Funny, but since the case and dial is kinda larger than the works, the bullet didn't bust anything. If you'd like, we'll clean and oil it and you can have it to remember the day by."

The lawyer continued, "The war ended before I got back into the air, and we all went home. I never flew again. I had a cabinetmaker here in Worcester make a desk stand for this clock. I do remember the day, and I don't want to sound corny, but each time I look at the clock I understand that each and every day is truly a gift. Will you take care of this?"

It was not a clock, but a rather large watch, and I was proud to repair it. This was the first time I'd wondered about the attachment to a timepiece as a memory of war. Over the years, I have lost count of the watches that had a military history with the owner. Some were civilian purchases that were carried to war, carried by a young man who crossed the world and went into harm's way, and returned. Some watches were made under contract with Bulova, Hamilton, Waltham, or Elgin…famous American watch companies. Many had been given to flight crew members and pilots, and these watches became "movie stars" in the scenes where the order was, "Gentlemen, synchronize your watches…Hack." This meant pulling out the crown, which stopped the watch with the sweep hand at "12" then the watch was carefully set, and at "hack" the watch was restarted. All watches in the squadron were now on the exact second time wise. The correct time was critical. Take off on time. Be over the target on time. Time. Time. The world was at war, and simple watches and clocks (which I wouldn't fix) told everyone on both sides when to carry out orders. The wristwatch that once had told the gunnery officer of a battleship it was time to fire the sixteen-inch 50s now told a civilian it was time for Uncle Miltie's program. Whenever and wherever, things happen and are done "on time."

Some watches were collected at the point of a gun, some collected in town squares, and some we don't want to know about.

In 1949, a gold watch was quietly given to me. It was from "somewhere" in the Worcester area, owned by a young Italian man. He waited while I examined the watch. I immediately noticed the engraving on the back of the case was in *Hebrew*. I turned around and looked at him. He saw the question in my eyes. Sadly, he nodded.

"Yes, I know it's Hebrew lettering. I had a rabbi translate it for me. It asks for blessings for the wearer. I told the rabbi where I got the watch, and before I knew it, he had both hands on my shoulders and was saying something in Hebrew. He said nothing else to me. I think he was crying and praying at the same time."

Quietly the young man continued, "In 1945, we had advanced pretty far into Germany, and I still don't want to believe what we found. My company broke into one of those concentration camps. We found bodies piled high from one end to the other. The worst was the people who somehow were still alive. One of our men screamed in horror and pointed, unable to talk. Here and there, some of the 'bodies' were moving arms and legs. We tried to help them, but nothing would have kept them alive."

I believed this soldier was little more than eighteen years old on that day in 1945. I said nothing as he continued softly, "I helped one man, took him off a pile of bodies, and laid him on a blanket. A small drink of water revived him enough that he smiled at me. Under his rags he had a watch, somehow hidden from the Germans. He took it off and then pressed it into my hand, but when I gave it back, he gestured an insistence that I keep it. I nodded and he smiled as I put it on. When I turned back to him, he had died, and I had a brief thought through my tears, 'Well, my friend, at least you died free.'

Every few nights, in my sleep, he comes to me and I show him I still have *my* watch. When I got back home, my parish priest said I should go to the rabbi and learn what the writing said. I did, and I'm glad. I guess you could say a blessing has come to me. I survived and made it home. That's enough."

The watch was repaired with love and reverence. When the young man came to pick up the watch, Uncle Abe had marked the tag "paid in full." The young GI backed up a step and asked, "But who paid?"

Uncle Abe's reply: "You did, some years ago."

A funny-looking watch was no longer running. When handed to me for examination, I saw the "numbers" were Chinese characters. "Where did you get this?"

A quiet answer, "Five miles south of the Yalu River," was the only information I get.

I cleaned a beautiful Patek Philippe, a watch really beyond prestige. It belonged to a man I knew couldn't afford a watch like this. I curiously asked its origin. I was willing to bet this was a watch "liberated" from some enemy in Europe. Wrong.

The proud owner of the Patek said, "I won it from an idiot on the *Enterprise* who couldn't read a bluff. I had a full house." Finally… a *happy* watch war story.

An inexpensive Swiss watch was brought in for repair. We always inspected a watch before repair. The customer, my dad insisted, must be told what was wrong, what had to be done, and, most importantly, the repair cost. Once a price was given, it was as set in stone.

"Never give an estimate," Dad said. "Estimates seem to end up twenty percent higher. Customers always resent a price jump, even if they say nothing. Get the price right the *first* time, but never increase it." Good advice.

This customer, George, was a relatively young man, but the watch was from around the late 1920s. I thought it could be another family hand-me-down.

As I carefully examined this "nothing" watch, I noticed there were no U.S. customs markings. No "Swiss" under the six and no stamps on the balance bridge. I was concerned that there wouldn't be a listing of the movement in the large reference catalog used by all watchmakers. This watch had been personally brought in from Europe. I wondered if this would prove to be another war trophy. It was, but not as I thought.

I explained to my customer the single concern I had about repairing his watch: parts could be a problem. I doubted if this movement had ever been an import. It took a mere four words for me to know that this was indeed another war memory. I asked where he bought the watch, and he just shook his head. No pun, we went back in time.

"We landed at Anzio. It was murder. Companies down to a few men, sergeants running companies...real bad." He paused for a minute, eyes focusing far, far away.

George continued, "When we finally broke out, we fought our way up inland. Along the way the destruction was awful, and the worst was civilian casualties. We fought our way into this little town with not many buildings unharmed. We slowly advanced up both sides of the street, covering each other. Kick open a door and either shoot inside or toss in a grenade.

"As I approached one house I saw a rifle barrel stick out a few inches and then retreat. I didn't bother with the door, but inched up and tossed my last grenade through the open window. When it blew, I turned and kicked open the door and quickly saw three dead Germans amid the wreckage. On to the next house, but no time to get more grenades for now. I kicked one door that wouldn't open, so a few rounds from my Thompson blew out the lock and latch, and in I dove."

This was like the story of the captain and the SS major.

The customer related, "There I was, a tired, dirty, and I admit scared American with a Tommy gun covering two old Italians. The old lady was crying, and I think the old man was too scared to cry or anything else. They just stared at my Thompson with huge eyes. I lowered my gun, just a little, and looked around, just in case. As I turned, I felt a painful tightness in my chest as I found myself staring at the picture of a young couple and a little boy standing in front of them."

I thought he was going to cry as he continued, "I was staring at a picture of my own mother, father, and myself—a little kid. A copy of that picture was on the living room wall at home in the States. I was holding a Tommy gun on my own grandparents, God forgive me. What if I had more grenades? I touched the kid in the picture with my finger then tapped my own chest. I touched my parents' pictures saying, 'Mama... Papa' and again pointing to me. I did not speak any real Italian."

I thought to myself, this sounds like a "two hanky" movie. Unreal.

George collected himself. "My grandmother screamed and grabbed me so hard I couldn't breathe. Grandpa ran out the door, yelling as loud as he could. One of my buddies, an Italian kid from New York, who spoke excellent Italian, ran into the house, saying some old man was hollering at everybody that his grandson was here to free them all. Everybody came out of what was left of their town and celebrated. You never saw so much wine in your life."

"My grandmother showed everybody the picture, and that was when I saw a studio stamping, like they all do. Believe it or not, it was from Morin's Studio in Milford. I guess lots of Italians had their pictures taken to send to the folks in the old country. Oh, this was my grandfather's watch. He argued and argued until I agreed to take it with me. I took real good care of it, and now you will too."

When my father opened his store, Morin's Photo Studio was upstairs over our jewelry store. Later, Mr. Morin's son, Clarence, moved the studio to its current location on Pine Street.

So many watches had stories that tugged at the heart. Often the third generation of a family was wearing a timepiece that *must* be repaired. A very pleasant woman came into the store with her husband's watch. I closely examined a man's Hamilton that needed a complete overhaul and some timing adjustments. When I explained to my customer the work to be done, she quietly said, "The accuracy of this watch is not too critical. My husband is losing his sight and really cannot see the dial or the hands. He wears the watch because it was his father's and nothing else will do."

She left the store, and "something" began to spin around in my head. A week later, while thinking over a cup of coffee (black, no sugar), I realized, "Wow, that'll work."

I called the customer, and she came into the store that afternoon.

I told her of my understanding regarding her husband's attachment to his father's watch. The watch was perfectly fine, and in terms of her husband being able to see the dial and hands, it had two easily correctable problems. One, the white dial had very thin gold bars at every hour except the "6," which was used for a small second hand. The minute and hour hands were also very thin and gold, quite stylish but "maybe" very tough to see.

I proposed changing the dial to one I had that had large gold *actual* numbers on the dial save for the "6." My proposal was to take a special enamel and paint the numbers black. Also, I had a pair of rather wide gold hands that I could also convert to black.

The watch would still be his father's watch and band, I explained, with the original movement and adjusted for accuracy. Additionally, I would return the original dial and hands for possible future use in case...She nodded her understanding.

Two days later, I showed the completed watch to my father and was quite surprised by his reaction. Gently he lifted his hand to cup my cheek and gently pinched me. Not a word, but I could sense a deep pride in his son. Ten minutes later, he came to my bench and said, "I bet you're not charging extra for the dial and hands. I'm really proud of you. I'm going into the back room to call Uncle Abe and tell him."

That afternoon the redesigned Hamilton was picked up. I assured my customer that the watch could be returned to its original appearance at no cost if her husband was in any way unhappy with what I'd done.

A couple of days later she marched into the store with a determined look on her face. Well, I thought, I had at least tried to help. I approached with my hand outstretched to receive the watch, but she grabbed my hand in hers. Then she stood on tiptoes and kissed my cheek.

"Young man, you have created the most lovable monster. My husband is announcing about *every* ten minutes the correct time. When he knows a relative is near, he announces the time. He will loudly inform the world that his TV show is starting in three minutes; that's how closely he can see what you did. There is *no* possible way to express our gratitude. All I can say is bless you."

For me, a great "people" lesson. To this gentleman, independence meant the ability to know on his own that his TV program was about to start. Maybe little things are really what counts.

Uncle Abe and my father had so often told me that I was taking care of *people*. Two smart men passed their humanity to a student watchmaker.

Many years later...

A nice lady brought her watch in for a new battery. As I wrote up the ticket, I mentioned that this was a very good quality watch that should last a good number of years into the future.

"It won't matter," she sighed. "My eyes are getting bad, and most of the time I can't even see the face, let alone tell the time. The watch was a present from my late husband and I just can't give it up."

I think I'd seen this movie. "Suppose I made it so you could see the time with just a glance? Would that be much of a help?" Of course it was another "modern" watch with a gold-colored dial and gold-colored hands. Someday I'd get the chance to shoot a designer. I'd hold out for a jury of people who must wear glasses.

Out came the black enamel; the hands were colored and a new battery installed.

Today, just after 3:00 p.m., the lady came to pick up her watch. I handed it over without a word and waited. "Oh my goodness," she exclaimed. "Look! It's seven past three as clear as day. I can't believe it. How'd you do that?"

"I just made the hands have a clear contrast with the gold dial. Just stupid designers. You should be okay now...no need for a new watch," I replied. A very happy woman left the shop.

A number of years ago, a gentleman, working hard moving into Milford, worked a little too hard and broke his watch. Late that afternoon he came into the store to see about getting the watch fixed. No problem, of course. I got one of our tickets and a pen and asked his name. The answer required many, many letters and several syllables to complete, and he started to spell his name for me. Suddenly he noticed that I was writing out his long Italian name without help from him.

He grabbed the ticket from me, looked at my printing, and exclaimed, "Good Lord, you spelled my name correctly. How did you do that? No one spells my name correctly."

This I could answer at once.

"Your name is no big deal, nor is it that unusual. You're really new to town. Get a phone book as soon as you can and look through it. You have moved into Italy, west...far west. There are two other families with your name, both our customers," I said.

When I was young and our store was new, my dad took the time to learn about Milford. Today, it would be called a marketing survey or demographic study. Milford was a town with a very, very large percentage of Italians living in it, my father had lectured me over a Coke (too young for coffee at the time).

"Barry, no man is more complimented as when you pronounce and *spell* his name correctly. Here you will meet and deal with many, many Italian people. They are a wonderful, hardworking, loving, and considerate people who have names that are very difficult for people like us. You have to learn their names and the spelling. I have a book that has a lot of the Italian grammar and pronunciation rules in it. I'm giving it to you to study, and I mean *study*. No tests, but I'll be watching how you do when you write up their repairs. Milford also has a lot of Irish residents, but their names are really easy."

Again, watches were the connection between people. I learned that many Italian names contained a silent *g*, and that a *cch* was a *k*, but *c* was pronounced as *ch*. I remember a prominent doctor being impressed that the young Jewish kid could spell his name perfectly on the first try. My father was right. Eventually I learned an extremely rudimentary Italian, enough to communicate a little with some of my customers. We had a couple of Eastern European customers, but their names were impossible for me. Still are, in fact.

Time for another lecture from my father: "Italians are almost all Catholic." I knew the word, of course, but I grew up in a neighborhood so Jewish the city closed my school on the Jewish High Holidays because there would be so few students in the whole building. So I learned something of Catholicism to better understand the people of our community. I learned what it meant when a customer would "light a candle" for my family when someone was sick. I experienced the kindness of people who would ask "the Holy Mother's help" for my father when he had a heart attack. I was grateful to the local priest who said a Mass of thanksgiving for the safety of my family after our home was destroyed by fire. When my friends and customers wished me a "Merry Christmas," I knew the good wishes came from a heart happy with the joy of the season. My only reply could be a sincere, "a Merry Christmas to *you*." I hear some of the nonsense that goes on today and I shudder. I'll do it my way...no, that is my father's way. (Another personal note...I'm proud that my own children have followed this tradition.)

We sold many religious articles in the store, and I learned the special meaning of each. I sold rosaries and learned their usage and somewhere learned the "Hail Mary" recited on each bead. I learn the special significance of the majority of the saints. We sold a crucifix to adorn the wall, but I learned to be serious when showing a "sick call."

What was I learning? How important it was to respect and learn the differences in people. People who just needed my help to fix their watches but who, along with their culture, became important to us.

Milford had the usual mix of young, rowdy teenage boys. After school, they congregated on the sidewalk of Main Street, only a couple of blocks from the then high school. In the warm weather, before we had an air conditioner in the store, we frequently had the door open and could hear when they got noisy.

One particular day a reverent hush suddenly settled on Main Street, so quiet one could hear the beating of a butterfly's wings. Young heads turned as the boys stood straighter and erased silly grins and smirks from their faces. Everyone be on alert! Sister Rose Concepta was coming. In silence the alarm went out as Sister walked slowly up the street. A nod of the head here, a frown there, and every now and then a smack echoed up the street. Sister had administered to another miscreant.

Sister came into the store, having broken her rosary again. The rosary was held together by thin wire links, unsoldered, that could and did get stretched until they opened. The rosary was put into my hands, and one at a time, carefully, I closed each open jump ring and secured each open wire loop.

"All set, Sister," I said, "each link and loop is secured."

It goes without saying that there was no charge for the repair. Ever. Sister left with a sincere, "God bless you, son."

Sister returned down Main Street, leaving in her wake a collection of very well behaved young boys.

L oves comes with a watch. I was seventeen, a high school junior, and progressing as a watchmaker when an old 18s Waltham came into the store for repair. By then, my dislike for "big" things had really taken hold, and I now wasn't happy repairing any pocket watches, so I told Dad he could take this one. Right...out came a quarter, and I was told to call heads or tails. Of course I lost. Funny...it was Dad's quarter, he flipped, and I always called it. Just my luck, I never, ever won the coin toss.

It was an18S hunting case Waltham...push on the crown to open the front of the case, open the crystal, and carefully remove the minute, hour, and second hands. Now hold the case front and bezel carefully and turn the watch over to open the back and...

The sun came down from the sky...I felt all warm and had trouble breathing, and silly as it sounds, time itself stood still. Seemingly three days later, my father noticed I was not moving. I was frozen in time, unable to move, just staring at the inside back of the watch. He walked over behind me, paused, and said, "Good heavens."

I sat there unmoving while I stared at the most beautiful young girl I'd ever seen. I never realized how homely the movie stars of my day were until I saw this angel looking back at me from the inside of an old watch. Eyes, lips, cheeks, jawline, hairdo, and shoulders exposed in the style of that era. I exaggerate not when I say she looked deeply into my soul.

My father, sensing my problem, gently said, "Barry, I think she is a little too old for you."

I didn't care; what were a few years? I looked to the other side and read the inscription on the interior case back:

Caleb
Come home from
this awful war
to the one who
loves you.
1863

But what was *her* name, for crying out loud? No name…the six lines of engraving, beautifully hand done, had taken up all the room. I'm sure Caleb knew *her* name, but a love struck teenager almost a hundred years later would never know it. I thought, "What do I call you, beautiful lady?" I remember thinking that I must be nuts. Anyway, I cleaned and oiled the watch, only to find it took extra time to get the timing as close as it should be. All that time the watch was in front of me, facing away, but with the back open, as I worked on other watches.

My father was quite impressed. "Most watchmakers have to look at the dial and hands to see if a watch is running properly. My son can tell from looking at the back."

Tragically, three weeks later, the watch was picked up. As I handed the watch across the counter, I asked, "Do you know if Caleb ever came home safely?"

The customer lit up with a huge smile and laughed. "Oh boy. It's obvious you saw *her*, didn't you? Don't lie to me. I spend more time looking at *her* than I do looking to see the time. I don't know who they were, I don't know *her* name. I bought this watch when I was in the army, down south. The watch ran perfectly, so I never looked inside until I was back here and it needed fixing.

"I took it to a watchmaker in Boston, and when he opened the back, he was stunned. He got up and showed me *her*, and I fell in love at first sight. He also asked if Caleb came home safely. I know you're just a kid, but I'll confess…my wife has never seen the inside of the watch…and won't. Thanks for taking care of *her*." He smiled like a conspirator and left.

I saw *her* just once more, because when I came back from the navy, *she* and the watch's owner had moved away. To this day, when, however seldom, I'm called upon to repair one of those very, very old 18S pocket watches, I spend a few minutes thinking about *her*.

(The following was added after the above was typed.)

This day, February 11, 2009, a "Date that Will Live in Infamy," was to be remembered as the date when my closest-held fantasy was for all time shattered. This morning, while getting ready for work, I watched a program on the History Channel about photography, an old interest of mine. Partway through the program, listening with only half an ear, I heard the words that broke my heart. I learned that the ability to preserve photographs on *photographic paper* did not come about until the 1880s. This meant that my beloved *her* could not have been the young lady who presented her token of love to Caleb. I had been betrayed. I shut off the TV and went to work much sadder but no wiser.

That afternoon, while working on an 1890s Waltham, I suddenly picked my head straight up. "Wait a minute," I spoke to my broken heart, "*she* hasn't changed. *She* is still the most beautiful woman I've ever seen...*her* face is still the most memorable, isn't it?"

Not only that...if the picture was taken perhaps in the Gay Nineties, there was still a chance that she was alive when I was born in 1934. Maybe I was nuts, but I smiled for the first time that day. My love had been redeemed and it became a fine, sunny day, this February 11, 2009. With a happy heart, it was time for a cup of coffee (black, no sugar).

(If anyone in the future reads this, check on the weather that day during the worst winter in many years. It truly was a bright, sunny day with the temperature rising into the upper fifties. A day to remember.)

A beautiful ladies' pendant watch came in for repair. Small hunting case (closed cover that sprung open) suspended on a 14K gold chain. Another Waltham model, and the case too was 14K gold; however, the metal was rather thin, I guess to keep both the cost and weight under control. The watch was in great condition with the sole exception of two dents on the front of the case, in a line. When I turned the watch over to examine the movement, I saw there were two corresponding dents in the back of the watch. I approached the middle-aged lady to discuss the needed repairs. As an afterthought I mentioned that I could easily remove the dents and give the watch case a mirror polish. In a voice that stopped traffic on Milford's Main Street, she yelled, "NO! Don't you dare touch that case! Don't even think about it!"

When she calmed down, I received the explanation. "This was my grandmother's watch. She always wore it. I never saw her without that watch hanging down. I've been told that as a baby, I always reached for it and played with it. She never took it away from me, even when I broke the chain once. Those dents you better *not* remove are from my baby teeth, from when I bit down too hard. My mother said it got rusty at the winder thing when I drooled into the watch, but Grandma never took it away. This watch, which I remember from babyhood, is all I have left of my grandmother besides memories."

She continued, with a sort of faraway look, "Now *my* daughter is going to give me a grandchild in a month or so, and another baby will someday remember a grandmother who always wore this watch." Just a watch, albeit a high-quality timepiece, but still a watch that had become a closely held treasure for multiple generations of a single family, not a reminder of war, or death, or close calls and near misses, but the earliest moments of the love offered for a baby's future memories.

What was it Uncle Abe had said to me all those years ago? Let's see…"Barry, we repair watches, but we are dealing with *people*, and many times their watches are of very special meaning to them." Something like that, but he put the stress on the word *people*. He was right then, and he is right to this day.

Watches are important to people for many different reasons. A man came into the store to pick up a repair. It was a nice quality Benrus Citation, identified by a red/yellow/blue strip just under the name on the upper half of the dial. As I handed the watch to the owner, I commented, "Must be a birthday or wedding anniversary coming next week. I see the date on the back is the beginning of next week." I smiled, proud of myself for being so observant.

"Neither," came the reply. "It was a present when I was released from jail." I thanked him, stressed the guarantee, and went back to work.

Some watches are more important than the people, it seems. A very cheery woman brought a man's Longines in for service. The watch was in bad shape, crystal broken, minute hand gone, balance staff broken, and the stem and crown were gone. I inquired as to the cause of all this damage, and she answered cheerfully, "It was sort of run over by a pickup truck."

I assured her that the watch would be as good as new, but that the repair would take extra time because parts had to be ordered from Longines. She smiled anew and said, "Take your time. My husband was wearing the watch at the time and won't be out of the hospital for another month. Bye." I stood there for several minutes. What to say? May I admit that I sort of wondered who was driving that pickup truck?

Some time ago, I added a "descriptive phrase" to the language. I'd overhauled and put a new balance staff into a handsome Longines dress watch. This translated into a non-water-resistant, non-shock-proof "dress" watch, not one that could take a pounding. I cautioned the owner about overstressing his watch, and off he went. I was quite disappointed to see him again two weeks later when he explained that the watch had stopped. I took the watch to my bench and checked it and…

"What did you do?" I exclaimed. "The balance staff is broken again and I think the upper hole jewel is broken too. I just replaced that staff."

"Well," he confessed, "I was doing some carpentry on the house over the weekend, and I kind of was wearing the watch and—"

"No, no, no. I told you that this watch was not to be worn for heavy use," I scolded him. "This watch is a *necktie watch*, for goodness sake. If you are wearing a tie then you can wear this watch. Otherwise no way. I'll be re-staffing this once a month for the rest of both our lives."

I made a mental note to remember that phrase, which I use to this day. And the conversation was not over yet. "What you have to buy is a 'who cares' watch," I instructed him. Wow, another good phrase for the English lexicon.

The customer asked, "What the heck is a 'who cares' watch? I never heard of that brand before."

"It's not a brand, it's a cost. A watch that if you kill it, WHO CARES?! You have old clothes you wear for rough or dirty work, and if you rip the pants...who cares? That's the kind of watch you have to buy for that kind of work. One that, if killed, you don't mind replacing for little money. You can buy a new 'who cares' watch for what it will cost you to repair your Longines again."

He left and returned for the once again repaired Longines two weeks later, and held out his wrist for me to approve his brand new "who cares" watch. I had to agree, it looked good and rugged, but if killed...well, WHO CARES? That made two new phrases I'd added to the language. I still use those expressions when discussing the proper care of watches. I guess the simpler the description the more it explains.

Did anyone ever suspect that a watch could quiet a very persistent salesman? Milford had a Cadillac dealer who was very unhappy that my father only bought and drove four-door Super 88 Oldsmobiles. Each year when the new Cadillacs were introduced, he came into our store to tell my father, "A prominent businessman like you should be seen driving only a Cadillac. The prestige and the quality reflect favorably on its owner."

Each year, my father would quietly turn around, reach in the wall case of men's watches, and take out a $35 or $40 Hamilton. Then he'd say, "Okay, you have convinced me. I'll be at your showroom in about an hour. You just show me a black Cadillac that will last as long as this Hamilton watch, and I'll buy it, but only in black."

Each year the Caddy dealer would look at Dad, turn around, and leave the store. Dad would put the Hamilton back and, with a grin, tell me, "Maybe next year I'll use a Longines." He never got that Cadillac.

I developed a deep pride in my trade and my own skills. More valuable were the lessons in "people" I had at the benches of my father, Uncle Abe, and the several watchmakers of Worcester who had helped the "kid." One in particular helped a young apprentice (me) despite a complete lack of the English language. I still cannot pronounce his name, and I knew neither his country nor his history. All I knew about him was the few hushed words that I had overhead. Sadness. Camps. At the time I did not know what that meant. Believe me, now I do.

Once, during hot weather, he had his shirt sleeves rolled partway up, and as he stood behind me showing a watch, I saw some numbers tattooed on his arm. At last I understood. Now and then, I'd see the reflection of some tears in his eyes. Finally I asked just who he was and why he paid attention to me.

Uncle Abe told me sadly, "He is—was—a skilled watchmaker in Poland when the Germans invaded. You will someday read where the Germans moved to round up all the Jews and put them in 'camps' where millions were murdered. He was lucky, if that could possibly be the word, because the Nazis kept alive some people who had needed skills, and watch repair was important. Eventually he was taken to Germany and forced to work at a facility in western Germany. After being freed by American troops, he found that his wife, two daughters, and son had been killed. He was hired to work for the Americans on their own military clocks and watches, and he then made his way, with the army's help, to our country.

"When Poland fell to Germany, his son was the very same age as you are now. He was also into his third year of his watchmaker's apprenticeship, just as you are. He keeps pretty much to himself nowadays, and of course he doesn't speak any English. Working with you now and then, I think, brings him back to a better time."

The Polish watchmaker found an effective way to communicate with me. As he stood over my bench watching me, a wrong action received a bop on the back of the head and a frown. Worse, and to be feared, was something he approved of. That resulted in a pinched cheek. I always wondered if my round face was due to too many approvals from a mentor.

One day when I expected him, he didn't come into the store. When I asked Uncle Abe, he said nothing, but looked quite sad.

One of the other watchmakers said to my uncle that my old mentor had really died in 1940. When you are thirteen you don't understand the meaning of this. I am happy to think that the young apprentice brought a lonely man a little bit of comfort.

A failing is my inability to cope with arrogance. I'd learned that the arrogant man is the one with the least reason to be arrogant.

We were, as always, behind in the watch repair. One man refused to accept the fact that we just had so many watches coming into the store and insisted that watch repair wasn't a great big deal. He boasted that if he had the tools, he'd do the job himself. Greatly impressed, I put the many, many loose pieces of his watch into a small lunch bag and offered the loan of the tools he needed. I heard nothing further.

A man brought in a Hamilton that had been repaired not too long before. Very few watches in those days were "shock proof" and the balance staff had been broken. Of course, all it required was the new staff, so the price was quite low, a reasonable (for the time) cost of $4.75. He was incensed at the huge price.

He complained, "That is outrageous. Just a little watch piece that could be replaced by anyone." That was the wrong thing to say.

I apologized, "I'm sorry I did not understand. You just want to purchase the balance staff so you can re-staff the watch yourself. That will be only forty-five cents. I'll put one into a little parts vial for you to take."

The gentleman looked at me and said, "I'll pick it up next week."

My father, who had opened the store in 1944, often said that he was "behind in the work" starting about ten days after he opened. As part of the setup, almost every store that had an in-house watchmaker had a "watch board." The one my father made was about two feet by five feet and hung on the back wall, visible to everyone who entered the store. This board had many, many rows of nails onto which were hung customers' watches. The right-hand section was for those watches that had been repaired and were being checked. The rest were watches awaiting pickup.

Before opening the store, Dad went up and down Front Street in Worcester, visiting each of the pawn shops located there. He had frequently helped them out by adjusting a watch to clinch a quick sale. Now he called in those favors. A "business lesson" for a young lad (me): Dad collected dozens of unclaimed and broken watches from each pawn shop and brought them to Milford. When Marcus Jeweler held its grand opening, the watch board was filled with watches awaiting pickup.

From that day to today, we have been behind in the work. A lesson in self-advertising. How to make a business grow. In truth, the volume of work became a serious problem. In the 1960s a critical problem developed. In the midst of the busy watch repair season, about thirty watches were "lost" by us. In the spring, people went outdoors after long captivity inside during the winter. Their watches, at the time not waterproof or shock proof, were very often, too often, "casualties of spring." People came to the store to pick up their watches and we could *not* find them. This was *not* possible because of the record system my father had designed.

One thing we both confessed to was a deep sense of paranoia over the safety of other people's property. Poor Dad was worried sick. There was not only the actual value of the lost property but the damage to our reputation to panic over. This was the time to panic. Over coffee (black, no sugar but two doses of poison) we tried to figure out what had happened. We searched and speculated for hours.

Finally Diane, a Milford High School junior who worked in the store, came in after school and simply asked, "Could those be the watches Barry told me to make go away?"

"What?!"

"Well," Diane replied to my father, "you and Barry were all upset about the amount of watches coming in. I had just written up about thirty (!) watches, and there was no room in the safe for them. I asked Barry where to put them, and he told me to put them where they would never be seen again." I thought she was going to cry as she concluded, "So I did what he said."

"Oh Lord," I thought, "she is going to cry, and I'm going to die... right now."

Before my father could erupt, Diane added, "So I put the box under the shelves way in the back room."

The opening into the back room was narrow enough that I had to turn slightly to enter. Nevertheless, Dad and I went through at the same time. Sure enough, carefully wrapped to protect them was a heavy box of watches, stored where they would "never be seen again." Need I say that I put in a lot of overtime catching up on the work?

When I related the sad tale of the "lost watches," my daughter Amy asked if I'd written up the story of the "*lost diamond.*" I admit, I'd totally forgotten about that incident. It was one that no one involved would want to remember.

A young woman came into the store to pick up her engagement ring, in for sizing and a prong replacement. It wasn't in the ready box, so I expressed a sincere apology for the ring not being ready and promised it in a few days. I explained that Marcus Jeweler took in an overwhelming volume of work and we were always somewhat behind. Thankfully she understood and even said that our inability to keep up was a tribute to our reputation for excellent work.

The following week she returned, and I went to the safe and...no ring! I double checked, tripled checked, and there was no ring. Now the friendly lady had no smile. The anger was apparent in her voice as she said that the ring had *better* be ready the following day or...

No further watch work was done while I took the store apart searching for the strayed diamond ring. I admit that a half-carat diamond is not the end of the world, but it was the half-carat engagement diamond of a young wife, and we were in trouble. There was, to put a point on it, no half-carat diamond ring in for repair.

I was upset, but my dad was sick over this. A store did not lose anything, let alone an engagement ring. One disaster like this would undo years of building up a reputation.

A month later, we'd been called to court. I was not too sure about the workings of the court system (thankfully) but there was a section called small claims court. This loss was in the jurisdiction of this court and it would be public record.

When the day of court came around I had to represent the store as Dad just couldn't go. I put on a good sport coat and my semiannual tie and walked to the Milford Town Hall where the court was held in a central hall. I walked along feeling the way Louis XVI must have felt as he strolled to the guillotine. I listened for the mocking applause of the crowd.

I walked into the courtroom, my heart in my mouth. I spotted the young wife in a forward row, sitting next to one of our long-standing regular customers. I screwed up my courage and greeted our customer, not making eye contact with the owner of the lost diamond.

Her reply froze my ears. "I am *not* talking to you ever again. You have lost my daughter's diamond ring. Wait till I tell my friends. You have broken her heart."

With whatever dignity I could muster, I went to the clerk and was informed that our case would probably not be called for at least thirty minutes. I had time to get to the store and back. I ran back up Main Street and into the store, pulled open the safe, and grabbed a box of completed jewelry repairs. I grabbed an envelope and actually ran out of the store without telling my father what was going on.

I was back in court for only ten minutes when our case was called. The proper procedure was carried out and it was my turn to speak. I took the envelope from my jacket pocket and began…

"Your Honor, the diamond ring has *not* been lost. What we did not realize was the ring had been brought into our store by one of our regular customers. When I took in the ring for sizing and a single prong repair, I naturally wrote my customer's name and address on the envelope…this is in my writing…but the ring is the property of her married daughter.

"When the daughter came to pick up the ring, she naturally asked for it under her name, her married name, which we never located in our store. This ring has been ready for pick up the entire time, but it was never looked for under *this* name. If her mother had not been in court this morning, I would not have known how we ever 'lost' the daughter's diamond ring. Even when I saw them sitting together, I did not understand. When Mrs. Titilo scolded me for losing her daughter's ring, it suddenly dawned on me."

I put the envelope on the judge's bench and asked him to show the enclosed ring to the plaintiff. The judge asked if the name on the envelope was that of the older woman, which it was, then held up the diamond ring for her daughter to examine. One glance and her eyes lit up as she put the diamond on her finger. Case dismissed.

The young woman apologized over and over and her mother also expressed deep regrets, which I insisted weren't necessary. Everything had worked out for the best. I also had to apologize as the whole tragedy was started when I, on my own, wrote the mother's name on the envelope. All's well that ends well, I guess.

I'm proud to say that not a single article was ever lost by us. Thankfully.

Watches, Uncle Abe always claimed, had the ability to "talk" to the watchmaker. Of course everyone knew that, I thought. After all, no one knows more than a sixteen-year-old with six years' experience. Eventually I learned that watches had the ability to "talk" to the watchmaker, but only if the watchmaker was smart enough to "listen." A person can communicate good health by a spring in his step or indicate problems by a careful, hesitant gait. A watch does the same thing. This is what Uncle Abe meant...listen and watch (no pun intended). Put the balance back in the movement and the watch starts to run...but it doesn't "look" happy. To the experienced benchman, there appears to be a lack of pep, of energy, as though the watch is trying to say, "I'd rather not run but rest for a while." We make an adjustment, tweak the hairspring or increase balance play, and the watch now says, "Whee! Look at me go. What a terrific day!" No one else would believe this, but it is true.

Watches are also very smart, as they communicate to watchmakers no matter the language they speak. As a doctor places his stethoscope to a patient's heart, so the watchmaker holds the repaired watch to his ear to listen to the sounds "spoken" by the watch. I understand that many auto mechanics do the same thing, only on something much larger. Turn the radio down, shush everyone, and listen intently. Oh, there is a little "something" every three seconds. Something is wrong with one of the escape wheel teeth. Less frequently it is a different wheel as they all turn at different speeds...escape wheel every three seconds, next a fourth wheel turning once a minute, and then the third wheel and the center wheel, which turns only once per hour. Listen as the watch talks to you.

My father told me that watches were tricky and sneaky and would play dirty tricks on the watchmaker. He came to watch repair later in life than was normal at the time. He'd been chosen by his family to be the *one* to go to college. He graduated from Boston University with a degree as a journalist, but that career was ended by the Great Depression and the birth of additional responsibility... starting with me. Uncle Abe taught him, finishing his training, and eventually my father passed his knowledge to me, adding another link to the chain.

Dad admitted to being hazy on some of the engineering and physics involved in building watches, but he always said he was not interested in either designing or actually building a watch...his job was repair. "Barry, a master mechanic may not know how to design the gearing for an engine, but he will keep it running. That is what we do...we keep the watch running."

"This watch is twelve years old. It is in for cleaning. Don't waste time counting the number of teeth on a given wheel...if it has been right for twelve years, and except for an 870 Waltham, watch wheels don't grow new teeth. (We hated that model.) If a tooth is broken, you will see it, but new ones don't grow. Sometimes you have to look for a solution that is really off the wall—stupid even."

That advice was how I figured out the problem with the tall case clock that I never saw, in the house I never went to, on the day I did not go out with the clockmaker. I found a solution that was, to be truthful, off the wall.

In the 1970s, a famous, respected, and revered watchmaker named Henry Fried wrote a column in the watchmaker's magazine. Watchmakers would write in technical problems of an aggravating nature, and Henry either solved the problem by mail or suggested an avenue of approach. In the summer of 1977, there was a questioning letter about a Swiss watch that, while only three years old, could not be adjusted to run properly. It was always slow, despite the fact that not a single thing was wrong. The writer had taken the watch to a friend who pronounced the watch perfect, but it just wouldn't keep time. Mr. Fried suggested many things, including checking the count of teeth on the train wheels and/or the dial train.

I sipped my coffee (black, no sugar) as I heard my father say (in my mind), "Barry, watches do not grow new teeth…ever. This watch came in for a cleaning and oiling. Something stupid is going on." Even if Dad was right, how could I find a "stupid" answer to a "stupid" problem? I couldn't even see the watch.

Another sip of coffee, and with a click, the solution came to me… think of something "off the wall." The watch in the magazine had a generic movement in it that I'd seen many, many times. Today the word "generic" is a put-down, but to call a "typical" Swiss movement of the day "generic" was a compliment. It took several hours before I had the courage to type out a letter to Mr. Fried. Who was I to suggest he was wrong?

There is an adjustment, critical in a watch, easy to correct, but a nuisance to correct. Swiss genius had come up with a way to affect the adjustment in a couple of seconds without even having to think about it. However, if something stupid happened to one watch out of several hundred thousand, that one watch could not be regulated, which was a different adjustment altogether. With a typewriter I put my good name and reputation on the line for the world to see—and possibly laugh at. I was truly nervous about making a public diagnosis of a technical dilemma being something stupid.

Two weeks later…a reply from Mr. Fried. I knew he thought my diagnosis of something "stupid" was itself "stupid."

Mr. Barry J. Marcus,

Thank you for your "stupid" idea. You thought it was "off the wall" but it was exactly right. WE NEED MORE LIKE YOU.

I've arranged to have this published.

Henry Fried

That letter was published two months *after* my father died. Having faith means I knew that Dad was aware of my…what word…triumph, coup, good job, whatever. He knew and, I think, was kind of proud. After all, not only was I his son, I was his pupil. One who heeded his

51

words. Now I confess…as a son I didn't always listen, but as a pupil I listened carefully. That worked out rather well, I think.

I've mentioned several times about my coffee drinking (black, no sugar). This went on all day, even when I was actually working on a watch. There was a railing around both Dad's and my benches, nicely paneled for looks, and the top rail was a two-by-three, which made a great place for me to keep my cup of coffee (black, no sugar). Dad didn't like me doing that and kept pointing out that one of these days I was going to knock a cup over and my entire bench was going swimming. Needless to say, that would be quite a problem. My father didn't give up easily, so for a little over a year he reminded me about what was going to happen one of these days. Yeah, sure, Dad.

Well, one fine day, I had just poured a cup of coffee (black, no sugar), and as I approached my bench, a customer walked into the store. I put the coffee cup on the railing and went to wait on our customer, actually bumping the rail as I went down front. Is it necessary for me to relate what happened, and all over the bench and the watches I was working on? (I didn't think so.) Without a word, I spent the rest of that day carefully wiping coffee (black, no sugar) from the bench and everything on it. The watches I had to run through the cleaner again as well as all the hand tools. When I was done, my bench was as clean as an operating room facility.

As an aside, my father did not finish a single watch that day as he sat at his bench quietly, his shoulders shaking in what I knew was silent laughter. He remained under control until he got home for supper. When asked how his day was, Dad couldn't get the tale out to tell my mother.

Exasperated, Mom called me to find out what was so funny that my father was sitting in the den laughing and with tears running down his cheeks. He had a weird sense of humor. Oh, I found a different place to put my coffee the next day.

Our benches were actually two feet apart with a walk aisle between. As we worked, we kibitzed back and forth about whatever crossed out minds. As the years passed, I noticed that he came to me for assistance on difficult things. I remember asking him if everything was okay, and he got serious.

"Barry, listen carefully. I am fine. Really. I come to you for help on some tough situations because you have become the one to go to for help. Remember Abe and I used to say that you were born knowing how to fix watches, only your hands were too small? That turned out to be true. I believe that to be a fact."

"Once, your uncle told me his intent to teach you the hardest of all things…hairspring work. But you were already adjusting and repairing hairsprings. When he pressed the issue, you said you were embarrassed to come to him and admit you bent a hairspring, so you just fixed it yourself so no one would know you made a mistake. Yes, you were born able to fix watches; just your hands were too small. Now I'll get a cup of coffee while you true up this Illinois hairspring."

One thing I will admit to is the fact that I had always seemed to understand mechanical devices, even at eight and nine. When I was *finally* introduced to the world of watches, I just truly seemed to understand them. In my mind, I could actually talk to watches and they talked back to me. When I started at the Instrumentman "A" School at the Great Lakes Naval Base, I seemed to have the same instant rapport with the typewriters I worked on. I could look at a machine and at once could trace the workings of varied sections and mechanisms. A couple of times the chief asked if I'd ever worked on typewriters before, and of course I hadn't. When I got to my ship, a huge destroyer tender, the USS *Frontier*, my instinctive knowledge of machines I'd never seen before came in handy. I didn't understand it and still don't, but I truly celebrate whatever mechanical instincts I was born with.

Dad and I went through a lot of coffee. I'd learned to drink it black, no sugar in the navy, and now I drank more cups of coffee per day than I'll put in writing. One day, after running through the raindrops to the Soda Shoppe for two coffees, I talked Dad into ordering a twelve-cup Farberware coffeepot. Now we perked our own, after our "wake up and get the blood flowing" morning coffee from the Soda Shoppe. Life was good.

The lessons we learn were often learned in the strangest ways. One day, while still getting coffee at the Soda Shoppe, I noticed Tulio, the owner, using two different coffee pots to get our coffee. Dad's coffee came from one pot, while mine came from a pot that had just finished dripping through. I asked about this extra work and learned a lesson about making a business *more* profitable.

Tulio quietly explained, "Your father drinks coffee with cream and two sugars, while you want navy coffee, straight black with no sugar. Your dad's coffee has sat around just about long enough for me to throw it out, but the cream and sugar flavoring will make the coffee taste just the way he likes it. Now your coffee, straight from the pot, had better be fresh, or you'll be back, or worse, will never come back again. I estimate I get three or more extra pots worth a day, and that is 365 days per year for my place. That would be a lot of money down the drain over the course of a year." Something to be filed away for future reference.

Now in 2009, I'd learned how to get an extra set of six watches cleaned in a given measure of ultrasonic solutions that cost $38 per gallon. It all added up.

Our benches being so close, my dad and I kibitzed back and forth while we worked. He told me about my grandfather, his father, born and raised in Lithuania, trained there, and owner of a jewelry store there. My father's father was some sort of super mechanic, because while he made his living as a watchmaker, he, a Jew in an area with many anti-Semites, was protected by the local police. The details I never knew, except that my grandfather was able to keep the police sergeant's motorcycle running properly. When he came to the United States and settled in Worcester, he continued as a watchmaker but made things for his own use. Grandpa Marcus did not know about patents. Too bad.

He taught the trade to his sons, although only Abe stayed with it. Uncle Jake didn't like it and did other things. My own father was charged with going to college. It was only during World War II that he became, under Abe, a watchmaker. Then I came along.

While we talked, a story developed. Our family name came down from ancient Rome. Our early ancestor, a free citizen named Marcus Timus, was chief sundial technician at the time of Julius Caesar. Tragically, Marcus Timus mis-set the large sundial in the central square, causing Caesar's bodyguard to be late for work that fateful day. When the reason for Caesar's assassination became known, Marcus Timus barely escaped safely out of town. We both thought this story was delightful and often blamed watch problems on Marcus Timus.

Years later, my daughter Julie, while at college, wrote about the legend of Marcus Timus in an English composition about her family. Big problem. While she got an *A* on the report, the professor, making the name connection, bought the story lock, stock, and mainspring. A nervous moment came when he told Julie that other people were going to be shown this "exciting family story." She managed to explain the family legend without insulting the gullible professor. The professor was disappointed, and we got a good chuckle out of the latest Marcus Timus development.

Did my grandfather's mechanical instinct come down to me? Who knows, but I too had ideas and made things for my personal use. I thought up and made an "automatic watch winder" before there was any such thing. It was a simple, twelve-inch-diameter X. Attached to a slowly rotating electric motor, it would test the selfwinding mechanism of a watch. It was run all day and unplugged at night, approximating the usage by the owner. It worked brilliantly, but it never occurred to me to seek out a patent for anything like that.

I had a close friend who was employed at a General Electric plant in Ashland. One Sunday, over more coffee (black, no sugar), he mentioned that GE was having a special "contest," for want of a better word. Employees were encouraged to put in their suggestions for new products that GE could manufacture and market. Any product actually brought to market would bring *great financial rewards* to he/she who suggested it.

At the time there was a late night TV show called *The Tonight Show.* This was the same NBC late night program that is still on, but now the name of the star is more prominently featured. Anyhow, Jack Paar was the host of a popular show that did not go off the air until 1:00 a.m. Millions of people fell asleep watching Jack Paar and had to get up some time during the night to shut the TV off. Of course, we got up to an alarm clock (which I would not fix).

Why, I do not know, but within half a minute I had what I knew would be a sure winner for my friend.

"Look, your company makes two products that we all use. They make a clock/radio that has a clock that can be set to turn the radio on or off, just like an alarm clock. The other is the line of smaller TVs people use in their bedrooms and watch Jack Paar on NBC. Tell them to make the molds for a TV set that has a clock/ timer wired into it. People could turn on Paar and set the clock to shut off at the end of his show. Wait a minute, they could *also* set the clock to turn the TV *on* in the morning as an alarm clock. The TV would already be set to the *Today* show on NBC. They wouldn't even have to change channels. The TV would turn itself on in the morning at their chosen time and they would shut it off with the TV switch when they go to work. Then turn it back on with the TV switch when they go to bed, letting the clock turn off the TV when Paar is over. Even if they've gone to sleep, the TV will be off. I bet that'll absolutely be a sure winner for you. I'll help you sketch it out and write it up."

I knew that such a finished product was not on the market at the time. I had plugged our bedroom TV into a timer and used it exactly that way. I knew people would buy them. GE already made clock/radios that worked in that exact way, and I was merely making an "electronic marriage."

"No," I was told, "no one is ever going to buy a TV to use as an alarm clock. That is silly. Thanks for the idea, but I don't think so." Need I point out that such a thing was introduced to the market about a year later by another company? My friend shortly afterward acknowledged his grave error. What could I do?

My girls grew up in the family store, Marcus Jeweler. Carol, Julie, and Amy grew up in an atmosphere that taught them much about the world. They learned about "people" as they waited on customers for many years. They learned from an early age that "there is always something to be done." Gift wrapping was an important service that we offered customers. Back in the day, we made all the bows that went on the presents. During Christmas season, I'd load a spool of ribbon into the bow-making machine, and the girls (starting at age five) would fill garbage bags with bows. Eventually we had two bow machines, and the race was on.

As the girls got older, each learned to engrave and do jewelry repair, which eased the workload for me. Having the girls work alongside me was a tremendous source of pride. Their presence and help enabled me to keep up with the watch repair, jewelry repair, and the engraving.

Julie was the only one of the girls who was interested in watch repair. I'll admit now that I was excited at the possibility of having the first female watchmaker in the family. I'm not sure how old she was, but she was in middle school when I started to train her. Every day after school, Julie would come into the store and sit at her grandfather Papa Rael's bench. I gave her a 16S pocket watch and we started the lessons. Oy, I was proud. She did a great job learning part names, which tools did what, how to take the watch apart, and, most importantly, how to put it back together.

It wasn't long before Julie could take apart and put back together the 16S pocket watch in running condition. Time to start really learning how to fix a watch. I gave Julie back the watch but I "adjusted" a wheel so the watch would not run. I don't know how many times she tried, but she worked on the watch for a quite a few days. The watch wouldn't run and she couldn't see the "adjusted" wheel. Finally, in frustration and tears, Julie tossed the watch on the bench (with quite a bit of force), thus ending the career of the first female Marcus watchmaker.

Ironically, it was Julie who later became the store pro at restringing pearls; a thankless job that takes a tremendous amount of time and patience.

The traditions of a watchmaking family continued. The phone in my store rang. It was my cousin Beatrice, wife of Cousin Marty, another watchmaker trained by Uncle Abe. Bea announced, "Bobby is finishing at Bulova this week. We are sending him to your store and he'll be there next Monday. Take care." End of conversation, and I had my own student watchmaker.

Bobby came, he sat, he learned. Today, I am rather proud of *my* student watchmaker. He is what I call—good. Rather often our phones now ring and one of us is at the other end, relating a triumph or asking for help with a watch that won't cooperate. Several times Bobby was amazed that I could solve a problem without personally examining the watch of the moment. I had to remind him that back in 1951 or 1972 I had the same problem with the same watch. Nothing is new under the sun. Bobby is keeping Holden, Massachusetts on time. There is another cousin, Alan, who has his business in Worcester.

Bobby's father, Marty, and I are the two of our generation who became watchmakers. Another cousin, Chick (not really his name, but most people never knew or even heard of his real name), did not have an interest in watch repair, but wanted electronics. Still in a family tradition, he apprenticed to his uncle Irving in the TV and radio field. Chick's mother, Auntie Anna, was heartbroken and worried about the economic future of her younger son. If he didn't get into watch repair, how could he ever support a family of his own? I did feel bad for him as we grew up. All he managed to do was be personally involved in the final assembly of the Raytheon electronics installed in the moon landing spacecraft. Poor fellow.

On a side note, it comes to mind that Auntie Anna must have been friendly with my grandmother, even though they lived fifty-five miles apart and seldom saw each other. My grandmother, who blackmailed me into repairing her clock, must have "ratted" me out.

Auntie Anna's oven turned out "tasties" that one would crawl over hot coals for. Since we lived just across a narrow alley, I often visited, especially when I knew there was baking going on. One day I went to their apartment to return a watch I'd adjusted and found her standing on a chair, trying to free a dust cloth from a snag on the top of a kitchen window trim. At six-foot-four at the time, I reached up and freed it and helped her from the chair.

When I went to the plate of cinnamon bulkies, my hand was gently slapped. There were more windows and door trim that needed dusting. I just knew she'd spoken to Nana.

From then on, there was a pile of dust rags on the top of the refrigerator, just waiting for a hungry teenager to come begging. Thanks, Nana.

My youngest daughter, Amy, went to school in Pennsylvania to learn and then master the trades of jewelry repair and hand engraving. Hand engraving, years ago, was a vital part of a jewelry store's effort to provide the customer with true service. Virtually everything that could be was engraved. From the huge watch adorned with *her* picture to smallish ladies' watches, beautiful engraving related messages of love, devotion, and pride. Many had initials and, to the extreme, masterfully done monograms. From one generation to the next, and then to the next, the engraving remained... to be read over and over again as a reminder of people and times long past.

As it turned out, the engraving on many watches assisted the watch-maker in solving difficult problems. As Dad and Uncle Abe often said, "the problem with a watch can be found in the owner."

We always had a problem with engraving, as the store was in Milford while we lived in Worcester. This meant that each article to be engraved had to be delivered to the engraver, Tony, in downtown Worcester. Tony was really an artist with his gravers, and I frequently asked him when my plates for printing $5 bills would be ready. When I was a twelve-year-old delivering and picking up, he laughed. By the time I was in my midteens, it was no longer anything to laugh about. Finally, a sternly delivered lecture broke my search for the "perfect" money plate.

In the summer of 1957, I, with assistance from my mother, prevailed upon a very reluctant father to make a purchase for the store of our very own engraving machine. The basic intent was to ease the burden of carrying repairs and engravings over to downtown Worcester virtually every day. At that time I was doing only watch repair, meaning everything else had to be "sent out." The "engraving department" I was going to set up was quite costly for its day…about $350 total.

I had a shiny new machine engraver, two sizes of "script," and one size of "block" type. Once set up, I spent each spare moment practicing on small pieces of brass stock. Again, for whatever reason, once I read the instructions on setting up the machine, I just seemed to know how to do the engraving. It all came automatically to me. I even came up with the idea of doing engraving, very lightly, on Scotch Magic Tape. With a strip of tape adhered to the (whatever) I could lightly engrave the tape itself, thus assuring me that the letters were properly centered and sized. This little trick prevented hundreds of engraving errors over the intervening years.

The first fall, then Christmas season, of our store doing all its own engraving was busier than I believed possible. As most service-oriented jewelry stores did back then, we engraved articles we sold without charge. To be honest, there were motives behind the free service. First there was the service itself, a reason for people to come to our store rather than a competitor's. Then there was the fact that the engraving on a gifted watch or locket or ring or bracelet or lighter would make the gift even more special. To tell the whole truth, it was a wonderful thing that an article, once engraved, was *never* returned or exchanged.

Dad was still unhappy about the high cost of the equipment, and he did have a point. Engraving only went to Tony if an article was sold, thus no engraving meant no costs. I had committed over $350 in expense, even if we never did another engraving.

During the busy season, I spent a great deal of time, overtime, and Sundays at the engraving bench, going through roll after roll of Scotch Magic Tape and pots of coffee (black, no sugar). Then my mother, who worked with us during the busy, busy month of December, would defingerprint each article and get it ready for delivery. With practice I had been able to really shorten the time each gift took to engrave.

Finally the season came to an end, and we smiled at having had a very good business month. Then a surprise. Mom called a business conference and smugly made an announcement. It seemed that she had been secretly recording each and every engraving job I'd done and entering the amount of money that *would* have been paid to the hand engraver. She always kept the store's books and really managed the family's finances. My father, a man of strong opinions and beliefs, would never argue or even discuss Mom's rulings money wise.

"Last year, we gave the engraver $390 between the beginning of November and Christmas Eve. This fall we paid $375 grand total for all the engraving equipment and stuff Barry bought," our bookkeeper/wife/mother announced. She smiled at me. "In November and December, Barry did engraving that would have cost us $430 if paid to the engraver. In plain English, after eight weeks, that engraving setup has become an absolute free item for the store."

Naturally, there were no labor costs involved in our new engraving department. This was a traditional family store, and work was over *only* when it was finished. No one counted hours or days, just work accomplished. Over the years, I've engraved thousands of articles of all kinds, and I'm proud to claim that I've made many of those articles into precious mementoes.

No matter how good something is, problems can and do develop. Sometimes the ability to read and the knowing of people can create its own problem. A large number of years ago, I sold a beautiful piece of jewelry, 14K gold and diamonds, to a longtime customer. This was one of the costlier pieces I'd ever sold, and of course I suggested making it even more personal with an engraved message. Of course, a great idea. Carefully I printed his exact directions. I stress "carefully" because any writing in my normal scrawl could well be misread and the article engraved wrong. That sad occurrence is one of my not too proud memories.

Martha
With all my love
12-25-XX

Uh-oh. We now had the potential for a great problem. This was a disaster just waiting to happen...to explode in someone's face. What was the problem? Why was I so upset...? I was being told to engrave an expensive piece of jewelry for a customer whose wife was named Sadie, not Martha.

The article was carefully engraved, and I hid the finished article in a drawer in my bench to prevent anyone from seeing the envelope. Doctors and lawyers are not the only people who must keep a client/ customer's privacy.

So long ago that no one involved can still be alive, a jeweler friend sold a 2.5-carat diamond dinner ring. This was a beautifully designed ring that contained many smaller diamonds than the solitaire found in a typical engagement ring. The stones in this ring were large for the style and weighed a total of 2.5 carats in an 18K white setting. The jeweler knew the wife's, shall we say, chubby fingers would require the ring to be returned for sizing, so he told the customer to have the missus bring the ring in quickly, in order that it be ready for wear on New Year's Eve.

Christmas came and went; New Year came and went; Valentine's Day came and went, without the ring being returned. During the last week in February, my jeweler friend and his wife were shopping and met Mrs. Diamond Dinner Ring. As a jeweler anxious to provide the best of service, he asked why the magnificent diamond ring had not been returned for proper sizing.

The answer, "*What diamond ring?*" stopped my friend's heart, and he shortly was treated for frostbitten ears. The tragedy played out in a divorce court, with my friend forced to describe the ring, the cost, and anything else he was asked. The betrayed wife took everything she could, the jeweler's customer was ruined financially, and most people turned against the jeweler, who had only wanted to service something he sold to a steady customer. For the next three years, the store barely survived, frequented by a much less financially able clientele. All too often he was admonished not to say anything about an article he'd just sold. My heart went out to him, but I learned his lesson.

As an aside, he once mentioned that he also sold watches and gents' rings that were engraved with initials *not* those of the husband. Occasionally a watch would come in for service bearing a tiny mark he used to identify his merchandise, but worn by a man positively not married to the purchaser. That is where I learned to "shut up."

A man brought an engraving job into the shop a year ago. Could I possibly engrave his name onto the slide of a .45 pistol? I explained that I could, just not really deeply as the steel was so hardened that I'd break the diamond point if I used too much pressure. Out of his pocket he took the .45, a US Army 1911 model, in what looked to be very good condition. I carefully wrote down the needed information, and he handed over the pistol to me.

I'd only done a stint in the navy and did not have real training in the handling of guns of any kind. Once, on an all-expenses-paid voyage to Hong Kong, several sailors were on the fantail (extreme rear) of my ship shooting at bottles and cans tossed overboard. I paid one of them for a full clip for a .45, as I had always wanted to shoot, at least once in my life. He showed me how to insert the clip, how to remove it, and how to pull back the slide to bring a round into the chamber. I followed instructions and then carefully assumed the directed stance and took careful aim at my chosen target. I must admit I do not know how many rounds that gun held, but I can proudly state that I put every bullet into my target…the Sea of Japan. My career as a gunman was over. I released the now empty clip and returned the .45 to its sailor. I would return to the machinist workshop.

So with an automatic movement that had its roots in 1955, I without thinking activated the magazine release…and a *fully loaded* clip fell onto the counter! Scared out of my head, I drew back the slide, and a round popped out of the chamber! In the name of God, this idiot had handed across the counter a *fully loaded* .45 with "one up the spout." I cannot type out what I hollered at that idiot, as the fines imposed by my daughter would be too costly, but the .45 was *not* engraved.

A week later, over coffee, I related this horror story to the Milford Chief of Police. He just looked at me for a minute then said, "If you had taken in that loaded gun for engraving, you would have been in serious violation of gun laws. In a sense, you were very lucky you threw the S-O-B out of the shop like you did."

A phone call. "Can you engrave something to the inside cover of a pocket watch?"

"Sure, just bring it in so I can look at it to make sure there's enough room."

The following morning a man about my age walked in and put a pocket watch on the counter. Without opening the cover, I knew it was an 18S Waltham, probably a twenty-year case, but it looked as though it had about 235,000 miles on it. The case was rough. As we chatted for a moment, I opened the case cover to check on available room and... uh-oh...I saw the itinerary of a lifetime's travel...

TEXAS MARYLAND

CALIFORNIA PENNSYLVANIA ARIZONA

ST. PAUL HOUSTON

MIDWAY

Wait a minute...this was not a travel memory...these were the names of US Navy ships!

Five battleships, two cruisers, and a carrier, but the *Arizona?* Oh Lord. I looked up at him, and he nodded. "Yeah, this was my father's naval career...every ship. Mostly battleships, just two cruisers, and the *Midway*, and I'd like the name of his last ship engraved. Is there room enough?"

"Of course there is. Most ships' names were rather short. Even tin cans were known by only their last name and hull number."

"Oh, if you know that, then you did a cruise or two yourself. Small world."

I took the job envelope and wrote out a name and address and asked for the ship's name.

It was carefully spelled out...*F R O N T I E R.*

FRONTIER...what the heck was this? Without a word, I went into my office and came out with a printout of a US Navy ship...named... *Frontier* AD25...my own ship!

He was delighted as I explained that I had also served on the *Frontier,* my one and only ship, and I pointed out the location of my repair shop on the aft port side on the main deck. Old home week for a few delightful minutes. His father had served on her in the late 1940s while I didn't show up until 1955 1956. His father, deceased for several years, had served from 1935 until 1965 and retired a chief on thirty years.

Quietly I asked about the *Arizona.* "Yeah, he was on it, on deck when it blew. He landed about a hundred feet away and got picked up later by one of the whaleboats that went out picking up survivors. He always felt a little guilty about surviving, but now he's back with his buddies." Nothing further to say...nothing at all.

He returned the following week, and as he reached for his wallet, I quietly shook my head. "Put it away. Just do me a favor…cherish this watch and what it stands for."

I am now reminded of another incident a couple of years ago. A man and woman came into the shop, and the first thing I noticed was his hat. At the front, above the brim, was a representation of a large ship and the name *Yosemite*.

I was delighted and exclaimed, "Well, well, a real Yo-Yo is here."

His wife got very angry and exclaimed, "We do not have to put up with such insults. I don't see how someone that dumb expects to stay in business. Come on, we're leaving." She tugged on her husband's arm, but he pulled away.

"Hold on now," he said and laughed happily. "What are you…a *Canyon* runner or buckskin wearer? Do you have your coonskin hat in the closet? Where's your Kentucky long rifle? In that closet?" And he reached over the counter to shake hands.

He turned to his wife. "Relax, a Yo-Yo to him is a crewmember of the *Yosemite*, my ship, and he's from one of the other destroyer tenders, either the *Bryce Canyon* or the *Frontier*."

I ducked into the back office and came back with the printout from the "net" of the USS *Frontier*, my ship. I proudly pointed out the location of my shop at the fantail, and he showed me the location of his place, which was up forward. We'd been at the same place, but at different times. A fun reunion…even the wife enjoyed the visit. When she left, she said she'd never heard that expression before spoken in friendship, and her husband grinned as he told her those were some of the more polite nicknames.

My father *never* retired from the bench. After I'd bought the store, he continued to repair watches, mostly at Uncle Abe's store in Worcester. On Thursdays he came to Milford and helped with the impossible task of trying to keep up with the work. I was, the store was, and had *always* been, behind with the repairs. There was no way to keep up with the volume.

There were other benefits also. My youngest, Amy, would "sneak" into the store after school on Thursdays and crouch near her grandfather's bench making kitty cat sounds. My father would be alarmed. "I hear kitties! I better feed them so they will be quiet." He and Amy would go into the back room to partake of the most absolutely awful milk crackers that they both loved. I tried one, half of one, only once and politely refused their invitations to the tea hour in our back room.

When he came to Milford on Thursdays, my father always had six or seven watches with him. He was doing trade work for a couple of jewelry stores in Worcester, in Uncle Abe's store. Abe, though, did not have a timing machine, so it took him three or four days to regulate a watch, a task that took minutes with a timing machine.

Each week, Dad timed his watches. His older brother, Abe, didn't really believe in newfangled things like timing machines, to the point that he didn't touch any of the new electric or electronic watches. We took care of those for him, of course.

I had purchased something new, an ultrasonic watch cleaning machine from Bulova. A marvelous invention that enabled the watchmaker to clean six watches at a time as opposed to the then normal three. Not only that, but with the ultrasonic machine, the watch did not have to be completely taken apart. A fantastic time-saver. In one step it both increased the amount of watches we could turn out and improved the quality of the work. My father loved working with this new machine when he came to Milford, mentioning his regret that Abe didn't go in for newer things.

I can be a good son at times. I showed up at Abe's store one day with my ultrasonic cleaner and all its accessories. "Dad, this is three years old. I just got a brand new one, also from Bulova. I only have room for one, so do me a favor and use this one here in Worcester. The only thing is, it is still *mine*, and if anything goes wrong with my new one, I'll have to reclaim this one quickly. Okay?" My father was a nice guy and agreed to safeguard my spare ultrasonic.

Another four months of Dad timing his watches in Milford. I asked if he ever considered getting a timing machine, but he couldn't afford one. I realized that I needed another favor.

Into Worcester with my "old" timing machine under my arm. "Dad, I need another favor, if you don't mind. I'm doing a good number of Accutrons, and this old-style timer will not work with them. There's a new machine from Watchmaster (Bulova) that translates the hum of the tuning fork onto a tape so I can read out the timing. How about if you use this one here? Same as the cleaning machine. If anything goes wrong with the new one, I'd have to come get this one. Okay?"

Dad thought it over and agreed to take care of my timing machine for me. He was always helpful, if you know what I mean.

Three weeks later he came to Milford. "Barry, your uncle actually asked me to time a watch for him…a man's Bulova. It was thirty seconds a day slow, and it took me about fifteen seconds to adjust and time it. Abe won't say anything, but he really is impressed. We are going to bring him into the modern world."

As the years ticked by (pun not intended), my father lost a good deal of his hearing and had difficulty listening to the watch speak to him. My brother-in-law Chuck, an engineer and good kid, took a cigar box and, doing some black magic, built a gizmo that picked up the sounds of a watch and amplified it to a great degree.

Dad worked at the bench until just a couple of weeks before he died. Some years later, Uncle Abe died. Abe was still going to his store every day, working on watches. With the exception of three friends who were forced by reasons of health to leave the bench, I have known only one watchmaker who willingly put aside the tools and retired. Only one.

In 1960, Bulova introduced the Accutron, a battery-powered tuning-fork-controlled watch. The tuning fork vibrated at a controlled frequency and powered an almost traditional watch train, and the whole thing told time to an amazing accuracy.

Many watchmakers at the time were reluctant to get involved with this new development, but the Bulova Company was infinitely helpful in training watchmakers to repair and service their new watch. Evening-long seminars were held in most major cities of the country, no charge, with coffee and danish provided. Other companies, notably Hamilton, also introduced electric watches, but those relied on a traditional balance wheel and hairspring, though they were driven by batteries. Personally I believe the idea of the electric watch was a prime example of a product that could be built but should *never* have been built.

Watches had been always powered by a mainspring, coiled in a barrel around a central arbor. Three steel gears facilitated the winding, and the watch kept time for basically thirty-six hours, more or less. This was a twenty-four-hour run with a power reserve. In the day, the customer was directed by the owner's manual to wind the watch *daily*, preferably in the morning on waking up. Thus winding one's watch became one more part of a daily ritual, done almost without thinking.

The battery-powered balance wheel watch replaced the very simple mainspring with a high-tech electronic circuit complete with a very fragile coil assembly. During the 1950s, the Elgin Watch Company introduced what they called the DuraPower mainspring. This was a traditional spring but made of a new material Elgin had invented that made the spring reliable enough to be called "unbreakable." This formerly ultra reliable piece had been replaced, with pride, by a fragile, undependable, high-tech piece of plastic with stuff on it.

One truth stands out: electronics die when they suddenly feel like it.

The Accutron replaced both the mainspring as a power source as well as the balance and escapement as a controlling device. Yet in the center were traditional watch wheels, levers, and springs. We learned to service the watches we sold.

I sold an Accutron to a local lawyer. He loved the watch and enjoyed announcing to one and all that he was the one with the right time. Sadly, his family was soon seemingly stricken with some health problems. They were edgy, slept poorly, and became very sensitive to anything said to them. Some weeks later he fell, and as he hit the pavement, the watch took the brunt of the force. The crystal was broken as were both the sweep and minute hands. Also a sharp piece of the crystal scratched through the finish on the dial. The watch was left for repair, but I told him I'd have to send out for new hands, and the dial had to go for refinishing, which would take about three or four weeks. I loaned him a wind-up watch and he left. I saw him a couple of weeks later getting coffee and asked after his family.

"Fine," he said with a smile, "sleeping well again, all calmed down. Even the little one doesn't hear the 'noise' anymore."

I thought, "That's odd," but only said, "I'm so glad," and went back to work.

At the time, I was wearing the only brand-new watch I'd ever owned, an Accutron diver's watch, costly for the day. A couple of nights later, my wife told me, "Take the darn watch off when we go to bed. You sleep with your arm against the headboard and the lousy humming noise is keeping me up at night." The watch came off that night.

A day or two later, I suddenly lifted my head from a very sick watch and thought, "The *noise* kept her up at night?" *His little one doesn't hear the* NOISE *anymore!* This was absolutely not possible. I called my friend and asked him to please come to the store at lunchtime.

"Look," I asked, "what do you do with your Accutron at night?"

"Are you nuts?" I was asked.

I finally got my answer. At night he carefully took off the Accutron and put it on the top of the toilet tank in their bedroom lavatory. He also mentioned that the problems at home began about the time he bought the Accutron, and they started to clear up when he broke it.

That evening I went with him to his home and, without much conversation, put my Accutron in the indicated place on the back of the toilet. Downstairs in the kitchen—this was surely not possible—I could hear a faint humming. My friend, following directions, stayed in the kitchen while I went upstairs and took the watch from the toilet. I counted to thirty and put the watch back. Downstairs I was informed that the humming had stopped for half a minute and then started again and he could still hear it.

His "little one" came into the kitchen, stopped, and started to cry, "The noise is back."

I didn't understand it; I never accepted the possibility, but that tuning fork Accutron somehow resonated from the toilet throughout the house, especially in the quiet of night. That was what my wife was talking about, but in my case, the headboard acted as a sounding board. I suggested placing the Accutron in the box on the dresser at night. For a while I thought he was going to place the watch in the center of the street that ran by his house, but he kept the watch.

Weird, that a watch could affect the health of an entire family. More weird is that Dr. Marcus cured the family.

The Accutron was a great breakthrough in timekeeping. I believe it ensured the future dominance, if only for a while, of the electronic watch. However, as with all new technology, it had its quirks. Several years after the introduction of the Accutron, I was at a general social gathering where the normal conversation consisted of, "What do you do?" Then, "What do *you* do?" And so on. The fact that I was a watchmaker caught the attention of someone I'd just met. I could sense he wanted to ask a question, but I said nothing.

After a few minutes, he reluctantly said, "Look, I own this Accutron, cost a bundle, but since the day I've owned it, it's been losing time. The store (a BIG one) sent it to Bulova three times until I gave up, and I now just set it ahead three times a month. They advertised it to be accurate to a couple of seconds a day, but this doesn't make it."

Many, many years ago, Uncle Abe said, "Barry, it is about the people. We must remember to listen to them...look at them...speak to them."

I listened...I looked...I spoke.

"Here's the problem," I replied. "None of the people at that store knew enough to see that you're a lefty. You're wearing your watch on your right wrist. Which is normal. Watches are always worn on the opposite wrist, to keep them out of the way."

"No way," he came back, "you haven't even looked at my watch, and you're telling me that the people who checked and serviced this watch didn't know what they were doing? Please."

"No, they knew exactly what they were doing. They adjusted your Accutron perfectly according to specs. But they didn't adjust the watch to you. I have a sheet that says, 'If worn on the right wrist of a left-handed person, gravity will so affect the watch as to require it be adjusted two seconds per day *fast* on the timing machine.' When on the wrist it will run properly, but no one knew enough to check which wrist you were wearing this watch on. Tell you what," I said, "you come to my store in Milford and I'll tweak the tuning fork regulators. No charge…it'll be an ego thing for me." I knew he wouldn't show up; no one would drive forty miles just to get a watch "tweaked."

Naturally, two days later, he walked into the store. What could I do but tweak the regulators? My directions to him were simple: "Leave the watch alone, don't touch it, but wear it like always. Check back in four weeks."

I knew I wouldn't see him again, so naturally he walked back into the store exactly four weeks later. The watch was precisely thirteen seconds off for the month. In my mind I heard my uncle say to me, "Listen to them, talk to them, look…sometimes the problem is *not* the watch." Smart man, my uncle.

A man brought a nice ladies' watch in for repair. Another nice Hamilton (all Hamilton made was nice watches) that had been giving trouble for some time. In due course, he came in a couple of weeks later to pick it up, accompanied by his wife. Uh-oh. A serious problem to overcome. The question was how to handle this.

"Please, while I write up the guarantee, will you wind and set the watch?" I asked the woman, a pleasant-looking lady who appeared to be in her early sixties. While she wound the watch, I made out the guarantee and then took back the watch.

"We have a problem. I have to keep the watch for an hour. Watch as I finish winding the watch that you just wound." Sure enough, it took a number of turns of the crown until the mainspring tightened. Now how did I say this delicately?

"You can't wind the watch. The years have passed by and you have arthritis in your fingers. It's quite obvious. Well, the crown on the watch is the exact one specified by the designers of the watch, but it's no longer good for you. Your fingers can't grip the crown to turn it. I saw your fingers actually slip over the crown without turning it. Like a smooth tire on a snowy street. Now that I see this, there's no more problem…I'll keep the watch for an hour, unwind it from inside, and put on a size larger crown. When you come back, I'll have you try to wind it and we'll see."

An hour later they came back and we tried again, but with no better results. "No worry," I said, "the crowns step up in size very gradually, depending on the size of the case. What I'm doing is fitting a new crown to your fingers, not to the case."

Back to the bench, and I jumped the crown from a 4.25 mm beveled crown to a 5.00 mm flat one. This was up two sizes and a little thicker in addition. I handed the watch to the lady, and as she attempted to turn the crown, I could actually see her face light up.

A few turns and she gave me the watch, grinning widely. Sure enough, the watch was completely wound and would run its full designated time.

"I could feel the difference at once," she enthused, "it was like magic. Thank you so much. This was my wedding present from my husband. Thank you; it would have broken my heart if I couldn't wear this anymore."

As they happily left the shop, my thoughts turned to my dad. "You know, Dad, it's like you said. It's not so much what you have to say… it's how you say it. I didn't blame her or her fingers. No, I said it was the years that had passed. It's important not to make a customer (or anyone) feel bad about something they cannot control."

Yes, I talked to my dad. I talked to watches…I talked to machines… I talked to my car…I talked to an uncle long gone. "You were right,

Uncle Abe, look—the problem can be the customer." Oh, I also talked quite a bit to my boat. And yes, sometimes I *did* get answers.

Years ago, in the nearby town of Upton, there was a multi-story sprawling New England-type factory building that housed a hat factory. The owner and chief assistant were up from New York City and I saw them often on Friday night at Sabbath services and at least monthly at B'nai Brith breakfasts. One Sunday morning, about six months after I'd met them, we were together at breakfast when I mentioned that I thought the colors in the coming spring line of hats were very pretty. Both men became very upset and quickly left the building. I shrugged and followed.

The following morning, the assistant came into the store and asked my father how I knew about the hats. Dad had no idea what he was talking about and said so. That only angered our visitor and he stalked out. That afternoon, "Mr. Owner" called and asked the same question, and he received the same answer, upon which he slammed down the phone. Poor Dad wondered what the heck this was all about, but I did not volunteer the information. I was just young enough to think this was fun.

Months later, at another breakfast, I again mentioned that I liked the rich and vivid colors of the new line. Same reaction. I paid no attention to fashion and did not know that in the world of fashion designers the new styles are very closely held secrets. I guess not only designs, but colors were held as "military secrets." To me, who cared?

After another year, and two more "bombshells," the hat people began to get desperate. Of course no secrets ever got out, but how did that wiseacre kid know these things? I had solemnly promised my father that I would never do anything to hurt the hat company, but to tell the truth, this really was fun. In reality, Dad honestly didn't know how I was guessing the colors. I continued to be a young man pulling the leg of a hat company.

After five years of driving the poor hat people frantic, I believe the factory was sold as the downturn in New England textile mills started. Before they moved back to New York, the two men came one last time into the store to ask for the secret source of my knowledge. Remarkably, this was the first time they asked *me* about the source. During all their other visits to investigate, the men had directed their questions to my dad.

"Okay," I said, "really, it's simple. Not a single person in the factory ever betrayed the company...that I promise you. Many of your women and girls at the sewing machines are our customers and they bring their watches in for service."

Now my father came close, wondering what watch repair had to do with his son's successful "industrial espionage."

"When I opened their watches," I continued, "they were most often full of fuzz and lint from whatever cloth they were working with. Especially felt. Pink, blue, black, whatever color, it was obvious." I could see looks of disbelief.

I told them that when they pressed Dad for my "secret" it became a game, but I assured them that I had told no one. The two men stared at me, then turned and walked from the store without a word.

"I don't think they like you," my father said. As a full-fledged adult now, I think that I don't blame them for being a little upset.

On the chance you missed it, I do *not* repair clocks. There was a time when a local pharmacist was a highly respected businessman. Usually owning his own store, he was known to all. My pharmacist, whose store was just down the street, was a man fully as big as I am. Two men, both six feet five inches and quite a bit too heavy, who when standing close together could cause the floor to sag. I drove an Oldsmobile station wagon that at least matched my size. However, my friend proudly drove a tiny MG sports car.

I think the word "drove" is not correct...rather, he "put the car on" in the morning and drove from Upton to Milford each morning. Often I wondered who helped him out of the car.

One day—betrayal at the hand of a friend. My pharmacist came into the store holding a clock in his hand.

"Barry," he announced, "this is the clock from my MG. I'm entering it in a car show in two weeks and I want the clock to work. Thanks a lot."

My answer was automatic, "Sorry, I don't do clocks. I can't help you with this. Sorry."

His reply came swiftly, "C'mon...this once. Don't I put everything aside and fill your kids' prescriptions the moment you carry them in? Now you won't help me out?"

My reply, "Did you ever meet my grandmother?" stymied him, but the clock was repaired. I consoled myself with the knowledge that it was a very small clock, smaller than many pocket watches.

The day after the auto show, he ran into the store. "Barry," he shouted, "you did it. My car tied for first place, but when I showed the judges that the clock in my MG was running and on time, I won first place! Everybody was asking who I got to fix the clock. No one will repair them."

I scooted down from my bench. "Look, I don't fix clocks...period. I repaired your clock for your car. If anyone finds out it was me, I'll know you squealed and you'll find your car with four flats one bright morning. I don't fix clocks."

No one ever learned who repaired his clock. Most likely I would not have flattened his tires...most likely.

About this time, a customer came in with an aircraft clock. I didn't fix clocks and was worried that word might get around that I did. I remembered the first military clock that I repaired in Uncle Abe's store. I had to admit that it was really an oversize Waltham watch, enlarged enough that it had to be called a clock. This was brought home after the war, taken by the pilot who knew that his fighter was going to be broken up for junk in the general disarmament following the end of the fighting. He was using it as a desk clock, and it was an hourly reminder of the fate that had spared him. I repaired the clock and was pleasantly surprised at the ease of the repair...just a big watch. Little did I know what lay in the future.

W atch repair has its social benefits. In the years before I was married, I generally spent weekends at Salisbury Beach in northern Massachusetts. I drove up Saturday afternoon with my friend Mal, alternating cars to even out costs. My grandparents had for years rented a small cottage there, and we never missed a Saturday night check-in with them. Nana most often mentioned how well her clock was still running. Thank the Lord for huge favors.

The sun at Salisbury was wonderful, the water freezing cold, and the girls very pretty. The only problem was my grandfather's constant "shame" that his grandson and his friend were sleeping in their car at night. Two bums, he insisted. Nana thought we were "cute."

One Saturday, Grandpa gave me a man's Omega Chronometer, which was an especially accurate watch. This watch belonged to the head of a state police unit stationed in the area, and it had stopped. Grandpa wanted to know if I could repair it. Of course I could; this was my forte.

As I took the watch, Grandpa insisted it receive "customer service, not family service. Understand?" I understood perfectly.

The Marcus family had a thing called "family service." This, in English, meant that there was a chance you never saw your watch again. I promised Grandpa that this watch would receive "customer service plus." True to my word, the watch was started on Monday morning and returned fully repaired and adjusted the following Saturday.

Three weeks later, there were notices that the police, local and state, were beginning a crackdown on young boys sleeping in their cars while trespassing on private property. This could crimp our weekend activities. I was driving a beautiful 1954 Oldsmobile Starfire convertible and didn't want any difficulty. I complained to Grandpa about such horrible treatment. He went to the phone.

"Captain, this is Abe Rappaport...fine...how are you? My bum grandson, the boy who did such a good job on your watch, is one of those kids sleeping in their cars. His is that two-tone blue Oldsmobile convertible you see around on the weekend. Yes, that one. When he gets into trouble, don't let him come crying to me. Thank you."

Shortly after, Mal went ballistic on me. "How could you let your grandfather do that to us? We'll end up in jail and my mother will kill me...you too maybe."

"Mal," I soothed, "my grandfather pointed out to the police captain that the kid in that Oldsmobile was the one who took such good care of his Omega. The kids in that car—us—will be immune from problems if we just behave ourselves." Needless to say, we truly behaved ourselves to the nth degree.

The concept of *family service* was not exclusive to the watchmaker. There was a legend that the "shoemaker's children went barefoot." The theory was that the shoemaker was too busy to fix his own family's shoes. The legend could be told using any recognized trade—tailors, painters, carpenters, and jewelers, among others.

I very recently was told, with a laugh, that years ago my daughter Amy had broken a piece of jewelry that required a jeweler's service. If given to me for repair, it would likely have never been seen again. With our store being so far behind in the work, we had to set priorities.

A fictitious name was entered onto a repair envelope, along with a made-up address and town. A note in red pen was scrawled, "Please Rush." The repair envelope was quietly put into the "to do" box and soon received "customer service." When the repair was completed, I merely put the envelope into the "ready" box and thought nothing more of it.

Well, it worked. I found out later when everyone had a good laugh at my expense.

"Customer service" sometimes was carried a little too far. One Friday in the 1960s, my father was having a great deal of trouble trying to repair a ladies' Bulova watch, the movement a twenty-three-jewel 5AH. This had been badly rusted, but as usual, a valiant attempt was required. This poor watch, originally a Christmas present sold by us, was beyond any help.

Dad was aggravated at the wasted time and, in the true Marcus tradition, solved the problem. He went to the front of the store, where my mother was showing a ladies' watch to a prospective customer. He pardoned himself for interrupting and removed the Bulova from Mom's wrist.

Within a very few moments, the rusted Bulova sported a nice new twenty-three-jewel movement and was, wonder of wonder, "saved." Watching this from my bench, I wondered what would happen next.

A few minutes later, after the watch sale was made, Mom came back to the bench area, but she stopped at my bench.

"Barry, would you please take a minute and size the band on my *new* watch so it fits a little more snugly? I'd appreciate it. Isn't this a pretty watch?"

I said not a single word. My father said not a single word.

The Bulova watch salesman called on us one day to say that somebody in Fall River was in big trouble over a watch and that my help was needed. Couldn't have been too big, I thought. Probably something wrong that their watchmaker couldn't square away. But it was an ego boost for a youngish watchmaker. I was no longer in the classification of the "kid watchmaker." I agreed to look at the "big trouble," but really without great enthusiasm.

The next day a very well-dressed gentleman came into the store. This was the owner of a very large and prestigious jewelry store in Fall River. We shook hands, and I received a long, sad story.

The watch in question was a platinum-and-diamond timepiece with a platinum-and-diamond bracelet...translation...big, big, big bucks. A ladies' watch of class beyond class. I was truly not too happy about this. Bulovas, Hamiltons, and Longines were one thing, but this was...*oy.*

The watch, given as a special present, would not run. Twice returned to the company, it was becoming a legal issue of well into five figures. I knew ahead of time the movement would be high quality, but normally it was the platinum-and-diamond case and bracelet that made the watch so valuable. Let me tell you, the diamonds were *large* for use on a watch. The customer, a very prominent Fall River citizen, was using the "R" word "REFUND." Oy vay.

All I could promise was to do my very best. I suggested he go out for coffee, but the poor man declined. I could understand…he was in trouble with this, and not only was his customer talking "money back," but the case was even engraved and…oh good heavens!

In my mind's ear (is there such a thing?) I heard Uncle Abe's often repeated instructions: look…talk…listen. Bingo. Things like this could give a young watchmaker a real swelled head, and I felt mine growing rapidly.

"Okay," I happily said, "give me a few minutes and I'll have you out of trouble."

He looked very unhappy. "Look, young fellow, I'm in no mood for bad jokes. Take the watch to your bench and give it a good look."

Young fellow??

Occasionally it was very hard to be modest, and this was one of those times. I went back to the gentleman to explain.

"Years ago, I was told by my uncle that quite often the problem with a watch is not the watch at all. Look, the back is engraved…

To Charlene

50 Loving years

6-10-XX

"She was a June bride fifty years ago. Let's say she was around twenty on her wedding day. Now she's around seventy." (I was always good at math.) "She's a seventy-year-old wife. How many thousand meals has she made? How many thousand dishes has she washed? Fifty years of marriage, I even bet she's got grandchildren…more work for woman's hands."

Here came an echo of past triumphs. Go, Barry.

"I don't know her, but I bet she has either arthritis or some other hand and finger difficulties. Look at the winding crown on this. It's tiny, of the right size for the watch, but the wrong size for her hands. I've run into this problem several times in the past. Anybody who looks only at the watch is not going to solve this problem. I'll put a larger crown on it right now and you take it to Fall River."

He still didn't look too happy; the solution had come too easy and fast. "I am sure," I continued, "that the people at the factory did a good job, but all they did was make sure the watch was up to spec. That spec was the whole problem. The crown that looks the best is just too small. The best part of this is that crowns come in several different diameters. If the one I put on is still too small, I can quickly go up a size. Like I told you, I've run into this before, and the solution is simple."

"But...but...but..." His motor wouldn't start.

I interrupted. "Look, you have, it seems, two choices...One, give them back their money. Two, explain to them what I've told you, and then have her wind the watch. When she's done, take it back and make sure it's wound fully. If it is, you are home free...but if it still takes more winds, get the watch back to Milford for the next larger crown. Trust me; this has been the problem all along. It's her hand, *not* the watch."

"How much do I owe you?" was the response. Oh boy, big bucks.

"Nothing is how much you owe me," I replied. "This is a huge ego thing for me. I wouldn't be surprised if I'm bragging about this in another thirty years. And the Bulova salesman now owes me a big favor...that I will collect on...that you can count on." I stopped him from saying another word. "I'm serious. This is a big ego trip. If you brought the watch for a true repair and overhaul, I'd really charge you what I deserve. This I really enjoyed, and it was a pleasure meeting you."

The next afternoon I got a phone call from Fall River.

"They picked up the watch this morning. I had her wind it, and the crown you put on worked like a charm. She was able to wind it fully, and I did check for further winding as you directed. Also, I looked at her hands, and again you were right. I'll also confess something, Barry. Two months ago our jeweler had to cut off her engagement ring and make it larger to get it on and off. I saw with my own eyes the problems with her fingers, but I never made any connection. The Bulova man was right—you are really sharp."

I could feel my head getting larger and larger. To be realistic, the credit went to Uncle Abe. Between my uncle and my father, I'd learned about watches and the people who used and abused them.

Several months later, the Bulova Watch Company brought out a set of technical books that contained all the listings of interchangeable parts for all their watch movements. Another listed all of their modern watches by case numbers, including the correct crystals, crown, gaskets, and other case parts. The books only cost $4 each, but I was not about to spend that much money when guilt would suffice.

I called Andy, the Bulova salesman, and reminded him of the "miracle" I'd pulled off for his customer in Fall River. Why should I have to put out that much money for Bulova books when I had two showcases full of his watches—let's be fair about this.

Also, if something was wrong, I repaired and adjusted his Bulovas myself, saving the company time and money, and I resented a charge of $4 for each book.

That night before I went home, I typed out four copies of a short letter of complaint to the Bulova president, sales manager, service manager, and parts department manager venting my indignation at the nerve they had charging *me* for tech manuals. Of course I knew that I had wasted time (no pun intended) and stamps, but I felt better.

The following Monday, the Bulova salesman walked into the store and put a complete set of manuals on the counter. "You are a nut," was all he said.

Maybe, but a nut with $12 in my pocket.

Trouble started the following day when a large envelope was delivered from Bulova, filled with, uh-oh, a complete set of tech manuals.

Later in the week, two large envelopes came from Bulova…more manuals. And the next day…and the next. Finally they stopped, but I had enough. I never told Bulova, but I gave away four sets of manuals.

One thing about Bulova, there isn't a company that did more to assist the bench watchmaker than Bulova. Besides the aforementioned

Accutron seminars, Bulova provided us with a steady stream of technical bulletins, covering everything from individual watch movements to instructions involving specific questions regarding specific movements and/or watch cases.

Bulova proudly introduced their *new* movement, the 11AN. This came in a number of variations...11AN, 11ANACD, etc. They took a basic wind-it-up-once-a-day watch, added different pieces and parts, and created an automatic wind watch, an automatic wind watch with either a date or a day *and* a date unit, or a wind-it-up with a date. The basic parts were the same in each variation, hugely simplifying the watchmaker's task. There developed one little problem: thousands of them would not run. That created some difficulties. To their credit, Bulova spent tremendous effort to solve this problem. To their detriment, they wouldn't listen to *me*.

I gave a new Bulova containing an 11ANACD to my father-in-law. I showed him how to set the day and the date, reminded him that a self-winding watch did not need a daily wind, and wished him good luck.

The following week, the phone rang. "My nice new Bulova stops every night. I have to reset it every morning. It doesn't wind like you said."

I picked up the watch on my way to work and super carefully checked it over...no problem that I could find. I wore it for the day and returned it the next morning. No luck, the watch kept stopping. This was my very own personal father-in-law, so no fooling around. I cheated, honest. I pulled a movement from another watch, changed dials, and gave Papa Doc (my kids' name for him) a new, improved watch. I'm so smart except that the watch would still not run. I had no other problems with this watch or any others in the series...just his.

A watchmaker friend called me to ask about the Bulova 11AN watches. He was having trouble with many of them. Worse yet, two refunds. Not good. Worse even, over the issue of the Bulova, Vinnie had lost a longtime customer. Vinnie was exactly my age and had a career that eerily paralleled my life. As a young Italian boy, nephew of a watchmaker, Vinnie's own training had started at age eleven. We'd been in high school together, then in the same naval reserve unit. I often did some work for him when he was too far behind in his own work. He was having the same problem with the same model watches. Something weird was going on.

Back to work, another watch in need of assistance. A couple of hours, a couple of watches, and—wait one minute—Vinnie had said a "long-time customer." "Hello, Vinnie, how old was the customer you lost?"

Vinnie protested, "C'mon, Barry, I checked out the old man. He's healthy and almost as active as you or I. In fact, more active. When we're working, we sit at the bench and don't move two inches an hour. That can't be the problem."

"Vin, I gave the same model to my own father-in-law, and it won't run overnight. This is strange. I have not had a single one back from any young guys," I insisted.

"Now this is really weird. Bulova has a watch that doesn't like the elderly? Can't be," Vinnie insisted.

No it could not be. How could a watch know how old its owner was? Something stupid was going on. Uh-oh, I heard Uncle Abe and my father again...something *stupid*.

Anything stupid in a brand-new watch had to be design. But what design flaw could be a problem only with older people...not elderly...but older? I started to take the movement apart. First the oscillating weight clamp and screw, then I carefully lifted off the oscillating weight. Reaching to put the weight in the parts cup, I suddenly, without warning, sneezed. The oscillating weight jumped from the tweezer, hit the edge of my bench, and then fell to the floor.

With two or three nasty words, I bent to pick up the weight, and a large flashbulb went off. The 11ANACD oscillating weight had *no* weight. It was of a very light alloy...very, *very* light. Wouldn't it take extra effort and force to get this to spin on its axis? The oscillating weight axle was really about four times the diameter of the original Bulova automatics, and the weight was much, much lighter than the original. There was a really large amount of direct contact between the oscillating weight axle and the weight bushing...could that create enough friction to be the whole problem?

I put everything back together and gently wiggled the movement. The weight wouldn't turn at all. I gently moved the watch back and forth with no apparent movement. With additional force the weight spun, and the attached gear operated the auto unit and the watch wound. Gentle motions and the weight sat still. Question: could the weight be so light that only a larger amount of force would cause it to turn?

"Vinnie, any problem with any of the watches you sold to younger guys?"

As I suddenly suspected…no problems with younger men, just as I'd had no problems with younger owners of this watch. Okay, now what? How did you prove that a light weight would not work where a heavier one would…on the same watch? As I sipped a cup of coffee (black, no sugar) my brain found the solution. An empty coffee cup was quite light, but fill it with coffee (black, no sugar) and it got heavier. Eureka or whatever that old gent said.

I hollowed out the Bulova oscillating weight and filled it with molten solder. Using a jeweler's balance scale, I found the solder/altered weight was three-and-a-half times heavier than the original. I put it back in the watch, I very gently turned the watch over, and sure enough, the weight stayed at the bottom. I gently swung my arm, and sure enough, the spinning force had the weight spinning and winding the watch. I had it, I think!

I put everything back together and then gave the watch back to my father-in-law. I really can't blame him for being less than impressed. I said, "Please wear this. I think I solved a national problem. Please." Nice guy, he put the watch on. Practical guy, put his old watch on the other wrist. Such confidence in me.

A week later, at supper, I dared to raise the subject and…surprise… the watch was running exactly as Bulova had hoped. It just had to be the light oscillating weight at the root of the problem.

The next morning I called Bulova and spoke to the service department. Nope, thank you, but that couldn't be the problem…yes, we are having certain difficulties, but our engineers are working on it.

I spoke to others, but apparently a watchmaker out in the boondocks could not have solved this dilemma. I called the Bulova salesman, and a few professional threats got me the name of the person I needed to speak to in whatever department was engineering and design.

Couldn't be, they claimed; the individuals in their department had personally worn watches with this movement and there were no problems.

I admit to raising my voice. "None of you are older or slower-moving men. That is the key to why the ultra-lightweight units won't work. I proved it when I made the weight so much heavier than you guys did. Listen to me!"

Six months later, Bulova proudly introduce a *new* model, this time the 11AO series. All problems had been solved, and the movement could be exchanged for the older 11ANAD's. Shortly after, I received in the mail Bulova's new and oh-so-informative tech sheet on the oh-so-new 11AO automatic models. Trumpets blared, hosannas rang out, and doves flew as I read the introduction for the "all new" Bulova 11AO self-winding series of watches. Its main feature was a (trumpet, please) "redesigned heavy alloy oscillating weight" that would ensure proper self-winding.

I guess "genius" is its own reward.

The following morning the phone rang. "Barry, it's Vinnie. Did you get a copy of the new tech bulletin on the 11AO series? You were right all along. Wow."

In the early 1960s I went to Warwick, Rhode Island, to be taught jewelry repair, sizing, and stone setting. I drove each Monday late afternoon to the store of an old-time "master" jeweler, diamond setter, engraver, and watchmaker...all in one man. This enabled us to keep more work than ever "in house" and to improve service as rendered by Marcus Jeweler. It also created a very difficult problem: *everything* was being done within the store, but by the same two people...Dad and me, with Dad doing only watch repair. The pressure was on, but it was good for business.

One advantage was my ability to reset a diamond ring, virtually at once, if it was required to clinch the sale. One sad day, while fighting a cold as I cleaned ten very small diamonds in preparation for setting them into a wedding band, I suddenly, without control, sneezed. After thirty minutes of searching in a darkened shop using the beam of a flashlight, I finally had four tiny pieces of gold, a worn-out watch crown, and *only* seven diamonds. Luckily we did have further inventory, so the wedding band was ready on time. As a side note, about six months later, I found, by flashlight, one of those tiny diamonds while searching for a small cultured pearl. Oh, I found the pearl too.

During a visit to my grandparents in Lawrence, quite happy to see that the "famous" clock was still running fine, I sipped coffee (black, no sugar) while Nana brewed a cup of tea in a way I never noticed before...no tea bag. Instead she took a measure of tea leaves and put them into a round mesh ball that opened like a shark's jaws. She put the tea ball into the small pot of boiling water, and tea was steeped. I couldn't believe my eyes when I saw that not the tiniest bit of tea leaf was lost. That tea ball snapped shut tight and...and...and I really thought it would work!

Ten days later, back in the store, I multitasked as I cleaned a group of diamonds for another ring while ordering some supplies from a "material house" salesman from New York. We never bought much from him, but we tried to give him enough business for him to justify his time in stopping here. He was a very nice guy and always a pleasant visit, occasionally going for a quick bite at lunchtime.

I suggested skipping out for coffee (black, no sugar), but he said no need to waste the time as he could see I was making tea on the jewelry bench. His jaw dropped as I explained I was finishing the cleaning of a group of loose diamonds and was ready to dip the stone basket in alcohol to air dry them.

"But that's a tea ball, like my mother uses all the time," he exclaimed, "not a diamond cleaner."

I smiled. "I know exactly what it is, but the thing is stainless steel, the mesh is very fine, and it closes up tight as a vault. I've been using this even for watch jewels, and nothing ever vanishes…ever. I love this thing, and I have another on the watch bench." I handed him the tea ball/ diamond cleaner and told him to very carefully open the ball and tap the loose stones into the tri-cornered stone holder. Fascinated, he carefully squeezed the handles, the ball opened, and he tipped the diamonds to the bench. We finished our business, and he went off to his next stop.

A month or so later, we received a new brochure from his company that contained a couple of pages of this month's tool "specials" and introductory new additions to their inventory. This month's Proud Introduction: a secure loose stone and miniature watch part cleaning device. It was very well made of stainless steel, and its finely holed steel mesh prevented "the loss of very tiny parts and/or stones." Strangely, the new wonder tool looked exactly like my grandmother's tea ball. Dad and I exchanged glances and just shrugged our shoulders. After all, we didn't actually invent anything, but it was a really good idea, wasn't it?

We noticed that the "Precision Stone and Miniature Part Cleaning Device" sold for twice the price of a low-tech "tea ball."

When next the salesman visited Milford, he was very thankful and openly admitted he'd earned a very good bonus for the presentation of "his" great idea. His boss was very grateful and sent a "thank you present" for us. Dad and I were each presented with a small gift-wrapped box and we were the proud recipients of our very own personal "High Tech Loose Stone Cleaning Device." In truth, I still have mine, hanging on a small nail above the ultrasonic cleaning tank. I think Dad's went home to make tea.

A woman brought in a high-quality Longines for service. Speaking with an Italian accent, but obviously in this country for many years, she explained that it was her present to her husband at their marriage in 1946. I walked to the bench to examine the watch and read the engraving on the back. I stopped in my tracks. At that moment I'd seen it all. The watch was nicely hand engraved...this couldn't be correct, could it?

YOU SHOT ME
YOU SAVED ME
YOU LOVED ME
6/12/46

I checked the watch and went to the counter to talk about the repair. She agreed to leave the watch, but of course I just *had* to ask...

"What is this about you being shot by your husband?" I asked.

She smiled...she actually smiled at me.

"It is our little, what do you say in English, a private joke? In 1944, I was a young Italian girl in a village occupied by the Nazis. We could hear explosions in the distance and knew the Americans were coming, but when? The Nazis were very cruel and we were supposed to be allies. They were bad trouble for young girls. One terrible day three Germans grabbed me and pulled me into a house and I knew what would happen to me. They pushed me into a bedroom and...suddenly there was much shooting and they turned from me and shut the door. The Americans had arrived and there was much fighting and loud bangs. I heard yelling and shooting and a...what is it...a throwing bomb came through the window.

"When it blew up, the three Germans were killed, and a few seconds later, someone kicked in the door. Through a little crack I could see it was one of your soldiers who checked the dead and then turned to leave. I moved to open the door and made a noise which startled him, and he spun around and shot through the door. Anyway, there was a lot of holes in the door, and two in me.

"I fell back, and as I landed on the floor, the door flew open, and there he was with another throwing bomb in his hand. He knelt beside me, opened my blouse, looked at me, and said, 'Wow,' which I thought was a word of sympathy. Then he put a white square of padding on my wounds, picked me up, and carried me outside and down the street. I spoke some English and thanked him for my life.

"I was treated, the bullets removed, and I was cared for by your army men in the town hall. The soldiers chased all the townspeople out and made it a hospital. The man who shot me came in the next day and sat with me for hours. The next day he brought flowers, and the next. A few days later, an officer visited me, telling me he had to check on the woman one of his men kept talking about. I didn't think the officer was an American because he didn't speak much English, I thought. He said he came from a country called Alabama and he spoke funny. Now I know where Alabama is.

"My American visited every day until his company moved away. He wrote to me often, and when he got leave he came to see me. As you can see, terror became concern; concern became friendship, which turned to a deep love.

"Now I am an American. My children are American. My most fortunate moment came when that American shot me. Today we laugh over it, but knowing…"

I repaired the watch, most carefully and respectfully. I was right, I'd heard it all…well, almost all.

Another Waltham clock came in. An eight-day "biggie" with two mainsprings. This was the first I'd seen, and it was taken as a souvenir from a Sherman tank that had shut down for the last time on the river Elbe in Germany. The sergeant in charge had shut off the engine during a quiet time, and an hour later the word came that the Nazis had given up and the European war was over. Somehow the clock turned up missing, but it didn't matter. I was learning the emotional ties with even "timepieces of war." The Waltham was technically a *clock*, which I never, ever repair. Of course I restored it to working order.

Uncle Abe talked about people-people-people and then looking at their watches. In later years, I became a trade watchmaker, doing repairs for various jewelry stores that no longer had an in-house watchmaker. I noticed that many stores didn't like to take in watches for repair. They said it was a nuisance. I tried to explain that watch repair gave the potential customer another reason to come into your store when there wasn't a need to buy something. If you gave a customer good service, they would remember it come gift-giving time.

A "prestige" store in a "prestigious town" sent me an 18K Omega for an estimate. A beautiful man's watch with a very typical sentiment engraved on the back. The estimate was in line with the value of the watch, but I was instructed to return it as the customer didn't want to put that much money into the watch. I could not understand it, but who was I to say anything. I mailed out the watch the next day.

The following Friday, I drove to a nearby town to pick up and deliver watches at a local jeweler. Among the watches of the week was an 18K Omega man's watch that looked like and was, in fact, the same watch that wasn't going to be repaired. What the heck? Yes, there was the engraving…not just a coincidence, it was the same watch. Whatever. The estimate was the same as the one I'd given the "prestige name" store. I earn what I earn.

Three hours later, I got a call. The Omega was to be repaired. "You take the time to do a super job, Barry. This man is the big, big cheese at the local computer giant, and I want him as a customer. I want an extra super job, understand?"

I wondered why the customer wanted the watch repaired now and not by the first store since the estimate was the same. Oh well, I was glad to have the work. I did an extra super job, returned the watch, and got paid. Did everyone live happily ever after? Not how you would think.

Two months later, the Friday after Christmas, I was again picking up watches, and the jeweler did everything but pick me up and hug me. But no one on this planet was going to pick *me* up and hug me, both at the same time. "Barry, remember that Omega that needed the special job? The owner was so happy he did his Christmas shopping *here*! He made my season all by himself and told several of his friends about us. He said a jeweler up in the fancy town he lived in wanted an obscene amount of money to repair his watch and that is how it got down here. He called and asked if I'd have a diamond heart for Valentine's Day. You did it!"

I think that somewhere Uncle Abe and my father looked at each other and smiled. Barry had absorbed his "lessons." Unfortunately, both the store and the computer company are history. Fortunately, I am still repairing watches, treating people as I'd want to be treated.

I've mentioned that I have only owned one watch that was new, brand new. It was that big Accutron diver's watch that made noise at night. From age thirteen to seventy-four and only one new watch ever.

At thirteen, on a Thursday morning before work, I was Bar Mitzvah. Later that day, Uncle Abe came to my bench with a cigar box and a small coin envelope. I was told, "It's time you had a watch to wear. Check with me as you make progress." Inside the cigar box were dozens of broken watch movements...all AS 970s. This was a medium-sized wind-up watch that was extremely common back then in the '40s. Either seven or seventeen jewel, not shock resistant, and usually not dust or waterproof but hugely popular as moderate-priced dress watches for men. In the envelope was a watch case and dial...put everything together and I would have my very own watch.

This was not as simple as I hoped. The train from a seventeen-jewel watch wouldn't work in the plates from a seven-jewel watch... the pivots were the wrong size. Some watches had escape wheels with straight pivots and others had a lower pivot that was conical for a cap jewel, and some had the same but for the upper jewel.

Finally came the day when I showed my uncle...my very own *first* watch. I was so proud. It lasted until my senior year in high school when I used the movement for the repair of a totally rusted customer's watch. I'm sure somewhere I still have the case, but I haven't seen it since I was seventeen.

For the next couple of years, I wore certain types of customers' watches after I repaired them…to "check them out." (I always told the customer that I would be doing this.) Very often, people looked at me strangely because very few people ever wore a watch on both wrists.

But I needed a watch to call my own. Two weeks before I left for the navy, my father presented me with a cigar box. As before, it was filled with damaged watch movements…this time AS 1187 parts. Again, a hugely popular and common "workhorse" movement. Rugged, shock resistant, and generally put into waterproof watch cases, they were the "Jeep" of watchdom. They had a sweep second hand and truly were faithful and dependable timepieces. They also utilized genuine and real *radium* in the hands and dial figures. When it was finally realized the peril radium put people in, there was a huge tumult around the country. Some stores went so far as to purchase a Geiger counter to check radiation levels of the watches people brought in.

It was September 2009, and I was working on five chronographs, a Zodiak, two Breitlings, an Omega, and a "no name" that had the same movement as a Breitling. This group of watches made me remember my *first* chronograph. It was a two-pusher, three-dial watch with normal hour and minute hand, a sweep second hand, a running second hand, a minute register, and an hour register….a model that I bought for three drinks in Yokosuka, Japan. It did not work, but I was curious about it. It could have been made to work, but I had no connections for parts. A week later, while reading a letter from Dad, I had a brainstorm.

The US Navy graciously provided me with three fifteen-inch-square pieces of half-inch clear plastic.

I borrowed a navy floor pantograph and ground out the center piece, removing the entire center but for a one-inch bar around the perimeter. I took the chronograph apart, down to the last tiny screw removed from around the balance wheel. Every jewel was removed. Each wheel, lever, spring, screw, jewel, cam, and the hands and dial were cemented to the rear piece of plastic. Later, the navy donated twelve small strips of plastic, which were engraved on the pantograph with varied slogans and ads for my dad's store. When the three squares of plastic were finally screwed together, I had a beautiful display that showed off each and every part of the highly technical chronograph watch, plus the slogan strip.

Of course I was afraid to have it shipped from Japan, so I kept it in my locker until I returned home to Worcester. That display today is still in the front showcase of the shop, still proudly proclaiming Dad's motto...

THE RIGHT PLACE

FOR

THE RIGHT TIME

About twenty-three years ago, I did some watch repair for the L. L. Bean Company. At the time their watches were built by the Hamilton Watch Company, and it was a truly great watch line. The dials, of course, indicated L. L. Bean, but the name Hamilton was on each dial, in much smaller letters. These watches came to Freeport from around the world and ended up in Milford for me to repair. My daughter Julie drove down each Wednesday from Maine (ironically) with my grandson, Adam. She (and Adam) became my receiving and shipping department, keeping all the records and logs books. Julie had the idea to keep track of the homes of the owners. She purchased two large maps for the walls of the shop...one of the entire world, the other of the United States.

We could not understand the number of watches that came in from communist countries, especially the Soviet Union. Julie guessed that these were almost assuredly owned by government diplomats or top officials from Iron Curtain countries, maybe United Nations or support personnel. It was very funny in a way to see how many of these communist people did their shopping in a store that was the absolute epitome of capitalist living.

We also kept track of the homes of watches from the USA. Eventually we had watches from all fifty states, the very last being Nevada, and that from Reno.

As a result, to this day, my business cards carry the motto:

KEEPING THE WORLD ON TIME

That is almost all true. As strange as it seems, with watches from virtually every country, there was never a single watch from South America…not a one. Weird, isn't it?

L. L. Bean called; they were moving the watch service desks to another building and did I have any use for a few "returned and rejected, get rid of them we need the room, not working" watches? I agreed to take them. I could cannibalize them for parts. A few days later the *few* watches came into the shop, a box that weighed almost *thirty* pounds. I couldn't believe it and called the company. This was merely an accumulation of dead watches over the years. They were for me to use for anything I needed.

In this treasure trove, I found about two dozen chronographs of a wonderful modern design. Chronographs had been around since, I believe, the 1930s. They were almost impossibly complicated, indicating not only the time but split-second timing as well as indicating the number of passing minutes and in some models the number of hours that passed. The push of a button and everything went back to "0."

At the time, I was again wearing whatever watch I grabbed for the moment, but I did not really own my own watch. These chronographs had three extra dials, a total of six hands, and, frosting on the cake, told the day and the date. On top of everything else, they were *self-winding*. As the wearer moved around during the day, arms swinging to and fro, an oscillating weight turned a number of gears that wound the watch. With great respect to my Italian friends, I called these "spaghetti watches" because looking at one was like trying to trace a *single* strand of pasta in a large dish of spaghetti.

Even though I have an old *Chronograph Assemble-O-Graph Encyclopedia* that has been copied onto a DVD, I take digital close-ups of a chronograph I'm about to take apart. Especially on a model that is new to me.

The L. L. Bean chronograph came to me before the advent of digital photography, so I worked with six file cards I'd drawn out as guides. This pile of busted pieces became *my* treasured watch, and most likely the last I will ever have. Although I admit that if the movement is ever needed to save a watch for a customer, it will be my *former* watch.

Here's an amusing clock story…not funny at the time, but amusing now.

I don't repair clocks, as you may have noticed, but of course I use them. Clocks can be very handy for telling time, helping my grandmother sleep, and keeping me happily fed.

When I was quite young, my father displayed, as did most jewelry stores, a large Telechron clock in the store window. The diameter was about fifteen inches with the dial white with large black numbers and hands, very easily readable from a good distance, even from cars passing on Main Street in Milford. It was even visible to the people having a "before work" cup of coffee at the Soda Shoppe diagonally across the street. One memorable (to me) morning there was chaos in downtown Milford. Traffic was a mess, people were hurrying along, yelling at one another, and store owners were out front scolding their employees for being so late to work.

Dad and I opened the store, and when I turned on the lights I noticed two strange things…the large Telechron store clock was twenty-five minutes *slow* and its "power interruption" disc was showing. A few minutes later, a local policeman, entered the store, very unhappy.

"Mr. Marcus, last night the power went out downtown for about twenty-five minutes. Your big clock that everyone looks at is twenty-five minutes behind time. People have been sitting in the Soda Shoppe waiting till it's time to go to work. Worse, people driving by thought they were extra early and dawdled before they went to work. Everything is upside down. Even the chief thought his watch was off for some reason and reset it to your clock, so he had an extra cup of coffee and was late to a special early meeting with the selectmen. Please have Barry reset it. This is crazy." The officer left, and to my best knowledge, no one else ever caught on to the cause of "Milford's Day of Madness."

The clock remained, and there was never a repeat...luckily. Every now and then the patrolman would stop in front of the store, and if he knew I'd seen him, he would, with a flourish, compare his watch to our clock. Then, with a smile, he'd continue down the sidewalk.

I repaired an L. L. Bean watch, but this one came with a request that I mail it directly back to the customer; he needed it quickly and this would save trans-shipping time.

I sent it out west via UPS, with my return address on the label of course. A couple of weeks later, I received a smallish box from UPS that contained an old and beat-up US military Hamilton. Attached was a letter thanking me for the good job on his L.L. Bean watch and could I take care of his favorite watch, one that...

(To the best of my memory, I paraphrase, but the meaning is clear:)

"During the war, I was part of a B-17 crew. It was as rough as they say, but we flew twenty-four missions over Europe without losing a man. A couple of the original guys were wounded but lived. We did not come back from mission twenty-five, which was to be our last. Over some damn German town our left wing was blown right off the plane and I was the *only* one who got out.

"The watch and I landed in some German forest, the wind having blown me a good distance from where the plane came down. Anyway, I managed to stay free for two weeks; how, I really don't know. Naturally I was eventually caught, but I had managed to hide the watch, so the German who got my wallet, pen, and pocketknife didn't get the watch." (Where do you hide a watch?) "I was put into a stalag with other air crew and sat out the last four months of the war as a POW. Some of the guards weren't too bad but others…

"Eventually we were liberated, repatriated, and celebrated…me and my watch. I hope you can understand why it is so important that this be repaired and running.

Thank you."

Again, repair a watch cherished because of memories most would be happy to forget. That bond again…man and a watch in a war.

I n the later 1960s I saw my first Seiko. One of our regular customers brought one in to have the band adjusted. His son had sent it to him from Vietnam and the band was too big. I asked permission to open the case to see the movement. I'd been in Japan years before and did not think much of their products. Mostly junk.

Uh-oh. This movement, a self-winding/day/date model was a strange engineering design. The movement was well thought out, well made, and going to give the rest of the watch world some serious competition.

My customer said that all the guys over there were buying these Seiko watches and a lot were sending them home to family. Largish, sturdy watches with brightly colored dials, they were being snapped up by the GIs, sailors, and marines like his son.

Four months later, he was back, but this time his nice Seiko was in bad shape…crystal broken, band bent, and in dire need of TLC.

I scolded him, "What the hell did you do to this?"

He sighed.

"I received this in the box with my son's effects. It came in the other day. Can you repair his watch? I would like to be able to wear it myself…this is all I have left of him." I stood there like a statue, frantically trying to say something…anything…but we just looked at each other.

I quietly went to the phone and called a watch material supplier. He had also heard about the Seiko watches, but as yet there were no parts being shipped into the USA. There probably would be before long, but nothing as of now. Oh boy. Now what? I looked at young Leonard's watch and back to Leonard. How could I tell this devastated father that there just weren't parts yet for the watch? I couldn't.

"Look, there are no parts in the country yet for this…but (I stammered a little) both of these watches are the same watch, even the dial colors are the same. How about if I switch movements?" I thought this would solve the problem.

He thought for a minute. "No. I want you to take good parts from my watch and use them to fix my son's watch. When I wear it we will be together in a way. Can you—will you do it that way for me?"

If you think grown men don't shed tears, you are wrong.

I think you know that there was no charge for the repair. Until my friend died, there was *never* a charge to repair that first Seiko.

I found it strange that over sixty years had passed while I sat at the bench, yet I still heard words from both Dad and Uncle Abe. "Remember, these things are only little machines that tell time, but we are dealing with *people*. You must listen, look at, and respect people. You may fix their watch, lots of men can do that, but you sometimes have to repair the *person*." I thank them, now and then, for giving me the example and lessons of what I try to be.

People. Wonderful people. My customers. People who come to the world's *biggest* watchmaker to have their tiny mechanism repaired. People…who can find a way to defeat the world's finest engineering. The Rolex Company had, for years, utilized a crown assembly that screwed down onto a threaded post to make the watch truly waterproof, and it worked. Other high-grade companies eventually adopted this crown design. The screwed-down crown became a sign of true "quality." These watches could be worn in the shower, while swimming, even while scuba diving. Some of them even had an outer turning bezel, used as an elapsed time indicator. After some years, the locking crown became much more common.

A Rolex was brought to me with a strange problem. There was water in the watch, enough so that I quickly opened the case and poured out the water, took off the dial, and dunked the movement into a cup of cleaning solution. I could not understand why there was no damage or signs of rust, but I was told the water was only in the watch about a half hour or so. Great luck. This was a Rolex, so I told the customer the end of the month…about three weeks.

While the movement was being cleaned, one of six in a rotary basket, I became curious as to how a Rolex, seemingly in very good condition, could leak like this. I put the case together, complete with the crown, and put the watch into the pressure tank. Pumping the pressure to a simulated depth of something over a hundred feet, I tested to find the leak.

Wonderful, there was no leak…none at all. The simple idea behind the test was to pump up the pressure inside the tank with the watch suspended in the air above the water. In theory, a leak would allow air into the case, and in five minutes the air pressure in the tank would equalize the pressure inside the watch case. With the watch case lowered into the water, releasing the air pressure would allow high-pressure air to escape from the watch case and…magic…bubbles if there was a leak. No bubbles meant there was no leak. This Rolex had *no* leaks, even when I left it in the tank under pressure for fifteen minutes before doing the actual water test. Strange.

Three weeks later, the watch was picked up; the customer paid me a lot of money and left happily. The watch ran fine, and I only saw the watch every few years.

Starting with that Rolex, I had been seeing an increasing number of watches with screw-down crowns coming in with water problems. It was a sudden realization about a year after the Rolex that too many of these watches were coming in with water damage. These problems were occurring in clusters and too often to be mere chance. Again Dad and Uncle Abe lectured me, "Barry, something stupid is going on."

Time (pun intended) to think about this. I turned again to my old standby, a cup of coffee (black, no sugar). No idea came to me, so back to work.

A couple of months later, coming back to work after a long Fourth of July weekend, I took in three (three!) of these watches, a Rolex, a Zodiak, and a name I didn't recognize. The last turned out to be a TAG, new to me at the time. What the hell? Of the three, only the poor Rolex was a real mess, and I told the customer it was back-to-the-factory time. I was not and am not on their "pure and noble of mind and spirit" list, so they refused to ship parts to me. I didn't like them either.

Time to think. More coffee (black, no sugar), and I suddenly caught the basis of the clustering of these leaky watches that wouldn't leak in the pressure tank. This was all happening during the first several days after the end of a short month. I couldn't believe the problem could be so simple. All of these watches were *calendar* watches that required the owner to unscrew the crown, pull it out, and advance the date to the correct one, then carefully screw the crown back in place. People, beautiful, wonderful, careless people who graciously made my living for me, were not screwing the crowns back in properly. Absolutely waterproof watches when pressure tested did indeed leak if I tested them leaving the crown loose or even not screwed carefully down. Of course I removed the watch movements before immersing the cases.

That must be it. Oh, such a smarty. I dug out the record on the very first Rolex that had come in with this problem. I remembered telling the customer three weeks, and he had picked up the watch at the end of that month. Sure enough, he had picked it up at the end of May, which meant it was brought in shortly after the end of a short month, April! That's it, I gloated to myself.

As I returned each watch to the owner, I delivered a very point-ed lecture on the securing of the crown, informing them that the water leak was their own fault. With these watches, this was a cost-ly lecture. I continue to receive watches that shouldn't have water problems during the first several days after a short month. At least I've never seen a watch with this problem a second time. My stern lectures must work. I love people. My own watch is kept waterproof by the use of two O ring gaskets. I like the design because the watch does not depend on the owner (even me) to do anything. Push the crown in, and two heavy gaskets grip the case tube and keep water out.

I was not alone in my strange world. Since, as you now know, I won't repair a clock, I was overjoyed to meet a real, live clockmaker who lived a couple of towns over. He'd heard of me, but I never knew he existed. We were kindred spirits. Why? This clockmaker would not repair watches! He explained that he left watch repair school because he could not stand working on little tiny things. The ability was there, but no willingness. He was fascinated with larger and even huge clock mechanisms, the ones you climbed a ladder to reach for service. What was the old rhyme? *Jack Spratt could eat no fat…his wife could eat no lean. Between the two of them they licked each platter clean.* Between the two of us, we could keep people on time. To my joy, this professional left me his business cards to give out to people inquiring as to clock repair. This allowed me to refuse the repair but still be helpful.

Progress, or what passes for it, cannot be stopped. The years passed, and the electronic age of watches became the norm. The newer watches that came to me for repair were only battery watches. I worried that I would become outdated professionally, all that practice, pride, and knowledge discarded like…like…like an old watch. Soon, however, I found the flaw in the thinking of those who wrote off the world of watchmaking. The flaw…*people*. Uncle Abe's favorite word… *people*. Wonderful, loving, careless, and clumsy *people*.

I had great trouble understanding the attitude of many modern jewelry stores. I was trained to respect people and to understand the deep attachment they had for their personal "treasures." I think Uncle Abe would clean out the roster of most mall stores. And Dad...he would explode at the lack of respect some stores showed customers.

A man entered the shop during our latest cold spell. He wore three notable items, a very warm-looking coat, an obviously 1930s Hamilton, and a notable frown. I hadn't seen the watch; correction, I had seen others like this, but not that particular one.

He put the watch on the counter. I picked it up to examine it and put it right back on the glass top. I asked how long the watch had been on the ground in the snow and ice and was told it had just been in his car.

"Three weeks now," he replied, "while I tried to find you. Not *you*, but someone who would fix my watch." The frown returned. "I took the watch into three fancy jewelry stores in the Natick Mall or whatever they call it now. Anyway, I was told that it was foolish to pay that much money to fix such an old, outdated timepiece."

I thought no one could be that dumb, but I did know that many stores believed they had only one reason for existence...to sell. Many could not even spell "service."

"This was my grandfather's watch. He, of course, is gone, and this watch is all I have of him. Great guy and a lot of fun. My own father died just before I was born. Grandpa took it upon himself to provide me with a 'dad' and did a great job. When he died, my grandmother gave me this old Hamilton to remember him by. The watch still runs, but now it needs something. Will you look at it?"

While he spoke I had picked up the watch, which was warmer now, and without thinking my fingers checked the watch.

I told the man, "The oil has long dried out, and it won't run because the mainspring is broken at the outer end. Give me a minute to check the rest and I'll fill you in."

"How can you tell that without even looking at my watch?" he asked. "I believe you, but how—?"

"Hang on a minute," I said while I opened the case, looked carefully, and rose from the bench.

"Look, sir, a lot of what I had to know my fingers told me while we stood at the counter. When I turned the crown, I could tell the mainspring was broken, and at the same time I could tell the wind and set gears were not rust-bound. I pulled the stem out to the setting position and they turned smoothly. That was a ninety percent indication that the watch had not been wet. As I walked to the bench, my eyes told me that the dial was not badly faded, discolored, or, on this older Hamilton, peeling. I just had to visually check the balance staff in an old watch that is not shock resistant. It is fine. So there is no major problem. When I finish your granddad's watch and put in a new mainspring, it will run like it's a month old.

"I understand the importance of his watch to you. To be honest, this subject was a frequent subject of lectures from my own father and the uncle who taught me this trade. One can never tell how important any article may be to the customer. An old watch, an old piece of jewelry, an old anything could well be a piece of junk, but priceless and precious to the owner. That's the category of this watch, except it's *not* junk. The Hamilton is, I think, the best of the American watches," I added.

He said, "But the other stores—"

I interrupted, "—Don't recognize that attachment you felt deep down to this particular watch. If it was a different watch, from someone you never met, you might not put half a dollar into it. This is beyond value to you. Unfortunately, it's the trend of the times. It's a new world full of disposable products. It's just not necessarily better."

The watch, of course, was successfully repaired, and a grateful customer took some of my business cards to give out. That is called "Word of Mouth Advertising."

The least costly kind, but absolutely the best.

As I described previously, an "electric" watch, while battery powered, runs with an old-fashioned balance wheel and escapement, but the watch runs in a completely opposite way. In the traditional mainspring-powered watch, the coiled spring powers the watch down through the train wheels, to the escapement, which furnishes power to the balance wheel. In the electric watch, a battery sends its power through the circuit directly to the balance wheel, which actually provides the power to run the watch. It is a design used by many quality companies. In between are the couple of hundred-year-old wheels, pinions, springs, and levers of "olde"...smaller, but looking the same and doing the same task as days of yore ("olde" talk). It still takes a watchmaker's skills and training to repair these timepieces, which will be mistreated by their owners. (Thank goodness, since I need to make a living.) I am at the same handmade bench, using the exact same tools, doing the same thing I've been doing all these years. I've added new devices, but they are only tools of the trade.

A modern watch came in for repair...a miracle of modern technology...a victim of historical mistreatment. The crystal was broken and with it the minute hand. The stem and crown were gone, and the customer didn't bring it in for repair until it was full of dust and lint.

An ultramodern pocket watch went overboard with its owner while he was out fishing. The watch was left in a drawer unused for so long that the battery leaked, and now we were into a major overhaul, because the "leakage" ate up part of the circuit.

Another watch, honestly a 14K gold Movado, was full of paint because the owner had way too much paint on the brush as he painted the living room ceiling.

I just love people who own watches. I love their watches, but I love the people more.

A friend brought in an electric watch. "There is a big problem," I was told. "Since I bought the watch, my brother-in-law told me there were no longer any mercury batteries being manufactured. Something about mercury batteries being against the law...the feds and all."

I opened the case to check the movement and—uh-oh—big trouble. I'd heard of a European-made electric watch that required a mercury battery of triple the normal size. It was a standard 1.35 volt, but very, very large. It seemed that someone had fitted the watch with a battery that technically fit but wasn't proper for the watch. The battery that was put in was a 3V lithium battery, proper dimensions, but twice the voltage, which would make the watch run crazy fast.

My customer/friend said, "I couldn't get in to see you, so I admit to taking the watch elsewhere. Now the watch is running really fast." Wonderful.

The watch was taken in, but without any promises made. I'd checked with my main supplier and was told "you got to be kidding me." That finished that.

I stripped down the watch and ran it with five others through the ultrasonic cycles. I knew I could be wasting my time, but this was a watch problem, and by instinct I was bound to be the one who solved it. I had called three other material people about this battery problem and was told to save both my breath and my time. After all, time is money (bad pun intended).

In its turn, I assembled the watch, having run electrical tests and finding all was well. In theory, there was nothing at all wrong with the watch, and sure enough, when I installed a three-volt lithium battery, the watch ran crazy. I went to work on other watches while my mind played with this problem. There was a particular battery required, but it was no longer available or legal. I think *legal* was more of a problem.

Time to think over a cup of coffee (black, no sugar). I set up the watch wired into my Accutron test set, which also provided power. Once I'd determined that the watch itself was okay, I put on the dial and the three hands so the movement was complete but for the battery. Without thinking, I automatically set not only the time but the date and covered the watch with a glass bell cover to keep it at least clean while it ran under Accutron power. The Accutron test set had a 1.5V silver battery installed, and that was not too much more than the 1.35V of the original. In fact, the Accutron watch itself required a 1.35V mercury bat—

The words I said cannot be typed onto my computer without being fined by my girls, but that was the solution...a 1.5V silver battery. When the entire line of mercury batteries was declared unclean and illegal, we were forced to adopt the use of 1.5V silver batteries. The voltage difference between 1.35 and 1.5 was not great enough to affect the timekeeping abilities of the Accutron.

When I had set the time, I had from habit set it according to the radio-controlled atomic clock on the front of my bench. After a week I checked the time, and the watch had gained a grand total of twenty-one seconds...three seconds a day on the fast side. I practically jumped up and down in joy, despite the shaking the building would have suffered.

There was still a problem: I had come up with a solution, but *no* silver battery was anywhere near large enough. The negative contact on this watch came up through a hole in the base of the circuit substrate while the positive contact was three springs that held the large outer rim of the mercury battery. The largest silver battery would rattle around like a marble in a tin can, although the thickness of a silver battery would be perfect. But that diameter problem...

More thinking was required as I had some coffee (black, no sugar). No ideas came forth.

Two days later, the watch was still running perfectly under glass, powered by the Accutron tester, and my brain was about to sue for abuse. To escape, I worked on a box of small jobs that had not only accumulated but brought in good money. I picked up a watch I disliked, a Skagen with a domed crystal. I'd found that the mineral-glass-domed crystals were much more susceptible to breakage than the normal flat ones. This one had a perfect circle broken from the top of the dome, with pieces of glass down in...that was it! The answer.

I took the electric watch off life support and checked the tech book for the needed diameter of the battery. In the crystal cabinet I found a flat Lucite crystal of the exact diameter required, and sure enough, it snapped right into place. I took the largest, although too small, silver battery of the right thickness and scribed a circle in the center of the Lucite crystal. I ground out the circle, and the battery slipped right into place, directly over the upward thrusting negative contact. As soon as

I shorted out the positive side of the battery, the watch started to run. I was off the wall and the ceiling...my brainstorm had worked. It was a simple matter to solder a contact spring onto the circuit assembly, and the new silver battery could be tilted and slipped into place.

With a mile-wide grin, I cased up the watch and kept a close eye on it for a week before I called its owner. I will admit my news was met with disbelief. He'd been assured that nothing could be done. It must be a miracle and so on. I will freely admit to being quite pleased with myself for this one—again.

The watch was picked up with many thanks and the news that he'd purchased two more similar watches. He had paid next to nothing after being specifically informed that there were absolutely no batteries available for this watch. Both sellers tried to discover why someone would purchase a watch knowing all the while that it could not run in the future. As usual, I'd extracted a solemn vow that that information was not to be given out...or else no more repairs.

This learned story began with the tale of a watch from 1857, badly "wounded" at Gettysburg but still running more than a century later. To this day, if the watch needed repair, most parts were still available. Today, all too often, the search for critical parts for a modern electronic watch is met with the disgusting reply of "discontinued model." In English...no parts anymore. Imagine a store saying, "Sorry, Mr./Ms. Proud Owner of a $400 Watch, there are no more parts for your nine-year-old watch. Time to get a new one." That's no way to win loyalty from a customer.

I am the "Master of Time" (pun intended). If I happened to stumble upon a DeLorean and went back in time, I'd go to the late 1800s, to one of the American watch factories, probably either Hamilton or the Waltham plant. I would speak to one of the foremen about their watches. I'd say, "Would you believe that where I come from, in 2009, these watches you are building today are still running?"

I am sure he would answer," What are you talking about…of course they will still be running. We build these so they last…period. Why get excited when they do what we know they will do? You are funny."

I'm back in 2009, and companies are proud when their products last beyond the guarantee period. This is to be proud of? This should be expected.

Happily, a few companies were going backward for the future. But I was afraid that costs today would prevent reintroduction of moderately priced mechanical watches.

(On June 30, 2009, I officially canceled that statement.)

The circle closes and history repeats itself. Today, I find that most of the high-quality watches are once again mechanical. From manual-wind models to self-winding/day/date beauties, all the way to chronographs that have the same movement as my own L. L. Bean watch…delightful, rugged, accurate mechanical watches are alive and well. Not only are mechanicals back, but the ills they suffer are back too.

A young doctor in my building came in. "I am disgusted with my new watch. I spent seven hundred dollars and it won't keep time."

So I asked, "What do you define as lousy timekeeping?"

"Every week this thing is two minutes fast. I sent it to the company three times, and it is still exactly two minutes ahead every Monday."

I carefully set the watch, synchronizing it to the radio-controlled atomic clock on my bench, accurate to the second. "Now go away and don't bother me. Come back next Tuesday, one week, at eleven a.m. like now, but don't touch the watch no matter what. Out."

We were friends; I could speak to him like that.

One week later, he returned in triumph. "See? This damn thing is two lousy minutes ahead of time. Junk."

"Are you through?" I asked. "Look, this watch is running perfectly, but only to its own adjustment. It never varies, you said, two minutes a week. Two minutes is one hundred and twenty seconds per week fast. One hundred and twenty seconds divided by seven days is seventeen seconds and a little per each and every day. On the timing machine it is perfect, but with you running around like you do the watch is picking up impetus and gaining time. I'm going to tweak the regulator and give it back to you. Come in again next week and we'll see how it's going."

A tweaking and he left, but with a doubtful look.

Next Tuesday, a chastened doctor walked into the shop admitting, "My atomic clock says the watch has gained only fourteen seconds since last Tuesday. I don't believe it."

Every now and then even a "genius" gets it right the very first attempt.

"I told you," I answered with all due modesty. "Wear the watch in the best of health, but remember, if you don't wear it for a while, the time will be off when it is off your wrist."

So technology has turned my world upside down and upside down again. After sixty-five years, I am still at the watchmaker's bench repairing whatever a customer may bring in to me. (But no clocks.) Some people are blessed in that they truly *love* what they do for a living. That is me, the little kid whose hands finally got big enough to hold the basic tools. And once again modern technology has put mechanical watches into my hands.

This morning history was delivered to the shop. Another aircraft clock came in for repair; someone was telling former pilots that I would repair these clocks (even though I didn't repair clocks). I realized this clock looked a little different as I took it to the bench for examination and read the accompanying letter asking me to send the estimate to the e-mail address listed. This clock was truly different, as was the BF109E Messerschmitt it was taken from. The war had been over for years, but I instinctively backed up two steps on realizing what I had.

"Where had you flown?" I asked the clock. "Over London or maybe the Russian front? Possibly you were a Luftwaffe fighter flying against B-17 bomber streams over Berlin."

I didn't want to repair this thing, and I put it back in the box for return to its owner. A couple of hours later, I suddenly remembered the Nazi watch from so very many years ago. The past was the past; at least fifty-five years had gone by and…fix the thing.

I e-mailed the estimate (actual cost), received the go-ahead, and repaired the clock. It was truly well made, but sort of over engineered as many German things were. After a week's running I proceeded to box the clock for return. I made out the mailing label. The first and last names were traditional German names, even though the watch came from the American South. I would have loved to have known the tie between the German "Southerner" and this particular BF109E. My best guess was this clock was a family heirloom. I would never know for sure.

I love receiving watches from around the country and the world. The Internet and e-mail are truly wonderful things. However, I do miss the opportunity to get to know the people behind the watch (or aircraft clock).

Technology can be humiliating at times. A very pretty young woman (VPYW) came into my shop with a man's Longines. Years ago Longines was a watch of unsurpassed prestige and truly deserved its place in the higher echelons of the watch world. This particular watch was a self-winding model in an 18K gold case, no date unit, but with a sweep second hand.

The VPYW related that the watch was the college graduation present of her late father and was to be given to her husband for his birthday the following month. It was a pleasure working on such a watch, and I admit to spending some extra time for what I realized was old times' sake. Three weeks later the VPYW came into the shop to pick up a completely refurbished watch. Can I admit I hated to see her leave?

As the fates had it, she was back in two weeks…the watch wasn't running properly, and she was quite disappointed. Accompanied by the proper amount of groveling, I had her leave the watch, because, after all, it was fully guaranteed, and any problems were my responsibility. I checked the watch carefully and set it up on the auto watch winder and watched it perform perfectly for three days, after which I waited until it ran down naturally, which was about forty hours after removal from the winder. Normal. I called my customer, and the watch was picked up by the VPYW.

The following week the Longines was returned by a now much more than disappointed VPYW. I was informed that her father *never* had a problem with his precious watch, and it was only since I'd worked on it that there was a problem.

She asked, "Is there a little possibility that the new battery you installed could be the problem?"

BINGO!

I tactfully explained, "This is *not* a battery-powered watch. It winds itself as the customer moves his arm during normal daily activities. See the word 'Automatic" on the dial? That is what it means."

Her reply came with wide eyes. "It winds itself *without* a battery or anything just from wearing it? Wow. Whatever will they think of next?"

The VPYW picked up the watch and with a wonderful smile walked from the shop, leaving behind a shriveled-up husk of a very old, old man. The passing years had finally caught up with me. Needless to say, the watch has not been back since. Neither has the VPYW.

Ten years later and I'm happy to report that most of the extremely high-grade watches are again mechanical...highly refined and quite high tech, but still and again mechanical.

Recently I worked on an Omega Constellation, of course a mechanical, automatic calendar watch. It required some extra attention, so I stayed a few extra minutes to finish it up. Just as I secured the case, the phone rang. "Hello, watch repair." The normal greeting.

"What the hell are you doing in the shop at quarter to eleven?" That was not the happy voice of a loving daughter. Quarter to eleven? At night? Couldn't be...so I looked at my watch. Uh-oh.

"I was finishing an Omega and stayed a couple of extra minutes." It seemed I'd lost all track of time. All I heard was "OUT" and a phone being slammed down. Sometimes you can get yelled at, lectured, and shamed with only one word. I left.

The phone rang. "Afternoon, watch repair."

A gentleman was calling from upstate New York. He has been recommended by one of my accounts.

"I've got a vintage handmade European watch that needs cleaning, oiling, and a gallon of TLC. My only question is how much insurance do you have?" I was asked.

I had heard of the watch, but *never* thought I'd see one, let alone be called upon to actually repair one. I worried about the insurance question.

"Why, what's the problem, and what is the watch worth? I do repair watches that come into my shop, but I don't pay attention to what they're worth."

I was quite startled when the answer came back in six figures. "I'm sorry, but I don't think I can help you. I appreciate you calling," was my instinctive reply. "I have to refuse the financial liability, sorry, but there is no way...no way at all."

"I'm sorry too. You were highly touted by my friend. Thank you for your trouble."

I began to say something, but just got a dial tone.

A six-figure watch. Oy! I wasn't worried about being able to fix the watch but of the money involved. I'd have to sleep in the shop while it was here in Milford. I asked myself, "What about the price of the repair, wise guy?" I answered myself, "Not that much money on my head."

Two days later, he called back. "Mr. Marcus, if I send the watch in the care of an armed, bonded messenger, would you take care of the watch?"

I didn't know there was such a thing as a bonded, armed messenger. My instinct was to accept the watch, provided, of course, I did not have to accept the financial responsibility. "I will do it next Saturday, but the watch will not be in my shop overnight. He will have to meet me about seven a.m. and wait here in the shop while I repair the watch. When I'm done, he can take it with him back to upstate New York." An agreement was reached, a verbal one, but enough to satisfy me. The messenger would have to show me his credentials and then I would look at the watch.

My new customer didn't know how lucky he was that boating season had not officially started.

Saturday morning a man came to my door, introduced himself, showed me his credentials, and handed me an ailing watch. I will be honest and admit that I should have been wearing my best suit, a tie, and good shoes rather than jeans and boat shoes.

As I worked on the watch, my guard read a rather thick book and shared coffee (black, no sugar) from my pot. Actually he was a pretty nice guy, and the conversation was enjoyable. Lunch was grinders delivered to the shop. I was too well known in Milford...the owner of the sub shop wanted to know why I was working on a sunny Saturday. A question came to mind...was I living a pleasant routine or was I in a deep, deep rut?

At 2:30 p.m. there was a knock on the locked door. I looked up and saw one of Milford's policemen peering into the shop and looking unhappy. Uh-oh. When I opened the door, he walked in rapidly, asking, "Is everything okay, Mr. Marcus? Someone called the station that your wagon was in the parking lot on a Saturday. You okay?"

I assured the officer that I was just working on a very special watch, and that was the reason I had company. I made introductions. He was relieved, shook hands, and left. My guard was quite impressed, said he'd never seen a person checked by the police because he *was* at work.

At a little after 5:00 p.m., the watch was completed, had tested out beautifully, and I carefully bagged it for travel. I escorted the watch to the parking lot. The messenger and I shook hands, I wish him a pleasant trip up the Mass Pike, and the watch was gone from my life.

I went back upstairs to my "little world" and finished the last of too much coffee. I thought of both Uncle Abe and my own father and their constant use of the word "people." This had been the *most* valuable, *most* prestigious watch I had ever had in my hands, and *so what?* There was no spirit attached to the watch...no grandfather or grandmother, no personal event, no memories, no emotions…just an impossibly valuable thing that told the time. Why was I not in awe of what I'd just fixed? I knew the answer, of course: I'd repaired thousands of watches over sixty-five years at the bench, but the individual watches that stuck in my mind all involved special people who cherished their timepieces. War, accidents, illness, more war, death, whether sudden or natural, even release from jail, those were my personal memories. Even clocks I didn't fix and guns I never saw in a clock I didn't work on in a house I never visited. I smile once again at the memory of *her.* Time to call it a day (pun intended).

T he more things change, they more they stay the same.

A very elderly man (even to me) brought an old Elgin in for repair. Gold-filled case, 8/0, seventeen jewels, from the 1930s. Could I get it to run?

"Sure," I answered. "I bet you had this a long time. Were you the original owner?"

"I was." (Now history came back to my story—war and watches.) "I was carrying this when I was wounded—bad—a very few days before the war ended. I was too bad to move, so I was put into a hospital in the town we'd just taken, and I was kept there for several weeks. This had been a civilian hospital, but our army took it over, lock, stock, and German nurses. I have to admit the German nurses took good care of me. Life was screwy because there were Wehrmacht soldiers there too. I hate to admit, but some of them were pretty good guys. Some of them. They were just soldiers. Like me."

I was surprised as the tears sprang into his eyes. "My grandson was recently badly wounded in Iraq. Of course he was flown to Germany for medical care and they saved him. Last week I found out that he is in the same town where I was. In a new US-built facility, but the same damn place. I was there in 1945. It is 2005 and my grandson recovers from battle wounds in the same damn place. Sixty years and how far has the world gone? I want the watch to go to him."

The grandson eventually came back to this country. I met him when he came to have the watchband adjusted as it was too small for him; this young man was a good deal bigger than his grandfather. I recognized the watch and asked about his grandfather.

"Granddad died three months ago."

Silence. War and watches. Watches and war.

My world of watches went on. As one tale ended, another crossed my bench. This morning I received by mail an 18K Rolex, the oldest one I'd ever seen. This was not an import; the word "Swiss" was not on the dial as required by US Customs. This was from Europe, and instinctively I knew the story. I phoned the customer in New Hampshire.

"This was brought home from Europe by my father," I was told. "He said that he 'liberated' it. My father was always sketchy on the details, but I know it came off of a German soldier. Can you fix one this old?"

I checked it with my fingers crossed. Even Rolex didn't have all the parts for these oldest models. Not that it mattered, since Rolex would never ship parts to little ole me. Luckily, no parts were needed so I could repair it. I'd send him a card when it was ready.

I sighed. Sixty-four years at the bench and nothing had changed. Maybe thousands of watches, repaired and long forgotten. And too many watches, some rather nondescript while others were magnificent examples of the watchmaker's art, all with a common thread—humanity's oldest pastime: WAR.

In early February a man brought in an obviously elderly Rolex. Before he would hand me the watch I had to "hear its story." In my mind I could hear the gunfire, but this time I was wrong.

Mr. Prout related, "I just received this watch back from Rolex in New York. They returned it without even opening the case to check the movement. They said they wouldn't even look at it because they had no parts to service this very old model."

I was not really surprised. Rolex had what I called a lousy attitude and couldn't care less about their watch owners. Naturally I agreed to at least open the case and carefully examine the movement to see just what was needed. As soon as I looked at the watch I knew there was a problem; there were no automatic unit parts available. Idly I moved the oscillating weight back and forth, and to my surprise, I could see that the watch was truly winding, everything was operating as it should, and each and every tiny spring, lever, gear, and gizmo was in good condition.

I asked, "Did they give you any kind of report on the condition of the watch?"

Bluntly he replied, "They wouldn't even look at it. No opening, no exam, no nothing."

I had to ask both Dad and Uncle Abe about this one. I had spent my life talking to watches, discussing things with my cars as I drove, and talking problems over with my sailboat as we sat out at a mooring. To me, talking over a people problem with Dad and Uncle Abe was just another part of the day. At Uncle Abe's "suggestion," I inquired as to any personal attachment to the watch. I needn't have asked, of course.

My customer related, "This watch was originally the college graduation present to my grandfather just before the war. He wore it all through the war, even though he never left New England. Eventually he gave the watch to my father, who just gave it to me. I sent it to Rolex to have it cared for before I started to wear it, but as I told you, they wouldn't even look at it."

Rolex makes high quality watches, but their customer service is pathetic. I told him, "Here is where we are. At this very moment there are no parts needed to repair and service this watch. Even the crystal is only surface scratched and will polish beautifully. I can service this watch the way a Rolex should be serviced and will even guarantee the repair. However there is a large 'but.' There is a spring that looks just like a swastika, with two opposing arms bent slightly downward. The other opposing springs are bent upward. Above and below are two gears that act as ratchets. When the weight spins in one direction the watch winds, but in the other direction the opposing springs just free turn over their connecting gears.

"That one part is the problem. Rolex doesn't have any replacements anymore, and if that spring or one of the arms breaks there's nothing I can do at that point. So even though I say I guarantee the repair, there would be no way to keep it a self-winding watch. Sorry."

The response surprised me. "But you said the watch could be repaired perfectly the way it is. Would you repair it for me?"

"Of course I will, but my obligation is to warn you about the potential problem if the crazy spring happens to finally break. That's why I dislike companies like Rolex; they didn't have the decency to examine your watch and let the option be yours to repair or not to repair it."

"I want this watch repaired, and if the spring ever goes, well, if it goes, I guess that will really be the end of the watch." He sighed. "I have to chance it."

My turn: "Look, I've spent my life not only thinking outside the box but, when needed, off the wall. If the spring does go, there's a way that will let you wear and use the watch for the rest of your life, but as a wind-it-up-every-morning watch, like in the old days, the real old days."

He stammered, "H-How can you convert a watch like that? Sounds impossible."

"Not really. Outside of the self-winding unit, the only part that differs from a wind-me-up is the mainspring barrel. An automatic has a smooth barrel with a torqued slip spring that allows the mainspring to be tightly wound, then slips around the inner rim of the barrel so the wind gears won't strip and break. All I have to do is change the slip bridle to one that is much, much too strong. It won't slip around the barrel, and when you have the watch fully wound, believe me, your fingers will tell you the watch is wound."

The look on his face was once again validation of my lessons and lectures from Dad and Uncle Abe. Maybe it was true that I was born already knowing how to fix watches...maybe. In the end, what made me what I was, was the most important lesson of all. That what I was servicing was people.

Weeks later I found I had been wrong. I'd contacted an old-line watch material company and requested the ability to purchase fill-ins for a large number of case gaskets needed for a material cabinet that originally was supplied through this company. Along with my order of gaskets, the company sent their latest catalogue. With a few moments to kill, I relaxed to scan through Borel's book of goodies. Suddenly I came across a large section of generic materials for Rolex watches, including, to my shock, the exact swastika-shaped automatic springs I didn't need for that vintage Rolex. Next to that one were pictures of two others I'd always thought were obsolete long ago.

There was a section that stressed that there was "no connection between the parts company and the Rolex Company." Somewhere, someplace, someone was making these generic parts. I'd used generic parts before, for Rolex and other brands, with 100 percent success, and I didn't understand the policies and attitudes of many companies. When I completed the repair of a customer's watch, it had *my* guarantee, so I couldn't take chances on the parts I used.

Two days ago, May 4, 2009, I got a phone call from a man who had a 992B Hamilton that could not be set. Over the phone I told him that the 992B was a marvelous railroad movement that was set by unscrewing the front cover and pulling out a lever tucked under the two o'clock position. He said he could not unscrew the cover, so naturally I suggested he bring in the watch.

In midafternoon, a middle-aged couple came in. Explaining that he was the man I'd recently spoken to, he handed across the counter a velvet bag containing what I could see was a large watch. This was indeed a *watch*.

I explained, "This watch is not a 992B Hamilton. It's a 4992B Hamilton, a watch made by contract for the government in World War Two. This is a navigator's timepiece and doesn't set as I said on the phone. The 'four' indicates the military application, and I've not seen one of this particular model for some years now. All the numbers and symbols on the back of the case are the contract and batch numbers, and from these letters I know this watch went to a US Army Air Forces navigator."

I took the watch to my bench, opened the case, and there it was... an absolutely pristine 4992B Hamilton. It did need service, but was obviously well cared for. I was a little surprised that there were only two repair marks, especially considering the age. I told my customers what I found and started to show them the features and operations of this very special version of a famous watch movement. I asked, "Is this a family heirloom?"

"Yes," the woman replied, "this was my father's watch, and he was indeed a navigator...on a B-17 during the war. He died last month, and we found this watch and his uniform in the very back of his closet."

I thought to myself, "This doesn't end, does it?" I waited for the story I knew was coming.

"My father talked very little about the war. He did tell us he was a navigator on a B-17 and he flew twenty-eight missions. Most flew twenty-five, but my dad wanted to stay with his best friend who had been wounded and had missed the last three missions. When he returned to duty, the rest of his crew was about to receive orders to stand down. The war was almost over, so Dad volunteered to fly just three more missions to be with his friend. He told us he flew the last three missions and the war ended shortly after. He came home to the States and here we are. It wasn't until he died that we found out..." She stopped speaking and just stood, looking into the past.

Her husband took up the narration. "Her father washed out of flight school and became a navigator. He went to England with what became his crew and went to war. That's all we were ever told. He went to war in a B-17. He came home and lived out his life. Did all the normal things, family, vacations, movies, TV, everything, but never, ever watched a war movie about the air war. Do you remember *Twelve O'clock*

High or *Command Decision*? He'd leave the room if anyone was watching them but never said why. He enjoyed *Victory at Sea* about the navy, but if a show included multi-engine planes, he was up and out of the room."

I held the watch in my hands and in my mind saw a young navigator checking the time against actual locations, speeds, and probable fuel time remaining. Another watch whose job was to help keep people alive and well. Yet just a watch.

The wife took up the tale. "When Dad died and we flew to Saint Louis to clean out his house, we found boxes sealed in a back closet. His old uniforms and what turned out to be his flight jacket, a heavy leather thing lined with sheepskin to keep the guys warm at thirty thousand feet. That's when my husband found the jagged holes in the flight jacket." She hesitated, and I fiddled with the watch a little more. I literally had goose bumps.

"I opened a zippered bag and there was his dress uniform. There were rows of ribbons on it...I mean rows. Multicolored ones, simple ones, a purple one with three things on it. I had no idea what they meant. I'd never seen that uniform before, but I knew enough to understand that my father had gone through four kinds of hell."

By now they were both sitting down and I'd brought around one of my wheeled desk chairs. I believe I was one of the first people to hear the father's story, a history not discovered until after his death.

She continued, "My husband opened a heavy envelope. It was full of official-looking papers, and as I read them I realized they were citations...citations for bravery in combat. My father, this peaceful, quiet man, had been awarded three Silver Stars. There were others, scary ones. Dad had stayed in the plane after a crash landing and went into the tail after the plane caught fire to save the wounded tail gunner... that was one. I couldn't read any more. My husband suggested we take the uniform jacket down to the army recruiter and find out what the other ribbons meant. We did.

"We went into Saint Louis and found the army place. When I showed what seemed to be the senior man the jacket, he came up out of his chair like a rocket. He actually stammered a little while he asked who this belonged to. He smoothed the jacket on his desk and said he

121

felt a lump in a side pocket, reached in, and took out this watch. It was the soldier who told us what he thought the watch was, and you confirmed it. Anyway, he said that the story told by the citations explained what I'd told him. My dad had gone through and seen things that no young man should ever experience. He found a way to live with them, but he could never talk about them. My mother never knew, because they met after he came home from Europe."

I had wound the watch and set it, actually without thinking, and for no particular reason put it on the timing machine. This was *not* possible, but the record looked as though I'd overhauled the watch an hour and a half ago. I asked how long the watch was in the pocket in the box, sealed up in Saint Louis and…she had no idea.

I carefully put the watch into a modern plastic sealed bag and gave it back.

"This watch needs nothing at all. It seems to run as well as it did the year your father was issued this. Put it away very carefully with your dad's things and look at it every now and then. If it's to ever be actually used, then bring it in for servicing. Beyond that, leave it alone."

We shook hands all around; they thanked me and quietly left. Now was time for a cup of coffee (black, no sugar). Just as I finished the coffee I realized…I hadn't taken in the watch for repair so I had no names, address, or even what town they came from. All I know is it was two hours between the phone call and getting to the shop. I haven't seen the watch since.

A problem that wouldn't go away had been haunting me. A year ago, in 2008, I overhauled a really nice Omega watch. Slim round case, made of 18K gold, really an example of the watchmaker's art. It went well, as an Omega normally does, and I watched it for a few days and returned it to the store. Life was good.

Two weeks later, the Omega was back…the complaint was the watch would not run. Well, it happens to all of us. I wound the watch and carefully set the correct time and put it in the checking box to examine the following day. To my surprise it was running almost perfectly, just a little bit slow, taken care of quickly with just a famous Marcus "tweak" of the regulator. I rewound it, adjusted the hands, and put it back into the box to wait another day. After a week everything was still fine, so I opened the case and rechecked the movement...maybe I could see something. No. Nothing, even with the double loupe. Nothing to do but return it to the store with confidence. Off it went.

A group of Rolexes came in for repair. A store that sells Rolexes had run into a group of customers that would *not* allow their watches to go to the factory. They said nothing, but I knew why. Four Rolexes really made both me and my bank account happy. The repairs were nothing out of the ordinary, just regular overhauls, but highly fussy work. When I work on a regular watch of average quality, I strive to do my best, but there is an instinctive increase in effort when the watch is a Rolex, Omega, or any of the really prestigious brands.

Everything was going smoothly until the mailman brought a present...the Omega was back. A note of complaint was included...the watch refused to run, yet it was completely unwound. I wound it and set the time and made a note to check it in the morning.

The following morning, I picked up the watch and—oh no—it was running fine. What the heck? I checked the movement and saw and found nothing once again. Something was screwy here, so I decided to clean and oil the watch again. After carefully redoing the repair job and finding nothing to repair, the watch went back in the checking box. It goes without saying that everything was fine, and after several days I returned the watch to the customer.

I received a ladies' watch. A modern quartz timepiece, but somewhat costly in a nicely made 14K yellow gold case and band. It had been running fine the previous night, but had stopped in the middle of the morning. The customer couldn't wait, so I took the name and address and off she went. The following day, during a lull in my busy day, I opened the case to change the battery and—a big oh no! This watch, a high-grade ETA quartz movement, required a Renata 44 battery. This is a special small-diameter, thin two-volt lithium battery. I began to get worried as all the battery catalog sheets that had the Renata 44 listed said "call for a price quote." This was not good, I thought.

I called for the price quote and laughed in my supplier's face...or rather in his ear. "Very funny," I exclaimed. "How much is the damn battery?" He was not kidding, and I was not buying. Thanking him politely, I called another supplier, only to be told that "you do not want to know."

Four phone calls to suppliers later, I gave up. I was forced to call my customer to tell her the battery would cost her (I still don't believe this) $145...for a watch battery.

Her answer, "Well, that's $25 less than the last time."

I asked her if she was willing to wait for the watch to give me time to think this over. She agreed, and I told her I'd be back in touch. In short order, I found that this *one* particular movement was the *only* one to take the R44 battery. The entire production line had to be geared up to make a very limited number of only the R44 battery. There was an equivalent 2V lithium battery of a size for a man's watch, but it presented the same obscene pricing problem. This would require some thinking.

For lack of any ideas I put the 2V R44 onto my battery tester. This was a normal battery tester I took apart and rebuilt for my own convenience. I could now test any battery with only one hand while the other was busy holding the watch of the moment. No matter the diameter or the thickness, the contacts were automatically made and I got my reading, for better or worse. Only one other watchmaker had ever seen my device...my cousin Bob. Anyway, the battery read out at only one volt...no good. No new ideas either, but at least the customer was in no hurry to spend that much money.

A week passed. Lots of coffee (black, no sugar) and no brilliant idea was at hand. I could come up with no alternative to an impossibly costly battery and I was getting angry—with myself. I should have come up with something by now.

My day was made...the Omega was back again. This time with a long note explaining how angry the customer had become. Not a surprising development. Again the note said the watch wouldn't work. This time I'd had it. Something weird was definitely going on here. I stripped it down for another cleaning and oiling. It became once again one of six watches going through the ultrasonic cleaning machines. The procedure here, instilled by Uncle Abe, was to pretend I'd never seen the watch before to avoid taking anything for granted. Checking every last little tiny thing...one piece at a time. With no undue modesty I did a superior job on the Omega, checking everything twice and then again. I even put it on the demagnetizer, just in case. When I finished, I was positive the watch was slightly better than the day it left the factory.

New angle. This watch was a thin model with a matching crown of proper diameter. Out of curiosity, I took the watch across the hall to the dentist office and asked one of the women to wind the watch for me...a test of fingers and the crown. Sadly, no problem... that would have been the easy solution. I ran and tested the watch for four additional days. Not a damn thing wrong with this watch.

Another day. Time for a cup of coffee (black, no sugar) and time to brood over the watch needing the R44 battery. I slowly drank the coffee, but not a hint of an idea. I was sure I was missing something...something that I already knew, but it wouldn't come to the surface.

Two productive weeks passed, and sick watches continued to come into the shop. Costly, cheap, famous...whatever...in the watches came. Thankfully, I was busy and productive until...the Omega was back again. Enough! I knew the problem was not the watch. Someone at the other end was running with a bent balance staff.

Onto the phone, and the volume was turned way up. Out of my personal norm, I read the riot act to the store owner, and of course he instantly went into Defensive Condition 2.

"I'm going to lose a good customer over this Omega. How long do you leave it on the automatic winder to check it?" he asked.

We paused for a long silence while I tried to "use the force" to melt his brain.

Totally out of character, I lost my temper. "You idiot, do you mean you are so stupid you can't tell that a thin dress watch is *not* an automatic!? I sweated for months over this damn watch, and neither you nor the watch owner ever had the sense to wind it up in the morning! Nobody in the business can be that dumb. You are worried about losing a customer. You should be worried about losing your watchmaker. I cannot and will not tolerate dumb."

Down went the phone, and I headed for the office and a cup of coffee (black, no sugar). It had been a long time since I was so angry. That was the end of any work for the day, and I left fifteen minutes early, which upset the owner of the building, who knew something must be terribly wrong. The whole town knew that Barry Marcus never, ever left work early. I had to assure him that I was okay, and he finally let me go.

The next morning I mailed the Omega out for the last time and went back to a world that was, for me, normal. Meaning I still had to solve the problem of the R44 battery. Still nothing.

I decided to begin the day with the overhaul of an original 1960 214 Accutron, a top of the line watch with a 14K gold case. This was the original Accutron model, unique in that the crown, used only for setting, was part of the back of the watch. When introduced, the Accutron utilized a mercury battery of 1.35 volts, which was expected to, and did, power the watch for a complete year. Additionally, if allowed to die inside the watch and then sit around until it leaked, the mercury battery would not corrode the inside of the watch. At the time, the 214 battery cost $1.95 installed, about double the cost of a similar-sized hearing aid battery, which used a different chemical makeup. Some watch owners took it upon themselves to change the batteries using the hearing aid battery they bought in drug stores. Changing the battery merely meant opening a hatch in the back of the watch, shaking out the old battery, and inserting the new one. The hearing aid batteries were not configured to last a year, and as they died early, the seals leaked. Result: a ruined Accutron movement in the watch.

As I took apart the Accutron, I chuckled at the hysteria when the federal government outlawed the use of mercury batteries. The only substitute was a 1.5V silver oxide battery, and the Bulova engineers had always warned the watchmakers that the stronger battery would make the watch run exceedingly fast. There was the same problem with the later introduced 218 model, or so they warned. When our backs were to the wall, we had to shift to the 1.5V silver batteries, and there were no problems with a properly phased Accutron. What we were so worried about turned out...

That's it! That's it! That's it! That's it! I was up out of my chair, trying to maintain my dignity and not jump around the shop. The R44 had powered the watch until it had weakened to a level of 1.0 volt. That meant the watch would run properly with a 1.5V battery, and there was a normal battery of the exact dimensions of the R44. With my hand admittedly shaking I got the battery and installed it in the watch. I put the movement onto the tester and ran for a cup of coffee (black, no sugar) and back to the bench. Every time the quartz circuit "stepped," the rotor turned a partial turn to drive the hands and the testing machine blinked a green light. Three times a minute the little green light blinked, once every twenty seconds. I turned on an electronic metronome I'd gotten somewhere along the line and sat counting "twenty" after each blink. I counted "twenty" over and over until I'd finally finished that cup of coffee.

On paper, it looked promising. The R44 started life at 2V and ran the watch until it dropped to 1.0V for $145. The 341 silver battery started life at 1.5V and would most likely run the watch until it too reached 1.0V. Obviously the R44 would, at $145, outlast three number 341 batteries that would cost about $10 each. I felt a real ego boost. Since I took in this watch, I had heard that many of these watch owners were putting them aside because of the impossible cost. A few who had sent the watch to the factories had been double charged as the companies insisted on doing a complete overhaul before putting in a new R44 battery.

I called and explained to the woman who owned this watch, and she was beyond delighted with my brainstorm. The simple idea of spending about $10 about three times rather than spending $145 once delighted her. The little inconvenience of driving to my shop an extra time or two was worth the cost savings.

(I am a little ashamed to admit that I decided to tell no one about this, with the sole exception of my cousin Bob, after the administration of a blood oath to secrecy.)

I went through a bout of the terminal smugs, which I deserved, I think.

Today, five weeks after I put the 1.5V battery into the ladies watch to sub for a Renata 44, the woman came in to pick up her watch. I went to the safe and took the watch from the envelope and...sure enough...it was running perfectly. It had been five weeks now, and I was truly smiling. Happily I explained my theory and my "experiment," of which she was a big part.

As I described what I'd thought up, her grin grew to the size of mine. I cautioned her that this new battery would not last as long as the original R44, but at the very affordable price of $10, it was barely an inconvenience to replace it more often.

As she took out her purse, I explained there was no charge for the battery I'd installed because I really did not know how long it would last. This "experiment" would only work if she promised to bring the watch in again as soon as it stopped running. I had to remove the battery to again measure the low voltage that stopped the watch. That way I could be sure of the expected longevity of the substitute battery. She happily agreed and went off to go shopping. I went into the back of the shop for a cup of coffee (black, no sugar).

A package came into the shop from the Chicago area. I located my box knife and soon beheld...I couldn't believe it...a World War II aircraft clock. There was a note inside, which included a request to phone the owner.

The person who answered was obviously very elderly...another World War II veteran, tied somehow to a timepiece, this one a Waltham "elapsed time clock." I know, I know, I don't repair clocks, but this was really a very large watch, a variation of a chronograph.

"I'm glad you called," the elderly voice said. "A friend who got your name from someone else told me to send you my clock. It is very special to me and you repaired a similar clock for him." He told me a man's name, but naturally it meant nothing to me. I can't remember a name beyond a half hour and never could. It's just how my memory works, allowing me to remember the details of a watch repaired thirty years ago but unable to recall the owner's name an hour later.

I asked why he wanted the clock serviced, despite already knowing. Yes, I knew the moment I saw the clock, lacking only the details of this particular story.

"It was just before the end of the battle for Okinawa. I was flying a Corsair on combat air patrol over the radar picket destroyers that had been badly hurt by the kamikaze suicide planes. I had just got another kill when the radio called the CAP back toward the carrier…some Japanese had broken through and the ship was in trouble. We got back in time, and I got my fourth plane of the day, but the last one got me. I was too close when it blew up, and a big chunk of him caught my engine. My engine was on fire and I was too low to bail out, so I had to ride her down. I was not far from the island and had enough control to head for the part of the island where the troops had landed on April first. I thought I could land on the beach, and I didn't want to put my plane into the water. We had been together too long for me to lose her now.

"Soon I realized that I wasn't going to make it to land. I tried to glide as long as possible. We hit the water just shy of the beach as the engine fire flared up real bad. She bounced after hitting with a huge splash and bounced again as the plane actually surfed onto the shore like some kid in Hawaii. The plane slid up onto the beach past the wings and stopped just as I noticed the splash had put out the fire.

"I just sat there, unable or unwilling to get out, just numb and completely unhurt. After a few minutes I heard shouting and pounding above my head and looked up to see a group of marines pounding on the canopy with their rifle butts. I knew they were afraid the plane would blow, and they were desperate to get me out. I released the canopy, and the knives came out as they cut my straps and hauled me out like a sack of flour. They carried me over the wing and onto the beach, and I didn't even get my feet wet. Someone pushed a sandwich at me, and I sat on the beach and ate a late lunch.

"Later I climbed back into the cockpit to get a couple of personal things, and for some reason I decided to steal the clock. Took a dime out of my pocket and unscrewed the two screws that held it in the control panel. It was still running after all that.

"An hour later a tin can (destroyer) sent a whaleboat onto the beach, and I hitched a ride on the can back to my carrier. There was quite a bit of excitement as I'd been listed as missing and presumed lost. I never told anyone about the clock. It didn't really matter 'cause the plane was totaled. Far as I know it's still sitting on that beach. Anyway, not long after that, 'the Bomb' was dropped and the war was over."

He paused then continued, "When I got home, I opened my office and had a wood stand made for the clock on my desk. It's been with me since, moving to my desk at home when I finally retired. It quit last week, and I need you to fix it up. Okay? That clock has been telling me the time since 1944 and has never failed me. I don't know how much longer I have, but that clock is important to me and I want to leave it in working order."

I gave him the price for the repair of a Waltham elapsed time chronometer and promised to mail the clock back as soon as possible. Hanging up, I went to my bench and sat there looking at the clock, trying to imagine myself in the cockpit, checking the clock to see how much flight time I had. A pilot once told me the elapsed time clock was more accurate than the fuel gauges at times. Time for a cup of coffee (black, no sugar).

At four o'clock that afternoon I got a phone call. He was calling from Worcester and had been given my name at a store I had done some work for. He mentioned that when he was a young man there was a jewelry store with a watchmaker on Main Street by the name Marcus…was there a connection? Uncle Abe had fixed his watch a couple of times. Another watch with a story…the parade of time really doesn't end.

This watch was a Hamilton version of a navigator's watch, and he had flown B-29s over Korea. The gentleman was just a little older than me. We chatted for a couple of minutes, and I learned that while I went to Commerce High, he had graduated from Classical High a couple of years before me, in time to end up flying combat missions over North Korea. The customer would make the drive out to Milford in a few days. I knew it would be another in a long line of war stories, a line I'd come to realize had no end. I guess no end until the end of time itself (no pun intended).

A month ago, a typical young *twerp* came into the shop. This one was a walking cliché. His baseball cap was brim backward, perched above a scraggly beard. His sweatshirt and jeans had lost the battle with the moths or whatever had attacked them. I couldn't see his shoes, but I expected I'd see toes sticking out.

"May I help you?" I asked, ever polite, as Dad and Uncle Abe taught me.

"Yes, sir," he answered as he placed a beat-up pocket watch on the counter, "I'd like this watch serviced as it needs. It's running well, but I'll need it, my dad said cleaned and oiled. Will you examine it, sir?"

My reply was easy. "I don't have to examine it. It's a 16S Waltham, most likely a twenty-year case, which is a very good quality, but with most of the gold worn off. The odds are that there is nothing wrong as you've said it's running well. The only thing I would do is to change the crystal; this one, frankly, looks like hell."

"That would be fine, sir. The only problem is I must pick it up in no more than three weeks. Will that be a problem, sir?"

A red light was blinking in my head, but it didn't register. "Three weeks will be plenty of time for me to do the overhaul and check it for surety and regulation." I grabbed a watch ticket and was surprised that this young *twerp* was from Sudbury, a good distance from Milford. "May I ask how you came to Milford with your watch?"

"Sir, a store in Sudbury doesn't take in watches but said I should bring it to Milford for proper service." Whereupon he gave me one of my older business cards.

I asked for and got a pretty good deposit on the repair price. A quick "thank you, sir" and out he went. I still didn't get what was bugging me.

A couple of days later, while I had a set of six watches in the ultrasonic tank, I took out the pocket watch, which had to be worked on individually because of its size. As usual, I opened the bezel, removed the hands, and turned it over to open the hinged double back. As I thought, I had a 16S Waltham from the late 1800s, in a badly worn but not abused case, guaranteed not to wear out for the indicated number of years. Also, as I had thought, the watch was in well cared for shape and just needed a good general overhaul. I was pleased to find a modern "unbreakable" mainspring inside. This watch had been properly cared for.

I took care of the set of six watches as I put the pocket watch through the cleaner. When I started work on the movement, I dropped the case and bezel into the ultrasonic jewelry cleaner for a super cleaning. The movement literally fell together without a struggle and then surprised me by timing out at only twelve seconds a day fast. I tweaked the regulator and watched it for a couple of days under a glass cover. It would be easier to do any additional work if the movement was out of the case.

Time to finish up the watch so I could wind and run it for a few days before the *twerp* picked it up. I fitted the new crystal to the bezel and sat down to case it up. On the inner cover I carefully scribed my mark and the repair codes, and then for the first time, I looked into the outer back cover to check for stains or dirt stuck in the corner of the rim and…

"What the hell is this!?" Line after line after line of engraving…mostly individual words or at the most two words. All the engraving was of varying print and size. Some was hand engraved, other words machine engraved, with a couple done by what was called a vibrating electric scriber. I couldn't accept what I read…word by word…line by line…

San Juan Hill

Argonne

Belleau Wood

Sicily

St. Mere Eglise

Falaise

Ardennes

Bastogne

Rhine River

Okinawa

Pusan

Yalu River

Hungnam

Kae Sahn

Hue

Kuwait City

Baghdad

I couldn't believe this. I sat back, stunned. This worn-out Waltham had been to most of the major battles of the last century and one at the beginning of this century. I anxiously waited for the *twerp* to pick up his watch.

Three weeks to the day, and I couldn't wait for the *twerp* to come for this watch. It was a normal day. People in and out…leave a watch, pick one up, battery repairs, but where was the *twerp*?

My shop door opened and an extremely sharp marine private marched in. I approached the counter. "Hi, may I help you?"

"Good afternoon, sir, I'm here to pick up my pocket watch."

A large light bulb went off in my head! This was what had been puzzling me—the constant use of the *sir*. Not normal for a twerp, but instinctive for a young marine. My *twerp* had become a US Marine Corps private. Can you imagine how stupid I felt?

I had to ask, "Would you mind telling me the story of the engravings inside the cover? I can't believe what I read. Please?"

He took a deep breath. "The watch belonged to my great-great-grandfather who carried it to Cuba during the war with Spain. Thankfully he came home okay, and the watch was given to my great-grandfather. He went to Europe during World War One. After the Argonne, he had the idea of inscribing the places the watch had gone. He had the printing done small to leave a lot of room. Anyway, he went to France as a young teenager and stayed in the army.

"My great-grandfather was still in the army when we got into World War Two, and you can trace his travels inside the watch, from Africa to France and even back to the Ardennes with Patton. This watch went to war *twice* in the forests of Europe. My great-grandfather came back from Europe and gave the watch to my grandfather, then a young marine. Grandpa had the watch when he landed on Okinawa in 1945. He was wounded a week before the island was secured, bad enough that he couldn't stay in the marines although, he healed up fine."

I could hardly believe what I heard. The young marine continued, "My own dad went from the Pusan Perimeter to the Yalu River and back during the Korean War. He was among the last taken off at Hungnam. When he got home, he had those names inscribed inside the watch cover. My dad carried the watch to Vietnam and saw quite a bit of combat. He came home badly wounded but did recover. My brother carried it to Iraq, twice. Now it's my turn."

"I'm deploying next Monday, I think to Afghanistan. Now when I come home, I'll be back with the watch for its new engraving. Now, sir, what's the balance on the repair?"

I stood there like a statue…unable to speak. I took a deep breath. I put an envelope on the counter that I had prepared earlier; inside was the money he had paid as the deposit. "We're calling it even. Please God I'll be here to engrave your entries into the watch." All I could do was smile at him.

The marine shook his head. "No, sir. I can't allow that. I must pay you for your work, sir."

"Look, in 1954, I too wore a uniform and had two more stripes than you. So listen up. I order you to convert that money into a supply of beers. One at a time, don't overdo it, ever. Every fourth or fifth brew, think of the old sailor who wanted to thank you for your service. Buying one for your buddies is okay too. When you bring the watch in for engraving, don't dare ask how much it will cost. Understand?"

The marine snapped to attention and barked, "Aye, aye, sir." He reached out to shake my hand. As he walked from the shop, I said a silent prayer for his safety. Sitting back at my bench, I realized I'd have to double check on the proper spelling of Afghanistan. (I am nervous about adding this to my tale. I don't know the final words and how it will end. I must think about this. My daughters unanimously agreed that the tale stays.)

I'd be laughing at myself, except in today's world this is no longer funny: This afternoon (early June) I carefully packed up the Waltham clock from the Corsair for shipping back to Chicago. Into the box also went a Swiss tuning fork version of the Accutron and an old wind-it-up Wittnauer. I crossed Milford's Main Street to the post office, said hello to the clerk, and put the package on the counter.

The clerk, new to me as I was new to him, froze, then backed up three paces and yelled, "This damn package is *ticking*! What the hell?"

Post office people ran, some toward us and some away, while I saw one reach for a phone. So the box ticked…uh-oh, this was 2009.

One of the older postal clerks reassured the newcomer. "Don't worry, Mr. Marcus fixes watches. These must be newly repaired."

Then, "Barry, are you nuts or just out of your mind? Years ago we would have marked the box 'Newly Repaired Clock' and everything would have been fine. This is now. This box will end up in a barrel of water or blown up by the bomb squad, and your shop will be filled with feds. None of them have a sense of humor. Get this out of here and bring it back tomorrow when it runs down and is quiet."

"But," I said, "this is an eight-day clock, and I wound it fully just before I packed the clock. It's too complicated to remove the clock from the case just to unwind it. I guess I'm stuck for eight days."

My friend said, "Free advice, Barry. Wait nine days, just to be sure."

Back to the shop, and I phoned the owner of the noisy timepiece. I think he's still laughing at me. At least someone thinks it's funny.

A man had brought a gent's Hamilton in with a broken glass crystal. This was a typical Hamilton of the late 1930s, and I actually remembered its likeness from many years ago. I, of course, quoted the exact price for the crystal, laughing to myself at the difference in price between 1938 (or so) and 2009. This entire watch retailed in 1938 for under $40. Now, in 2009, the cost of the crystal was $35…just the crystal. He left and I went back to work…the watch would be ready in a couple of weeks.

A week later, time to work on small jobs, and I came to the old Hamilton. I grabbed the G. S. Crystal catalog and measured the case, already knowing it was classed as a CMH, a code for a particular shape of crystal. Oy, no crystal in the catalog. Could this be *that* old? I dug through the pile of old catalogs, and deep in the stack, I finally found a G. S. catalog from the 1940s and started hunting.

There it was, but a PMH listing; indeed, an old crystal of a flat plastic from "3" to "9" but curved from "12" to "6." This was so old it could only be in the crystal cabinet originally obtained by Dad in 1944 when he bought the store. I opened the proper drawer and dug through, and there it was. However, it was a MH, not a PMH or a CMH. This was an original plastic crystal of a much older formula and softer surface, but actually made for this particular watch. I took it out of the envelope, and with just a small amount of filing, it fit perfectly. I was thankful because this crystal was long ago discontinued.

I am not a philanthropist, but the price I quoted was really too high considering the age of the crystal and what was paid for it in the late 1930s. I decided to drop the price to $25, which still gave a good profit for the crystal plus the time I spent on it. I took the ticket and with a red pen crossed out the $35 and wrote in $25. I stapled the envelope to the repair tag to show the customer. He'd be happy.

On schedule my customer called about the watch, and I happily reported that the watch was ready, except I told him I had "adjusted the price."

"*Bullsh*

**!" was all I heard, and the phone was slammed down. Oh well, I'd explain when he came to pick the Hamilton up.

Only he didn't.

Yesterday (date not important) I received a letter from a lawyer. It seemed my customer went to a lawyer about my "adjustment" of the price. For crying out loud.

I read through all the nonsense and decided to call the lawyer's office, which maybe I should not have done.

The lawyer told me I should not have called him but referred to my own lawyer. I had given his client a quoted price, in writing, he said, and then without warning raised the price. The watch owner had showed him the stub with the price written on it and—

I interrupted, "Your client swore at me and hung up before I could tell him that it turned out the crystal I'd used was so old that the thirty-five dollars was too *high*. My ticket shows the thirty-five-dollar price crossed out with a red pen and the lower price of twenty-five dollars written on the tag. If your client insists on his legal right to pay me the extra ten dollars, I'll gladly accept the donation."

A smaller voice asked, "You lowered the price?"

"Yes, I adjusted the price down, but I will take the extra ten dollars. Get a lot of coffee with it too. I didn't call my own lawyer because I don't believe in throwing away good hard-earned money."

"Mr. Marcus," the lawyer said, "now I have heard everything. Good day."

The finale came today, when a younger man came to pick up the watch. He passed over the counter the claim stub for "lawyered-up

Hamilton." When I came back from getting the watch out of the safe, there was actually $35 on the counter.

"I'm sorry; my dad sometimes acts before he thinks things out. I hope you weren't too upset. He said he agreed to the thirty-five dollars, so he sent it along."

I strongly refused the extra $10. No matter what, I wasn't taking that $10. The man smiled, picked up the bill, shook hands, and left. As he walked from the shop, I knew it would be added to the "Papa Chronicles" before I turned in for the night.

A few days after the Marine formerly known as the *twerp* had left the shop, the phone rang. "Good afternoon, watch repair."

Man's voice: "Good afternoon. We must call you to tell you how very grateful we are for your treatment of our son. He was in your shop a few days ago to pick up a family pocket watch that you serviced." My marine private.

Woman's voice: "He left yesterday and will deploy to Afghanistan soon. He was teary eyed as he described how you refused the balance payment on the watch repair. He actually stammered as he told us how you returned his deposit, pulled rank on him and ordered him to convert the money to beers. I'm not too thrilled about the beer, but thank you for 'ordering' him not to overdo it. Bless you."

Man's voice: "Now dear, our son is a marine as I was and his grandfather and his brothers. That money is not going for glasses of milk. Right, Mr. Marcus? Thank you again and God bless you."

My turn: "Let's all ask God to bless your son and bring him home safely so I can engrave the latest entries into the watch."

Just before the connection was cut, I heard a mother…softly crying.

At midafternoon the door opened and an elderly (to me) man entered the shop, accompanied by a middle-aged woman. I admit there was a very vague familiarity, but I couldn't place the man's name. How could I, with the defective chip in my "name memory" circuit?

As he handed his watch to me, my face lit up like a flashbulb, and I reached across the counter to shake hands with a long, long retired Milford policeman. The instant I'd seen the watch, I knew exactly who the man was. As usual in my mind people did not own watches; rather, watches tolerated the people who frequently abused them.

I was to service a Bulova automatic, twenty-three jewels, in a sculpted stainless steel case.

I had personally sold this man this very watch on June 20, 1954, one day before I took the train to navy boot camp in Maryland. This from a man who needs, from his daughters, a ten-day early warning regarding family birthdays but can remember a specific watch even from fifty-five years ago. I think I have a bent balance staff.

The watch was to be overhauled and prepared for use by my friend's daughter. The watch was somewhat large for a woman's wrist, but this was her *father's* watch, and it would adorn her wrist. In time it would be handed down to her older son.

"As long as you keep it going, Mr. Marcus," she quipped, "this Bulova will keep telling my family when to get going."

The phone rang; a man was seeking directions to the shop. He'd made his way down Route 495 and got as far as the corner of Main Street and Cedar. "Easy," I told him, "I'm just farther up Main Street." I described my building and went back to work. Twenty minutes later, a man my own age walked into the shop, muttering about the traffic, which was merely in its normal jammed state. I was handed an old Bulova "23" automatic and asked if it could be repaired.

While I opened the case to check the movement, the customer looked around, and at a picture on the wall, he exclaimed, "Twenty-five...that has to be the *Frontier.*"

Up I jumped, excited that someone had recognized *my* ship from a printout showing the bow number, which in total was "D25." That stood for AD25...Auxiliary Destroyer Tender # 25. I asked if he'd served on the "twenty-five ship," and he shook his head no.

"I was on the USS *Thomas*, and we frequently tied up alongside the *Frontier* in Japan. My ship was one of—"

I interrupted, "Four tin cans that were often alongside. *Maddox*, *Moore*, *Brush*, and *Thomas*. We spent a lot of time keeping you guys afloat. A whole lot of water has gone under the keel since then, hasn't it? I was an IM in the typewriter shop in '55—'56."

We shook hands as he replied, "I was a yeoman clerk on the *Thomas*. Went aboard the *Frontier* on each tie-up taking typewriters to the main deck for repair. Wait a minute...there was a gigantic third class in charge...scary big but quiet and nice. Is it...?"

"Yes, that was me, a lot of years ago. There's less of me here on top and more of me in the middle, but it's still me. What a small world. How's it going?"

He couldn't believe it either...the world can be a small place. We visited for a half hour, and I went back to check the watch. The watch just needed a good overhaul, which my new shipmate agreed to. I picked up the case back to close the case and...

"I see you had this watch repaired on the *Frontier* in November 1955, just before we came back to the States. I recognize the repair mark inscribed inside the case back. An IM2 fixed this in the watch shop. The world just got smaller."

"I remember that, cost me twelve dollars for that repair, and twelve dollars was a lot of money then. How come you weren't in there?" he asked me.

I smiled. "The senior IMs always went into the watch shop because they could repair crew and officers' watches on their own time for *money*. The navy owned the machines and timers and all the cleaning solvents, but on their own time, money could be earned. If I had the rank, I'd have been in there. But in fairness, I was a twenty-year-old single guy, and the two IMs in the shop were married with kids to raise. They should have been in there. Oh, the repair in 2009 will be a bit more than in 1955." Actually it was a lot more in 2009.

We shook hands again, and he left. The watch was, of course, carefully repaired and picked up two weeks later. When he walked once more into the shop, my "shipmate" carried in two Dunkin' Donuts coffees. He figured I'd drink it black, no sugar, so we sat and talked about the old navy. That's something old guys do.

Several times I've sat down thinking that this story was at an end. Once again, today, June 25, 2009, a new chapter opened. Lately I had been seeing Chinese-made watches more frequently. Last week one came in, a mechanical, self-winding model that was called a skeleton watch. The plates were cut out, with as much metal removed as practical, and the case had crystals, both front and back. It only needed a stem and crown, and by ordering a small selection of varied Chinese stems, I found one that fit perfectly. The crown, being just a crown, was easy to replace. When completed, the watch didn't work.

Of course I had to have a brainstorming session. Just as I had with that first overhaul on that early Seiko, I wanted the learning opportunity on this Beijing special. I called the store and offered a complete overhaul for way too little money, but I wanted to do the job.

That afternoon I stripped down the watch and was quite surprised. I didn't run into any problems taking it apart, the engineering looked well designed, and several little things pleased me. This, of course, was no Omega or TAG or ETA movement, but we would be seeing more of these in the future. As of now, few parts were coming into the country, but as with the early Seikos, I was pretty sure I'd be seeing these in years to come.

(Not many pages ago I'd said the lower-priced mechanical watch was truly a thing of the past. This evening I went back and deleted that statement.)

The Chinese watch was reassembled, adjusted, and cased with practiced ease. No problem whatever, and I was delighted. These movements, installed in low- and moderate-priced watch cases, would become much more familiar in years to come.

Today, July 2, 2009, the Omega was back, like a boomerang. Into each life something must be wrong. The watch apparently ran well for several days in the store and then suddenly stopped dead. I sighed, went to the bench, and opened the case. Carefully examining the watch, I found nothing wrong...oh yes, I did. The hairspring...the coils all stuck together. Couldn't be; this was a sign of oil on the hairspring, causing the clinging, but how? I brought the points of my number three tweezers close to the hairspring, and to my surprise the coils shifted to the tweezers. The watch was magnetized, and suddenly I remembered having to demagnetize it once before.

I put the watch, dial down, on the bull's eye and pushed the button...and the watch instantly began to run with vim and vigor. Putting the watch on the timing machine without further adjustment, I watched the tape come out with a perfect record. That was the problem. But how was the question.

I called Worcester to figure this out and was informed that the watch did truly run, manually wound and kept on my customer's desk so he could keep a constant eye on it. He did this for several days, and then, convinced the watch was finally okay, put it back in its envelope and into the safe where it would be protected. The watch was put in the repair box on the top shelf, running perfectly. The next morning the watch was dead, having stopped about ten minutes after the store closed.

"Your safe has two doors. Does each door have a wired-in alarm unit at the top of each door so they're in the center of the safe when the doors are closed?" I asked.

"Of course, you've seen it. If the doors are opened when the alarm is set, everything goes off, and the army comes running. Why?"

"Because your top shelf box for the watches puts them almost in contact with the magnets in the top of the safe. The watch, with no anti-magnetic protection, is getting magnetized when you put it away so carefully. The modern quartz watches won't be affected, but this solid gold Omega doesn't even have the protection of a stainless steel case back. It's all set and I'll mail it back after the holiday, and don't put it in the safe again, or at the least, put the watches in the bottom of the safe…far from the magnets."

Another watch problem solved…one having nothing whatsoever to do with the watch. Uncle Abe was smiling down on me…his pupil had remembered that in the final analysis the problem could well be something stupid.

The mailman delivered a box containing eight watches of surpassing complexity and value. Four chronographs, two Rolexes, a Patek Philippe, and a Vacheron Constantin. Instructions were to repair them. Period. No estimates…just fix them. One watch, a square Rolex, had a special note inside the envelope.

"This watch is a very, very vintage Rolex that has not run since the mid-1980s. Four watchmakers have attempted to repair it, but it will not run. This <u>must</u> be made to run."

This was not a time to be flattered; this was a time for trepidation. What possibly could four qualified and professional watchmakers have missed? I named the Rolex as number four and got to work taking apart six watches. Watches are usually repaired in a group of six. The ultrasonic cleaner basket is divided into six and the basket must be balanced to spin properly. I was too smart to read the directions when the tank was new in 1963 and launched into orbit parts that may not have landed yet.

The Rolex was taken apart one piece at a time, with each part being carefully inspected with a double loupe. Everything looked perfect until I got to the balance. I was thankful, because re-staffing a vintage Rolex watch can be a true challenge. I twisted the movement to put a spin on the balance, and it oscillated back and forth several times until inertia was spent and it stopped.

I moved the watch to a forty-five-degree angle and the balance stopped dead. Holding my breath, I checked the balance wheel and… the staff was broken…This was all I needed. I e-mailed out an order for the staff and called it a day. Tonight was the night before the Fourth of July, and I was heading for a restful weekend on the boat. I'd probably not get the part before the ninth, so no need to hurry.

After a happy Fourth of July long weekend, I put the watch through the cleaner and decided to do all the work required up to the balance staff. As I began to put everything together, I spent time over a cup of coffee (black, no sugar) to do a little thinking about this watch. Others had worked on it as long as twenty years ago and it still wouldn't run. A familiar voice from many, many years ago came into my head, "Barry, there is something stupid going on here." Every part was put into the watch, the train ran by "tweezer power," and then ran with a wound mainspring, every way perfectly smooth. No matter which way I positioned the movement, it was perfect. Finally I put it aside to wait for the balance staff.

As expected, the new Rolex staff arrived on the ninth, and taking a deep breath, I started. The voice still prodded me to keep an eye out for something stupid…okay, enough already. I took the balance, still attached to its bridge, from the watch and released the hairspring stud, and the balance staff was not broken after all. Both upper and lower pivots looked perfect. Visually, I could tell the balance staff matched the new, costly staff. Uncle Abe was right…something stupid was going on here.

Removing the hairspring, I put the balance into the watch, secured the plate, and used a puff of air to spin the balance in the "dial down" position. As it slowly lost motion, I turned the watch to "dial up" and gave another air puff, which had the balance spinning like an airplane propeller. Yet when I shifted the position only a few degrees, the balance stopped dead. The otherwise "perfect" balance was flopping around. Something was definitely screwy here. Now I was into problems that were normally seen in modern times. This watch was made in the late 1930s, so I went back to the methods of that time.

I removed the upper cap jewel and regulator, and when I lifted the jewel setting, the cap jewel remained on the bridge. It was supposed to be friction fit into its setting, but this one just sat on the bridge, held in place only more or less by the beveled recess in its setting. A rigidly set jewel limited the vertical movement of the balance assembly and this *stupid* thing let the balance bounce up and down beyond allowance. Stupid…do you hear that, Uncle Abe? Way back when, someone didn't bother to properly set the jewel, or didn't have the exact right one, and caused this watch not to run for almost thirty years.

Just in case, I removed the lower cap jewel and checked it and the lower hole jewel. Nope, everything was…not right! The lower hole jewel was in perfect condition, properly set, but the actual bearing hole was four times larger than it should have been. No wonder the balance was flopping around…loose jewels and way too big pivot holes were something I'd never run into before. Balance staffs break, they bend, they wear away, but this perfect balance showed no indication at all of being the problem.

I truly believe that I haven't had to change a balance jewel in almost forty years. This one went easy. I gauged the jewel setting diameter and found that pivot hole ten was what I needed, not the fourteen that had been in the watch. I properly set a new upper cap jewel and put everything back together.

Screwing down the balance bridge screw, I said a short blessing on this watch and wound it. Instantly the balance began to oscillate, with a very happy motion, and to my surprise when put on the timing machine, it did not require so much as a single tweaking. I really believed the mystery of this poor watch had been solved, but I'd run it for a few days outside of the watch case…just to be sure.

Strange, if I had not been told of the other attempts to fix this, I too might have missed this *stupid* series of mistakes. Under normal conditions, these were things not only just not seen but not even suspected, and I admit I wouldn't have looked for them. I would have eventually found them, but after a lot of valuable time had been wasted.

This evening, I saw for the 123rd time a rerun of *M*A*S*H*, in which there was a close-up of a medi-vac helicopter instrument panel. There on the right-hand side was the exact model Waltham panel timepiece I'd repaired and mailed off to Chicago a few weeks ago. I admit I felt a little proud of me.

Thankfully, watches continue to come into the shop. Over and over, I hear the same refrain…this was Dad's…this belonged to my grandmother…this saw me though the Pacific…this was my wedding present long ago. The people are the same. The watches are the same. And the watchmaker is the same, older, more experienced, but still enjoying the challenges of each day. Tomorrow I start, or attempt to start, the resurrection of a badly rusted Breitling Chronograph. I wish the watch lots of luck. I wish me lots of luck. We will both need it.

Today, July 28, 2009, I successfully completed the "resurrection" of the Breitling. The watch was truly quite rusted, but the rust was only surface rust. This was a chronograph that featured the normal sweep second, minute recorder, and a twelve-hour recorder in addition to a calendar window. As I took the watch apart, each wheel, lever, cam, spring, and plate had to be cleansed of the coating of rust. This watch, of mid-1940s vintage, decided to behave itself, and I discovered that no parts were required. This was a stroke of luck; parts for these magnificent watches were getting quite difficult to find.

After a normal trip through the ultrasonic cleaning machines, the watch was reassembled with surprising ease. To say surprising ease is to understate the case. It was as though the watch tried to make amends for the extra work it required. Each section and part went in without problem, each section worked perfectly as assembled, and I found no adjustments were needed. The dial was installed, the many hands put into their proper synchronization, and the watch was wound to run under a glass cover, but outside of the case. It was much simpler to time, check, and adjust such a watch without the restrictions of the movement being cased up.

As the Breitling went "under cover," it was time to finish the casing of another extra-complicated chronograph, this one an Omega Navigator Chronograph. This was a much more modern model, complete with shock proofing for the balance jewels. The newly overhauled and perfectly running movement was put into the case and secured carefully. As a final check of the chronograph units, using the case push buttons to actuate the time recording, I casually wound the watch. Just as I reached the approximate halfway point in winding the mainspring, I felt a sudden lack of resistance in the crown.

It was beyond the ability of my mind to accept, but the modern "unbreakable mainspring" had broken. In a chronograph, no less... beyond belief and no fair. The entire watch would have to be taken apart again, just to get the mainspring barrel out of the watch.

I had but two choices...either take a coffee (black, no sugar) break or...plan B...jump out of the window. I checked...it was looking like rain, so I opted for coffee while I sat in the office and sulked like a petulant four-year-old.

There was a time, before the 1950s, when the broken mainspring haunted all watchmakers. The steel of the time could break whenever it took the mood. It was not uncommon for a newly installed mainspring to break on its very first winding. That was in the past...my current disaster was totally unexpected and for that reason alone was the cause for my despair. I did not have another spring in stock, so I had two or three days before I would have to deal with the watch. Sadly, I finished my coffee and ordered a new spring.

A woman about my age came into the shop an hour later, putting her non-running watch into my hands. With a smile she asked if I recognized the watch, or if I recognized her. With my world famous lack of memory, I confessed to not knowing either the watch or the owner.

"I'm hurt," she replied. "You sold my father that watch for my high school graduation in 1949, and I was there with my father. You told me the watch would last for many years, and it has."

I had sold that watch sixty years ago, a ladies' Bulova with a 6AH movement inside a rolled gold plate case, and it was really still wearable. It was now in the shop for a complete overhaul. Today, in 2009, the cost of the repair was double the original sales price of 1949. Such is progress?? I have often said, sometimes jokingly, sometimes quite seriously, that I would buy "whatever" if only I could be sure it would last as long as a watch.

An extremely thin Movado was brought into the shop, once the property of the customer's mother, even though it was really a man's watch. This watch model was made extra thin by the company using a flat steel plate as a case back, held in with casing screws rather than the traditional case back. Inside I discovered that someone had actually broken the circuit assembly in two pieces. When I showed the damage to the customer, he did not seem surprised and agreed to the repair, no matter the cost. I ordered the circuit assembly and cleaned and oiled the movement itself while I awaited the circuit.

In less time than I thought, the circuit came in; it was installed and tested on my ever-trusty Accutron test set. Everything was fine until I looked up the listing for the right battery. Uh-oh...this watch was listed as needing an R44! The dreaded two-volt lithium battery. This time I only spent seconds being upset as I remembered my prior solution. I installed the Renata 341, and sure enough, the watch ran, stepping once in twenty seconds. I'd explain to the customer, but out of curiosity, I called for a quote on a R44 and, frankly, was sorry I even asked.

It was now the beginning of August, and my very first task of the new month was to replace the broken mainspring in the Omega Navigator Chronograph. The reason I considered jumping out of the window was that the watch had to be completely taken apart before I even could reach the mainspring barrel. Screws, levers, springs, cams, each to be removed...one at a time...in addition to the plates and wheels, both train and chronograph.

I often believed that watches were, in their own way, *alive* and able to be spiteful. Once again I received proof. Just as I removed the holding screw for a pair of actuator springs, the topmost one suddenly flew up and out. I felt it hit my shirt and "calmly" put the tweezer down so I could scan for the spring; thankfully the piece was an inch and a half long. For a watch, this was a large and long piece, so it wouldn't take long to find. Lift-off for the missing spring was 9:25 a.m., so by 11:45 a.m., the trip out the window was again looking good.

I spent two hours on my hands and knees, with a tiny brush and flashlight, finding nothing but dust bunnies, dead batteries, two broken balance staffs, and six inches of an old mainspring. I had to give up the search and get back to the new mainspring. The rest of the disassembly went well, as did the installation of the new mainspring in the barrel. The reassembly of the watch went surprisingly easy, up to the point of requiring the missing actuator spring. The great hunt was on again, but to no avail. There was no place for the spring to have gone, but it was not to be found. At 2:00 p.m., the world's biggest watchmaker gave up. I'd have to try to order the part, but first…time for a cup of coffee (black, no sugar).

As I stood up to retreat in humiliation to the office, a sharp, stabbing pain radiated up my right leg, almost costing me my balance. Now what? I plopped into my chair and pulled off my right shoe and sock only to discover I was bleeding from my inner heel. I was just able to turn my foot enough to see a puncture wound, which I managed to clean off and put a Band-Aid on. This was a day I couldn't believe.

Suddenly I had a thought…what had stabbed my heel? Gently I examined my sock, hoping against hope, and soon virtue became its own reward…I found the errant spring, in perfect condition save for a little bit of blood. The shoe and sock went on, and it was happily coffee time (black, no sugar). I poured a cup and phoned Amy, demanding she provide two reasons for me to not go out the window. She reminded me that it was boating season; reason enough to soldier on, so I went back to the Omega.

By now the Omega had learned its lesson, and everything went smoothly. Since my fingers were busy, I crossed my toes and wound the watch, and all was right with the world again. I would run it for a couple of days and then case it up for return. If I was lucky, I'd never see it again.

E ighteen months ago, a man brought in a vintage American pocket watch, a classic railroad-grade 16S watch in a 14K gold case. The watch, I was informed, had been sent to an unnamed firm about three years prior and had never run properly since, gaining as much as a half hour per day. I believe that I've written before that the faster one finds the problem, the more difficult the repair. In that vein, I spotted the problem in about ten seconds and knew I was in deep trouble.

Whatever happened in this watch's past, I was never to know, but I saw a horrifying sight for a watchmaker…one of the balance timing screws was missing. The balance wheel was much too light, so the watch gained an impossible amount of time. It was time to face a hard truth…this watch was vintage 1880s, and the manufacturer went out of business *before* World War I. Besides everything else, the watch had been made to the specifications of a particular railroad, and the railroad's name, Burlington, was on the dial. Nowhere on the main plates was the name of the original manufacturer. There was, to copy someone else's pun, two chances to find a timing screw… slim and none. Nonetheless, I had to at least try, so the great hunt was begun.

Phone inquiries to several material dealers elicited the expected replies. These "polite" answers ranged from "no" to "you've got to be kidding." I was searching the United States of America for a screw not quite as long at this comma (,) and just about the diameter of this period (.)! Another problem was the high quality of this watch; people kept and treasured them, so the movements were not available to be cannibalized for parts.

A year and more passed, and admittedly I had yet to put even a single minute of work into this poor watch. The customer was beyond patient, but I was ready to admit defeat.

The owner picked up the Movado watch that I had saved by fitting a battery that didn't belong in the watch. As I walked to the bench to continue work on a Rolex Datejust, a bulb went off in my idea box— that which most people call their head. What I needed for this vintage railroad watch only had to fit physically and be of the correct weight. I was not to be marked for symmetry or appearance but for accuracy and durability only. Digging through an old Clorets Lozenges can that held about eight thousand assorted American screws, I eventually found a timing screw that had the correct threads. I had to shorten the length of the head and the balance. With a puff of canned air, it spun as freely as it was supposed to. I timed the spinning out at seven minutes plus.

Placing the balance wheel on my poising tool, the *new* timing screw rolled rapidly to the top, meaning it was too light, even though it was larger than its new mates. It took a minute for me to realize that the original specification for this balance wheel was for gold screws. What I'd installed was larger, but quite a bit lighter, hence the imbalance. If the balance was of the correct net weight, it would run well in the flat, but if this correct net weight was improperly distributed, the watch would run very fast in one position and equally slow in the opposite. That is where the term "balance wheel" originates.

I located a long-unused cabinet of timing washers, date of sale marked 1939, compiled by a once huge and leading watch material supplier. I added three washers to the light side, onto the poising tool, and then had to remove a microscopic bit of metal from my substitute screw and...perfect balance. I ascertained the beat position and put the hairspring onto the balance assembly, mounted everything in the bridge, and returned the balance to its honored place. Visually, the balance was a disgrace, but the watch ran happily, talking to me joyfully. Crossing my fingers, I put the running watch on the timing machine and...beyond belief and luck...the watch was running precisely fourteen seconds per day fast, and in all six positions as well as the flat. I must honestly admit to a fair portion of luck, being so close. I "tweaked" the regulator, and the watch timed out to railroad specs once again.

I just had a funny thought. For a watchmaker, life's triumphs seem to come in tiny ways. Really, really tiny ways. Of course, any purist would have a fit as this balance sort of looked like a railroad wreck rather than a railroad watch. Naturally I didn't care, being interested only in superb performance. I phoned the owner, ran the watch for three days, and proudly returned a perfectly functioning watch to him today, August 13.

Seemingly there was no end to the mysteries I had to solve. This time it was a 16S Waltham pocket watch. Seventeen jewels…twenty-year case…precision regulator…this had all the bells and whistles. It also had one rather aggravating problem…the hairspring was making me nuts. Overhauled not long ago, but returned three times with a hung up hairspring.

My first thought had been oil on the hairspring, which would make the coils cling and also cause the watch to run extremely fast. The first time it came back, I was mildly annoyed at myself, taking blame for a careless moment. The second time it came back was an embarrassing event, as I cleaned again the complete balance and the bridge assembly.

When the owner picked up the watch he accepted my apologies and left a gent's Rolex for a complete overhaul. He "understood" that things can happen and trusted me to take proper care of the high-grade Rolex, his pride and joy. He promised to take good care of the pocket watch and said he'd be back in two weeks for the Rolex.

As expected, two weeks passed, and my customer returned for his newly restored Rolex. He also had a surprise for me, as with a shake of his head he placed the Waltham on my counter.

"It's doing it again," he said, "running crazy fast. It was great for about ten days and then…off it went."

I swallowed so much humble pie that I wouldn't have to eat for three days and put down the little paper project I was working on at the counter of separating the little parts cards from the small pile of paper clips. As I feared, again the hairspring was hung up, which I re-cleaned while Mr. Owner answered a call on his cell phone. This had now gone quite a bit beyond curiosity, damaged pride, and embarrassment. Now this was personal.

As I returned to the counter, he finished his call and put a very sturdy cell phone on the glass. It was a different type of phone from what I was used to and had a metal flip cover that was just a thin sheet of metal that snapped closed. As the phone was placed on the glass, one of my paper clips slid about two inches across the countertop and stuck to the phone. I commented on the heft of his phone.

He explained, "This is a heavy-duty phone. I work around and on very heavy machinery on board a supertanker. I'm the chief engineer. Sometimes I find myself leaning on one thing to fix another, and I've squashed quite a few phones, like the plastic model on your belt. The metal lid is a simple plate that's held down by a rather strong magnet."

He picked up his "adjusted" Waltham pocket watch and put it into the traditional "watch pocket" in his jeans. Alarm bells rang throughout the land as I realized the watch pocket was located *exactly* where his cell phone holder was attached to his belt.

Gently I asked, "You mean to tell me you're carrying that eighty-seven-year-old pocket watch a mere half inch from a powerful magnet…a magnet? Your poor hairspring is not getting oil on it, it's being magnetized, and heavily, from proximity to the phone on your belt. Let me have the watch again."

Sure enough, I put the watch, newly cleaned, on the timer, and it was running crazy fast once again. I motioned him to come around to the timing machine so he could see for himself how fast the watch was running. Then I placed the watch on the flat surface of the old-fashioned "demagnetizer" and pushed the button. With a wry smile I put the watch back on the timer, and as I expected, the watch timed out perfectly.

I instructed the chagrined engineer to put the watch in his jeans next to the cell phone and then return it to me. Naturally on the timing machine it was running crazy fast once more.

In triumph I explained, "You are between voyages and you don't normally carry your working cell phone, so the watch can go a week or so without a problem. But just put on your cell phone case and the watch goes blooey. It's that easy…just keep them apart…far apart."

The modern watch of today, which uses a powerful but tiny magnet as its motor, would not be so affected, but the very old Waltham had no need of such technology, which of course didn't even exist when it was made.

Another victory after struggling with something that was in a sense "stupid." My customer tried to pay me something for a problem that was his fault, but I waved him off. The repair of the Rolex was sufficient, and I'd come through another learning event.

His ship sailed next month and the Waltham stayed at home… thankfully. For working hours in the engine room, he now wore a "who cares" watch rather than beating up the Rolex. Thankfully.

One time I was clicking channels and stopped on a rerun of M*A*S*H. It was the episode in which a Korean peddler tried to sell one of the doctors a "real" bargain watch. The peddler pulled up his sleeve to show off his wares and…I broke up laughing remembering a "not at all funny at the time" story.

When I was in my junior year of high school, I was on an early release schedule. When I was done with classes, I headed straight to Uncle Abe's to practice my trade. At work the previous day, I had completed repairs on four self-winding watches. In those days, before the modern watch winder, it was normal for a watchmaker to check the winding function and time by wearing the watch. When

I first showed up at school wearing extra watches I did get some strange looks from teachers and students, but they got used to it.

It was a warm spring day, and I was wearing five watches; two on my right hand and three on my left (it's hard to do school work with an armful of watches). I left school and headed down Maple Street, crossed Main Street, and just had to go a couple more blocks to Harrington Square and then left down Front Street to Uncle Abe's store. All four watches were running fine, as was my own watch. It was going to be a good day at the bench.

I had just passed Woolworth's when someone grabbed my right arm. I was brought to a sudden halt and turned around to see a Worcester policeman sternly looking at me. The fact that I towered over him made no difference. I had taken root on the sidewalk and he was in charge. I noticed the cruiser at the curb and was ready to panic.

"Kid, you may be the dumbest crook I've ever seen. Bad enough you steal all those watches, but you're stupid enough to wear short sleeves to advertise them on Front Street."

"No. No," I protested loudly as people stopped to watch the "arrest." "I repaired these watches yesterday, and all I'm doing is making sure that they wind and run good."

The policeman looked at me as if I was crazy. "You are really dumb if you think I'm going to buy a story like that. You fixed them," he said, dripping with sarcasm.

"But my uncle is expecting me at his jewelry store. The customers will want their watches. I didn't steal anything!"

The policeman from the cruiser walked up and pulled the first officer aside. "Do you remember that Abe Marcus has that huge nephew of his in the store now? The kid goes to Commerce with my son. This kid looks like a Marcus. Take him down to Abe's. I'll bring the car down to meet you out front."

The policeman never let go of my arm as he marched me down to Front Street. As we entered the store, Uncle Abe jumped up from his bench. "Michael, what's happening? What did my nephew do?"

My arm was quickly released as an apology came rushing out of the policeman to...Uncle Abe, not to me, the former suspected felon. "Abe,

I'm sorry, but with all those watches hanging on him he looks like a thief. Any cop in the city would've grabbed him for looking like a roving fence."

The policeman and Uncle Abe shook hands. I was given one final stern look. My criminal career may have set a record for brevity, and I never wore more than two watches again.

A number of years later, not too long after my release from the navy, I had a backlog of automatic watches to check and I still wouldn't wear more than two watches at a time. The proliferation of automatic watches was becoming a problem. Being too busy is a good problem to have but a problem nonetheless.

The solution to my problem came one night while watching an old war movie that was set in Holland. As the soldiers were marching, I was excitedly staring at the windmills in the background. The windmills were slowly rotating. A bright light bulb went off in my head as I envisioned a collection of self-winding watches attached to the arms of a miniature windmill. As it rotated, gravity would keep the oscillating weight at its lowest position as the gears wound the watch. Not only that, but I could copy a pretty normal active day by plugging in the unit during the morning and pulling the plug as we closed the store. The day's activity would/should wind the watch enough to run overnight through the sleeping hours. If the watch was properly regulated, it would be right on time in the morning.

I was in the shop early, anxious to see if I could make my idea work. I took apart a rotating display, salvaged the motor, and fashioned an x with each arm about a foot long. I thought each six-inch section would hold three watches. With my fingers crossed, I fastened my invention to the wall next to my bench and plugged it in.

Just in case my brainstorm didn't work, I had been careful to put the rotating display together minus the motor. When the display was reassembled, it wasn't apparent that the motor was missing. My dad was quite upset that the display had stopped, so he told me to try to fix it. I "tried my best" but just couldn't get the display to rotate. In the meantime, Dad was quite delighted with "our" new invention, the Marcus Automatic Watch Winder. I made the first one in the late 1950s, and I believe the fancy auto winders for "home use" didn't come out until many, many years later. Oh well, Grandfather Marcus didn't know about patents, and I guess his grandson didn't either.

An Illinois 18S pocket watch, vintage 1870s in a 14K gold case. This poor thing was a disaster...the crystal broken, minute hand missing, and half of the hour hand broken off. Worse, the "sunken dial" for the second hand was missing completely, broken out of the dial. This would require a new dial, which of course meant finding parts probably made 130 years ago.

As the watch was of "priceless status" to the owners, I started the repair while beginning the hunt for the dial. The movement was in a condition that approached that of the dial. The balance staff was broken and the upper hole jewel was mostly gone. Most scary was a bent hairspring. The only piece of luck was the new mainspring in my material cabinet. The mainspring was the easiest part of the repair.

To my surprise, the repair went quite easy...a balance staff in my supply fitted perfectly, and the bent hairspring responded to my tender efforts without problem. With the installation of the new upper hole jewel, the movement was adjusted as to time, and we settled down to wait for the dial.

Three weeks of repairing watches, and I had received the last negative response to my search for a usable dial for the Illinois. Several people did indeed have dials, but on very good watches that would not be broken up for parts. Illinois watches, like Hamiltons, were often greatly cherished and very unlikely to be either traded on a new watch or just abandoned to the watchmaker for parts. Now what?

I had a wild idea of using, as a very last resort, an 18S dial from a Waltham watch. I had a very good one that was 90 percent the exact duplicate of the Illinois. Naturally, however, nothing could be this easy...I measured the distance between the center of the dial and the hole for the second hand, and the Waltham was a single millimeter too small, much too great a variation to use. It was a good idea, though. The customer had indeed indicated that she was primarily concerned with the watch running properly and looking as it should. She admitted to not knowing the difference between the Illinois and the Wyoming (of which there is no such thing).

Disappointed, I scooped up the pile of unusable Waltham dials, idly noticing the circles of solder on the rear of the dials. That was where the varied designs of "sunken dials" for the second hand were placed in a precut recess. Now I'd have to figure out something else. I couldn't give up because I'd already repaired the watch, even finding new and matching hands. Just because something can't be done doesn't mean that I won't find a way to do it anyway.

Once I read that aeronautical engineers had conclusively proved that bumblebees cannot possibly fly, but since bees cannot read, they continue to fly around. Time for coffee again (black, no sugar).

Three nights later on TV, someone using a propane torch heated a machine unit just enough to soften the solder that held in part of the device. As the mechanic lifted off the newly released piece, my problem was solved. I think I slept with a smile all night.

The following morning, I was in the shop early, determined to do the impossible for the Illinois. Carefully I measured the diameter of the hole in the dial of the Illinois and then the diameter of the "seconds dial" of a pristine Waltham dial and...perfect! I sharpened a small screwdriver blade into a graver sharpness and very carefully cut away the solder holding the Waltham dial together. Finally, holding my breath, I gently pushed the seconds dial out of its "home" onto my bench. A fine file cleaned up residual solder, and I placed the small porcelain disc onto the Illinois, and we had a perfect fit. I could hardly believe my good fortune. Now I just had to solder in the disc and revel in my triumph.

Wait. When the dial was made in the 1870s, solder was the "high tech" of the day. This was November 2009, and I would be turning to the "high tech" of this day…high-strength epoxy. Not only would the epoxy do the job, but the "working time" of the epoxy would enable me to ensure the proper lining up of the seconds dial into its new home.

I got ahead of myself with the self-congratulations. The Illinois had a sunken dial recess for the second hand. The Waltham piece was the exact size, so it would make a completely flat dial. Time to think. I carefully scribed a scratch line from the "60" to the "30" on the seconds dial and did the same on the main dial from the hour hole to the "6" on the bottom of the hour scale. All I had to do was epoxy the disc in perfect alignment and finish the watch, after a proper period of congratulating myself. I still was trying to think of a way to make the seconds disc a bit lower than the face of the dial.

In the interim I completed the assembly of a 2003 Japanese quartz watch, all the while thinking of a problem regarding an 1875 vintage American pocket watch. The maker of the quartz watch would be proud to learn that his product had lasted for an entire half dozen years. The maker (Illinois) of the American pocket watch would have taken for granted that his watch would last for over 134 years, with many more to come.

The quartz watch, of course, had broken dial legs, so I utilized four dial dots to secure it in place. I had a so-called "ah-ha" moment. I'd solved the problem with the Illinois pocket watch. The quartz marvel would have to wait. I put four dial dots on a plastic disc, which I'd secured to a mirror. Carefully I placed the seconds disc *upside down* onto the dial dots, and by looking through the plastic, I could see the reflection in the mirror. Looking sideways, I saw that, sure enough, the seconds disc was raised above the plastic just the right amount. I placed the large dial section over the disc and matched the alignment scratches…perfect.

Gently I used a toothpick to place three small dabs of epoxy on the fifteen, thirty, and forty-five second spots. Since I was using five-minute epoxy, I let this set for ten minutes then carefully lifted my creation off the plastic, and it was perfect. The disc was "sunken" the proper amount and the numbers on the disc were in perfect alignment. A new batch of five-minute epoxy finished off my bright idea, and I could proceed with the overhaul. For the Illinois's family, this would indeed be a timely Christmas. (I apologize for the terrible pun...I just couldn't resist.)

As I relaxed in my dial transplant success with a cup of coffee (black, no sugar), a tiny bell rang in my head. A thought was trying to emerge from deep down, something I saw but did not register. Something that had to do with a watch, but I couldn't remember. I admit to not being able to remember my daughters' birthdays, customers' names, holidays, and other *secondary* things, but I never forget something concerning a watch. Something I saw a couple of days ago, while I was...I forgot what it was.

Enough...back to work on a Rolex, and I gently moved the Illinois pocket watch aside until later. I'd get back to it and its "new" dial later, after—

Bingo! That was it! While I was looking for a Waltham dial to steal, I looked into a very old box I'd ignored for years. There was a watch in it that caught my eye for a split second before I shoved it aside, but what had caught my eye? Not only that, where was the box now? An Olympic record was set...it took me only fourteen minutes to find that box of old useless pocket watches. It was behind another box of old watches. Now what was sticking in my mind?

I sat at the desk with the box of watches and another cup of coffee (black, no sugar) and began to search one watch after another looking for...I wasn't even sure what I was looking for. I put aside a very large, badly tarnished watch and reached for the next. Wait a second... tarnished! Many metals discolor, but only *silver* tarnishes.

I grabbed the watch again and popped open the outer back case, and sure enough...coin silver. Turning the case over and pushing the button to open the hunting case cover, I saw the name American Watch Company. This pocket watch predated Waltham. It was a treasure. Checking the serial number, I realized I had a screwless balance, fully jeweled American pocket watch of about 1862 vintage. Beyond belief…where did this come from and when did this arrive, and where was I when I got it? This 150-year-old watch could have come down from my grandfather, Dad, or Uncle Abe and had been sitting around for how many years?

Gently I turned the balance wheel to its limit and released it, watching happily as it oscillated for several seconds perfectly. As badly as the silver case was tarnished, the case, crystal, and dial were in wonderful condition. This beauty would be given lots of tender loving care. I would figure out what to do with it later, but…wow. For years I'd told myself to search through all the watches here in the shop to find just what was hidden unsuspected in each old box. It was about time I listened to me, wasn't it?

An old, old Rolex came into my hands. Even as I slid the watch from its plastic envelope, I knew I was in for a tough time. A series of loud "clunks" were heard as the watch slid dial down onto the desk and I turned it over. Clunk. Clunk. No watch should ever clunk. Certainly Rolexes are not supposed to go clunk.

The data sheet told me that the watch was "No longer supported by Rolex." There were no parts available. Could I possibly pull off another "miracle"? This watch was from my special "collector" account, my source of Pateks, Breitlings, Rolexes, Vacherons, and others of that ilk. As I handled the Rolex, removed the band, and set it into the case opener, each movement produced a solid "clunk." Carefully I set the opener and slowly unscrewed the Rolex "oyster" case back.

I held the watch in my left hand and upended the watch into my right to release the case back. Surprise. There was no oscillating weight in this watch. Puzzled, I put the case back onto my bench and saw that the oscillating weight was in the back…broken loose. Of course, this meant the real end of this watch. There were no parts to be had.

One of the reasons I do not properly respect Rolexes is the—in my opinion—foolish over engineering. If a broken oscillating axle belonged to a Bulova, Benrus, Hamilton, Eta, A. Schild, and so on, two or three screws were removed, the broken plate was pushed out, and a brand-new oscillating weight axle was screwed in place. Simple as could be.

Rolex weights had a plain round hole in the center. The axle is a round plate that sort of looks like a rook in a chess set, round with openings for the battlements. There is a special punch, with projections to peen the battlements to friction fit the hole in the weight. When the axle has broken a few times and the round plate knocked out, the center hole in the weight can and does get enlarged.

This was the problem with this watch. The hole in the weight was so enlarged that the axle plate could not gain the friction needed to hold in place. This watch was dead. No question about it. Even if I could find a new axle, it could not be made to hold in place.

I e-mailed the bad news and went to the next watch…a chronograph. Just as I finished taking apart the chronograph the phone rang, and I just knew who was calling. I barely got my "Hello, watch repair" out when I heard a voice literally pleading with me.

"Please, do anything…anything off the wall or over the edge…one of those wild ideas of yours. I do not care what it costs…just do something. I know I can count on you. Bye." Then all I heard was a dial tone. Now what?

Before I was willing to begin work on the problem at hand, I wondered if the watch itself was going to work properly…never mind wind properly. I took it apart, making it next after the chronograph and a couple of quartz movements, and ran the six through the ultrasonic tank. With the cleaner buzzing in the background, it was time for coffee (black, no sugar) and a deep think. I had to admit that inside I was somewhat pleased that it was *me* who was turned to in desperation. On one hand I was flattered, but on the other hand I was nervous about the pressure of being "the last, very last hope for this multi-thousand-dollar watch."

With a shock, I suddenly realized that a good deal of *fun* had been taken from my repair of watches. For sixty-five years I had been sitting at the bench, from Uncle Abe's in Worcester, to Dad's store in Milford, until it became mine. For forty-five years I'd sat at my own handmade bench, higher than normal by six inches because I was too tall to use the traditional watchmaker's bench. Now I found myself working on watches of such value and rarity that each one became a nervous job. True, I got a tremendous sense of satisfaction when I pulled off a "Barry miracle," but this wasn't the easy fun of years ago. However, I told myself, this was a great way to make a living and there isn't anything else that I would rather do.

I saved the Rolex until the last of six, and as I already suspected, the watch went together perfectly and timed out as a Rolex should after just the tiniest possible tweaking of the regulator. We were down to the oscillating weight and axle, broken, unrepairable, and irreplaceable. Hopeless. I wound the Rolex, and as I set the time, I realized that this day had been long enough. I'd think about this at home.

That night I sat facing the TV, not seeing the screen but instead visualizing an oversize hole and the last "good" oscillating axle on earth. I went to bed having failed to think of anything promising.

The following morning, my Rolex was exactly on time, so the watch demanded a true brainstorm from me. While I tried to think, I finished casing the newly repaired Illinois pocket watch with its epoxied dial. As I fitted a second hand to the fourth wheel post, the solution to the Rolex came to me. The Illinois disc did not do anything but sit in its recess decade after decade as the second hand turned around once per minute, also decade after decade. The original disc had been securely soldered in place so...

I called the "hopeful" Rolex collector and explained my brainstorm. Just as I had asked a customer about fifty years ago, I asked, "Do you care how I fix the Rolex, and do you care how a perfectly functioning movement looks?"

The answer: "I knew I could count on one of your screwy ideas."

With a barely sincere apology to the designers of this Rolex movement, I prepared the piece for repair. In only slightly more time than it took to tell about it, I had soldered the axle to the oscillating weight. Pure blasphemy, but it would work. With a heavy tweezer, I put pressure on the axle and determined that the repair would truly hold.

Using a very sharp graver, I trimmed away the excess solder and bright cut the exposed solder to improve the general appearance because, after all, this was a Rolex.

Another benefit...a mere application of sufficient heat would enable the removal of the axle from the weight, which would *not* further enlarge the hole. I did the final assembly, and as I turned the movement over and over, the weight remained static, thus winding the watch. No more clunking. I smiled to myself; once again the stubborn problem was solved by the simplest effort. I even admitted that when the automatic unit was part of the watch, the repair was not even visible, which was a pleasant surprise.

I called my customer to, I will admit, boost my ego a little, but as soon as my name came up on his caller ID, he picked up the phone, loudly proclaiming, "I knew that you'd pull it off. Wait until you see what I just mailed to you. Got to go and close a sale. Thanks a lot." And with a click, all I heard was another dial tone. Oh well.

This morning, even before I took off my coat, I checked the "miracle" Rolex as it turned on the auto winder. Perfect. I noted the hours run, turned the winder on for the day, and went into the back for a cup of morning coffee (black, no sugar). Relaxing early in the morning, I sipped coffee and waited for the computer to boot up so I could read the news online.

A woman brought in a better grade ladies watch, an Ulysse Nardin. It was a brand I'd seen before but not too often. The watch was left for an overhaul, repaired without a single issue and picked up a few weeks later. The woman left the shop happy.

Two weeks later, the woman was back. She held out her watch to me. I ensured her that the watch was under guarantee and I would take care of any adjustments.

She put up her hand and stopped me. "My fault. I reached into a file cabinet at work and caught the watch on the edge of the drawer."

Sure enough, the crown was missing. I wrote up the watch for a stem and crown with the promise of the repair being done sooner than later.

Later that afternoon, I telephoned Ulysse Nardin to order the stem and specially designed crown. I was told that they would not send out parts for their watches. The watch must be returned and repaired to their standards. I told their *customer service* person that I had just overhauled the watch and only needed the stem and crown. My repair made no difference, in fact I was told that the factory would have to overhaul the watch to include the stem and crown repair.

I don't handle stupid well so I took a deep breath and started over (maybe the person on the phone didn't understand me the first time). "You don't understand, I just overhauled the watch and the woman broke the crown afterwards. It wouldn't be fair to charge her for another overhaul."

The answer and attitude was the same. A mere bench watchmaker was not qualified to service the Ulysse Nardin watches. Sixty plus years of experience counts for nothing. Definitely time for coffee (black, no sugar). Time to call Carol...she would, as she says, "talk me off the ledge."

Calmer, I called my customer and explained what Ulysse Nardin had said. She was disappointed and didn't want to get a new watch. "The watch was a gift."

I explained that I could do the stem and crown as long as she wasn't concerned with having authentic parts. I could hear her anger as she told me to fix the watch to *her* watchmaker's standard. I appreciated the vote of confidence.

A week later, my monthly issue of the *Horological Times* arrived. The *Horological Times* is the trade periodical printed by the American Watchmaker's Institute, a group I had belonged to for many years. Time for a coffee break to see what was new.

"What the hell?" I asked myself.

An officer with the AWI, a fellow Massachusetts watchmaker had written an article approving and supporting the watch companies' policy of refusing to sell repair material, parts and data to the bench watchmaker. "Et tu, Brute?"

There I sat, a watchmaker with over sixty years bench time dedicated to servicing watches and the wonderful people who abuse them. My *own* organization claims that I'm no longer qualified to service a high quality, generic, Swiss movement. I wondered what Dad and Uncle Abe would say. I finished my coffee (black, no sugar) and began to mentally compose my letter of resignation from the American Watchmaker's Institute.

One afternoon, a very elderly man slowly walked into the shop. He asked if he could sit down. I couldn't help but noticed his size. The gentlemen was a bit taller than my six feet five inches. I approached the counter and pulled up a stool too (my knees thankful). The man took an old, stainless steel watch from his pocket. The watch was a manual wind, its case beyond scratched. My first thought... watches and war.

"Will you please service this for me? A couple of stores that I've been in won't repair anything this old. One guy said it wasn't worth the effort to toss it out. I couldn't understand his attitude. Can you, or rather, will you? My son found you online and he's driven quite a ways to get me here."

Oy. I need to buy a new dictionary and see if the word service has been expunged. The watch had a dial name that I hadn't seen before. I carried the watch to the bench and opened the case. The watch was a European made wind up watch, typical of the 1930s and 1940s. The case had received rough treatment but the movement was just in need of some TLC.

"The watch will be good as new when I'm done with it," I assured.

With a sparkle in his eye, "Thank you so much. This watch was a birthday present to myself. I won it in a card game. In fact, I put it on for the very first time in a landing craft heading to Omaha Beach on D-Day. The guys even sang "Happy Birthday" to me."

I gasped, "You celebrated your birthday on the way to Omaha Beach! Good Lord, how old are you?"

The old veteran sat a little straighter, "I turned seventeen in that landing boat. Thousands of us enlisted despite being underage. I grew early and it was easy for me to lie my way in. I was the best goody two-shoes in the company. I was afraid that if I got into trouble, I'd be sent home. By the time it was all over, I'd been wounded three times. Throughout it all, the watch never missed a second."

"It would be my honor to service your combat tested watch."

I n January 2010 the mailman brought a box into the shop, a box that was really too cold to handle. I amused myself by saying the watches needed to be thawed rather than overhauled. The following morning I removed the box, now warm to the touch, from the safe and, locating my box cutter, opened the box to find that…

I had another tale to tell the grandkids. There were four watches in the box, and I was stunned by what I saw. I was now seventy-five years old, and I was looking at a box of watches that would frighten a "youngster" of forty.

The first watch took my breath away. In my hands was a magnificent pocket watch in a case that had to be, and turned out to be, an 18K gold Swiss beauty. I opened the back cover and noticed a peculiar slide lever in the outer rim of the case. Wondering what this was, I slid it down, which resulted in nothing happening. Odd. I returned the lever and was astonished to hear a series of melodic *dings*. As the dings ended, I heard a series of *dingdongs*. I nearly dropped the watch I was so startled. After sixty-five years at the bench I now held, for the very first time, a "Golay *Repeater.*"

A Repeater watch could tell time from inside a pocket. As the slide lever was moved downward and then returned, a very complicated mechanism caused the watch to ding once for each hour, following a dingdong of a different note for each five minutes after the hour. I couldn't attempt the repair on this watch, a type I had only seen in museum display cases. Without undue modesty, I acknowledged my own limitations, even though I did not know what they were. This movement was in itself a work of art, levers, wheels, springs, jewels, and two circular wire "bells" that made the music that told the time. Sadly, I admitted to myself that I was afraid to tackle this wonder; the watch would have to be returned not repaired.

After all, I consoled my wounded pride, a leading cardiac surgeon would not operate on the brain. This watch was out of my league. I went to the computer and typed out a "defeatist" e-mail. This watch was beyond both my experience and my confidence and I was going to return it undone. I was truly sorry...

Time for a quick cup of coffee (black, no sugar) and on to the next watch. This was—uh-oh—another 18K pocket watch, but this one a Universal Chronograph. Manual wind, of course, and with six hands. Six hands! These were the hour, minute, sweep second, running second, minute minder, and twelve-hour hand. I read the "work sheet," and this was in for a new mainspring. Not possible to do. I laughed because this kind of watch required the total disassembly of the *entire* watch just to get to the mainspring barrel...every last little piece had to be removed. Back to the computer to send out another e-mail.

Next envelope, and oy! This one was an Angelus chronograph, but in addition to all the usual timing devices, it was extra thick to allow for day, date, month, and moon phase windows around the dial. I wondered who was doing this to me. I sat for a couple of minutes just gazing at the back of the last envelope...kind of too nervous to look.

Taking a deep breath, I turned over the last envelope and will admit to being greatly relieved to find a simple manual-wind mechanical watch that just required a normal overhaul along with a new crystal and a stem and crown. I didn't recognize the European brand, but I held the watch carefully while I read the rest of the customer's notes. I should have remained in bed that morning. I read that this watch, of a rare German make, had not worked for forty years. There were *no* parts for it, as no one available had ever heard of this really fine timepiece, and it needed a new stem. How was I supposed to find a stem for this?

There was a time when watchmakers actually had to make, from scratch, parts such as a watch stem, but I hadn't even seen the raw materials for many years.

While brooding over another cup of coffee (black, no sugar) I checked my e-mail. If lucky, I had been called back to active duty in the navy. No such luck. Possibly as punishment for past sins, I read, "Go ahead and do your best on the Repeater. We have more confidence in your 'attempt' than the best of others. Keep in touch, please. There is no time pressure on this one. Have fun." Someone had a sense of humor.

The—pardon my sarcasm—"easiest" of these watches seemed to be the Angelus chronograph. Extremely complicated, but I'd seen these before and was somewhat familiar with the chronograph unit and had a good idea of the calendar mechanism. As part of a precheck, I pulled the stem and advanced the hands as a check of the day/date/month unit. Oh no…The date hand advanced right at midnight and the month advanced as the date went from "31" to "1," but the day disc didn't move at all. I hoped the "day jumper" wasn't broken; maybe just the screw came loose. I pulled the six hands and removed the dial and immediately saw the problem with the "day jumper." There wasn't one…no jumper, no screw, loose or otherwise, just the day disc itself.

Checking the *BestFit Encyclopedia*, I located the schematics of the Angelus movement and had at least the official numbers and sketches of the missing part. I called my normal supplier and got a "you got to be kidding" answer. Next was plan B, and I e-mailed the specialist who had saved the day before. He was down south, so along with the description of what I needed, I sent "greetings from the Frozen Northland." Time to bail out for the day.

In the shop on a cold Sunday to see how the Angelus was running minus the day jumper, and it was perfect. I checked my e-mail, and to my relief, the part was available and would be shipped out Monday for a healthy sum of money. Included in the e-mail was a suggestion that I go to "an extremely hot place," as his southern town was buried under ten inches of still falling snow and the temperature had fallen to eighteen. Terrible to say, but "better him than me."

I had used digital close-ups printed at 8 x 11 as a help in working on a prior Angelus. I'd been taking individual photos of other chronographs to aid in final assembly. The Angelus had extra sections fastened to the top of other sections. A series of pictures, studied in reverse order, would be a requirement for this watch. I decided to start building a "photo studio" as an aid by punching holes in the Angelus pictures and starting my own technical manual.

I should have done this some time ago.

Monday morning arrived, and the Angelus was running perfectly. As a final test I cycled the chronograph unit several times, on and off, on and off, and every four times pushed the "reset to zero." Absolutely perfect, and now I just had to wait for the day jumper to arrive. Over a cup of coffee (black, no sugar) I checked the e-mail and read that the day jumper had been shipped. Also included was a comment that anyone who actually enjoyed snow was running with a "bent balance staff." I smiled at one of my favorite "put downs."

Next was the pocket watch chronograph, but only after I finished a set of six "normal" watches that required full overhauls. True, the Angelus would bring a good deal of money, but I had spent more time on that one watch, which was not even finished yet, than I would spend on the six "normal" watches, which included a Rolex, an Omega, and four other mechanical models.

Monday night and I was killing time watching TV as the Allies approached the coast of France on D-Day. I'd seen this before, of course, but it was the best thing on. The landing craft neared Omaha Beach, the fleet continued its bombardment, and a German officer checked the time as...hold it! Suddenly I remembered that a retired watchmaker friend had given me a very large supply of watch materials to use. In the middle of one of the many, many cartons was a wooden multidrawer cabinet that contained only European parts of early 1900s vintage. The cabinet was actually from Germany, compiled in the 1940s, and it also contained French and Swiss parts of the era. The TV show had tweaked my memory... I couldn't wait to get to the shop.

Tuesday morning I was in early and on a mission. I located the cabinet. Of course, every word was in German, but the company initials were virtually the same. I scanned the cabinet's catalog, and in one of the 2,800 little tubes I found what I needed; or rather I found six of them. Toes crossed (can't fix watches with crossed fingers) I gently tried to insert the stem into the movement. I had a perfect fit and screwed an old, worn-out crown onto the much too long stem. Now I could check the winding and setting gears without the need to take the watch apart.

My fingers told me that the gears were working fine, without any problems beyond a broken mainspring, a very common and easily correctable problem. When I pulled the stem into the setting position, the hands turned properly and easily, once again telling me that everything was operating as intended. In fact, as I set the hands forward, I noticed the second hand moving as it should in a properly running timepiece. Amazingly, this would now be just a normal overhaul now that I'd eliminated the need for long lost parts. A minute later I realized that not only did I have a stem, unseen for many years, but I had five more. In fact, I'd have to check further into that material cabinet.

I then checked the performance of the chronograph awaiting the day jumper, and everything was fine. I rewound the watch and noted the time on a scrap of paper, in order to check the total running time.

The mail arrived. I put the bills in their drawer and checked to see what treasures had arrived. Uh-oh…this was trouble. Here was a man's Hamilton Swiss automatic calendar watch, its crystal missing, as was the minute hand. There was no crown, the sweep second hand was bent, and the upper part of the case near the "12" and the band was covered with (I think) dried blood. Instantly I knew the story with this one. Hesitantly, I unfolded the enclosed note.

This watch was brought into a store in the Boston area by the parents of the wearer. He was recuperating at Walter Reed Hospital from wounds suffered in Afghanistan. Could I possibly repair the watch and, if so, e-mail out the estimate? Opening the case, I found just a normal high-grade Swiss ETA automatic that looked virtually undamaged but for the obvious. I pulled off the badly bent sweep hand, which was caught down against the hour hand...and the watch started to run. Okay.

Without a second thought, I e-mailed the estimate. I would repair this watch, but only under two conditions:

1. I would *not* charge anything for the repair...nothing.
2. The store would not charge anything for the repair and would e-mail me an acceptance of those terms.

I clicked "send" and went back to work.

I finished the last of a set of six overhauls and gathered the next group. Three heavier watches to balance off three light ladies' models, heavy and light alternating. For some reason the six were stripped without revealing any problems. I put the basket of watches into the ultrasonic cleaner and ducked into the office for a coffee break (black, no sugar).

At the computer, I checked my e-mail and found one new message. "Terms accepted. Repair the Hamilton watch. You shamed us with your generosity." Quickly I grabbed the watch and opened the case, and sure enough, I had any and all parts needed in the shop, even new hands and a typically generic crystal.

The first repair out of the "six set" was an automatic Rolex that decided to fight back. It took about fifteen minutes to locate the problem, which of course was quite easy to correct. I replaced the balance and...the phone rang.

"Good afternoon, watch repair."

I heard a woman's tearful voice saying over and over, "Bless you, sir, bless you and thank you so much."

"I'm sorry, I'm afraid you've reached the wrong number. It does happ—"

"No, Mr. Marcus, I'm calling you. The jeweler just called with the 'estimate' for the repair of my son's watch. He is recovering at Walter Reed and is well enough to be anxious about his watch. It was his grandfather's and went with him to Korea. Anyhow, the store said you demanded there be no charges for this repair, and I wanted to thank you. When the store wouldn't give me your name and number, I threatened to go to the store and create a scene that would make the nightly news. So I'm calling you to thank you for your kindness. Again…bless you, sir. We have been assured that he will have a complete recovery, and none of his many wounds will be life altering."

"You are most welcome. This will be my honor. Let us just hope and pray for a complete recovery and a long life for this brave young man. You be well too."

I sighed. Over the past sixty-five years, how many watches had passed through my hands that had a common history…war and all its horrors? Someday, when this is truly finished, I am going to make a score sheet and a roster. From a Hamilton pocket watch that floated in the Pacific, a watch presented by a dying man in a German concentration camp, to a watch (wow, another Hamilton, I realized) that was "wounded" in Afghanistan.

I wondered what the next package would bring.

Saturday, February 6, 2010, was an upsetting day as I spent a solid hour sitting with the Golay Repeater in my hand. My customer's confidence notwithstanding, I didn't want to do this watch…I didn't want to even think about doing this watch. Yesterday I had called Cousin Bobby and sought his opinion. I didn't get the answer I wanted because Bobby said he was sure I could do it. He wouldn't try it, but he *knew* that I could.

I was stalling for time, so I called Maine to check in with Julie. I told her about the repeater. She reminded me that today was the anniversary of the Blizzard of '78. Oy! Thanks for nothing, kid. To make a "Marcus story" short (which is virtually impossible), the Blizzard of '78 had a devastating effect on Marcus Jeweler. So much snow had piled up on the roof that we had a cave-in, setting off a chain of events that could have been its own book. Needless to say, it wasn't a happy anniversary.

Procrastination continued. The next phone call was to an old watchmaker friend. A true master watchmaker, German born and trained, in the "old school manner." I knew that he'd repaired many of these, and I valued his advice and had for years. He was just a little over a year older than me, and our careers matched closely. Unfortunately, seriously failing health drove him from the bench several years ago. What was this master's advice? "Be very careful."

Well, I hung up the phone committed to repairing my first repeater. First I made a pot of coffee (black no sugar, of course).

Finally at the bench, I wound the watch, and to my great surprise, it started to run, even though the balance motion was not at all good. I stopped the balance wheel, and when I released it….nothing. I twisted my hand, and the balance again turned back and forth, just not happily. Removing the decorative hands and releasing the stem and case screws, I oh-so-gently removed the movement from the 18K gold case. OY.

No dial screws, so I pried the dial from the movement and beheld…a compilation of smooth levers, saw tooth levers, racks, cams, stop levers, springs, normal wheels, star discs, jewels, and I didn't know what else. I didn't know I could hold my breath that long.

I turned the watch "dial down" and was relieved to see a normal lineup of train wheels, pallet, and traditional balance assembly. My heart fell as I gazed upon an additional collection of wheels, gears, two hammers, three springs, two cams, and two circular gongs that circled, in opposite directions, the entire movement. I knew I was in trouble. I forgot to mention the "quiet the thing down" lever and spring. I was in real trouble.

I turned the watch over once more and slid the activating lever to see the workings of the chiming mechanism. If possible, worse than I thought, many things going round and round, others going back and forth, and a couple just sitting there doing nothing at all…nope, there they go. At the same time, I heard melodic chiming, but in a peculiar pattern.

Setting up my temporary "photo studio," I carefully took a series of extreme close-ups of the movement, three of each side. I covered the bench and went to the computer to load in the pictures. With a feeling of thanks for the ability of my computer, I edited the pictures, closely cropping each until the movement itself filled the entire monitor. When I printed a full set of pictures, I printed them 8 ½ x 11, with a very thin border. In the prints the balance wheel by itself was larger than the actual watch. Homework for tonight.

I said goodnight to the repeater and bailed out, looking back at my bench as I shut the door. I remember leaning against the wall before I got on the elevator. I was in trouble.

All evening I couldn't get the repeater off my mind. I stared at the computer monitor and then at the TV and then back to the computer and so on. As usual, I clicked onto this, the "adventures of a young watchmaker," and as usual found a couple of typos to correct. As I read of past puzzles and "triumphs," an idea began to form way back in my head. I couldn't quite put my finger on it, but there was something about the repeater being the product of the 1890s and this being 2010. It was there, but I had to find it. After I went to bed, I twice found myself wide awake thinking, reaching deep to get to that idea. Was it an idea or was it one of "Barry's Brainstorms"?

Six o'clock the next morning, my eyes popped open with a sudden realization. It was something I'd reread last night about the ultrasonic cleaning machine I'd "loaned" to my father. The special ultrasonic cleaning waves required that much of the watch mechanism be left *assembled.* Could that be the key to this? The span of a hundred years separated the making of the repeater and its repair. Two varying technologies from two vastly different eras. Back to sleep for a while.

In the shop I made another pot of black coffee and thought over my "brainstorm" of last night. Once again I moved and released the operating lever and carefully watched the chiming mechanism, even as I listened intently to the chiming. I couldn't make sense of the musical pattern, but everything seemed to work properly, without hesitation or halt. The balance still was reluctant to oscillate, but that didn't worry me.

I turned the watch dial down and with extreme care disassembled the running part of the watch. Balance and bridge, pallet and bridge, and the three train wheels and their bridges were gently removed and the moving parts prepared for the cleaning machine. The plates I screwed back onto the main plate for their own safety. The complicated mainspring barrel assembly required the removal of the center wheel bridge as well as its own multilayer bridging. I had already removed the circular chime rods, but returned them to their place of honor for the cleaning.

As I worked, I frequently referred to the large photographs and found the visible details very encouraging.

The movement main plate assembly had to go into the pocket watch basket, of course, while the much smaller moving parts went into three of the thimble containers from the wristwatch cradle. Into the cleaning machine, filled with brand-new solution, my latest adventure went, five solutions, one at a time. In the meantime... into the office for another cup of coffee (black, no sugar). Needless to say, I was worried about what I was doing.

With a deep sigh, I realized it was time to put everything back together. What was the motto from years ago at Mal's frat house at Clark University? Oh yeah, "Onward, upward, and throughward. That is the word of the day." Nonsense, of course, but it fit.

First, to protect them, off came the chime rods...I'd take no chance of bending them. With utmost care I put the proper oils on every visible friction point on the dial side. I oiled and siliconed the winding and setting gears that were on the watch. Manually I pushed the controlling lever and all the moving parts; wheels, levers, cams, and everything else were apparently working properly. So far so good. My brainstorm must have worked, as everything seemed to work easily, without effort. Now the rest...

Dial down, off came the plates, and the train wheels and drive mechanism were replaced piece by piece. First that crazy mainspring assembly, which was completely and securely attached to the bridge. Took a deep breath and carefully slid it under the center wheel, which even without its plate could not be removed from the main plate. Then the rest of the train wheels carefully mounted and their plates gingerly screwed down. I pressed the tweezer against an arm of the center wheel, and the four train wheels spun as free as I could hope. Next came the winding wheel and crown wheel plate and I, with a glance toward heaven, slowly wound the mainspring, but only three turns. Again the train wheels spun freely, and when

I turned the watch over, the chime control units, spring, and cams, both smooth and saw tooth, appeared to be completely free.

I returned the pallet and the completed balance to their places of honor, and then came the moment of truth. I couldn't face it, so I walked into the back office to calm down.

Back at the bench, another deep breath, and I wound the watch, probably halfway. I let out that breath and relaxed as the balance began a very lively oscillation. Onto the timing machine, and I admit to being completely amazed. This 120-year-old watch was timing out with a tiny gain of twelve seconds per day, and in five positions.

I put the last pieces of the chiming unit onto the watch and secured the chime rods.

Now I approached the real "moment of truth" as I slid and then released the actuator lever. Saw tooth racks snapped to position, wheels spun, cams pivoted, and I saw the hammers swing back and forth and...heard nothing. My heart sank as I tried again then again with no sound coming forth. Everything appeared to be working perfectly, but not a ding to be heard. Now what do I do? I just cannot have lost this much time for nothing.

One last push of the actuator, and everything spun, but there was *no* sound until suddenly I heard it...a single "dong." My head swiveled around and I stomped into the office to sulk. I had been listening to the final movement, the "Ode to Joy," of the Ninth Symphony and had turned it enjoyably loud. It had masked the chiming of the watch, until the last note of Mr. Beethoven's piece allowed me to hear that one dong. Back to the bench, and now I heard the watch as well as could be expected considering a certain loss of hearing.

However, what did "dong, dong, dong" followed by "dingdong, dingdong" followed by "ding, ding, ding" possibly mean? I pulled the stem, reset the minute indicator a little, and once again "dong, dong, dong" followed by "dingdong, dingdong, dingdong" followed by...silence. What in the...? Oy! I've got it!

Two chime rods gave three musical combinations...the *dong* was the lower note, the *ding* was the higher, and *dingdong* was a rapid strike of each. A slight reset didn't affect one but did the other two.

1. A "dong" indicated the hour.
2. A "dingdong" indicated the number of quarter hours since the dong.
3. A "ding" indicated the minutes since the last quarter hour.

Thus: three dongs plus two dingdongs plus two dings meant the time was three hours plus two quarter hours plus two minutes, or 3:32. It was up to you to know if it was day or night. This beautiful piece of machinery was built before electric lights were the norm. The chime sequences would allow the repeater's owner to know the time in the dark. This watch was the plaything of a very, very wealthy man. I wondered who.

Happily I replaced the dial and replaced the hands to indicate 3:32, then pushed the lever. What I heard was 3:34 not 3:32, so I had a problem. Now what? Now nothing. This was a minute repeater, and the watch was running while I put the hands on. I put the running second hand on, pushed the lever, and counted out 3:36. Quickly I put a finger on the second hand to stop the watch and with the other hand reset the minute hand to "36."

I carefully set the hands to the then correct time, 5:45, covered the watch and then the bench, shut of the lights, and called this a day...a very long, long day.

I'd check the watch in the morning. Good night.

Hurrah! The Golay Repeater was running, too fast but running. The watch was regulated and put back into the safe to check.

Hurrah once again...the day jumper for the Angelus chronograph was finally in. Oh, it was delayed by the big storms down south. My supplier couldn't get to the post office. Carefully I removed the six hands and the dial and finally the day disc itself. Using great caution, I place the day jumper into place and...it was the wrong part! It couldn't be, but it was really the wrong part.

With a sinking heart, I checked the *Bestfit Watch Parts Encyclopedia* and…I couldn't believe it. There was the part I had received, but with the wrong number. I was looking at a 575-page huge book and one entry in the book had a misprint on the piece I was looking for. The drawing of the part was correct, the factory part number was correct, but the "ebauche" part number had been listed on the wrong part. The part number I ordered and received was for the *date* jumper, a part twice the length of the *day* jumper. What were the odds of this happening? Time for coffee (black, no sugar).

Sadly, I went to the computer to check a special CD that contained about three thousand pages of chronograph data. This was a modern scanning of an out-of-print manual that was the "bible" for watchmakers that really specialized in the servicing of chronographs. It covered about twenty-nine different watches, with each watch having its own "volume," each volume ranging from 90 to 110 pages. Most pages in each "volume" were actually transparencies showing a single part, so as pages were turned one at a time, the chronograph and (if present) the calendar unit were "assembled" one part at a time. Notes and cautions pertaining to each part were printed on the outer edges of each page.

After finishing half a cup of coffee while I scanned the CD, I finally located the Angelus movement and then the picture I needed. I was right…the number printed in the *Bestfit* book was wrong.

It was now time to be nervous. On the strength of the original e-mail telling me the needed part was soon to be mailed, I'd gone ahead and spent extensive time and trouble repairing the chronograph, complete with total assembly to test it while the post office mule plodded north to Milford. Now I had to e-mail my supplier, explain the problem, and then hope and pray he had the correct part. The e-mail was sent, and I put the movement into the "Wait and See" box. Oy.

Life goes on, and there were more watches to repair. I chose six larger men's watches as I was in no mood to fight with extra tiny ladies' models. As I took each watch apart, I went to the computer to check for an answer to the e-mail. Nothing. Finally, at 5:00 p.m., I was listening to the news on the radio and there was another huge snowstorm in the Mid-Atlantic states...where the e-mail went. Accepting defeat, I prepared to call it a day. Of course, I couldn't help checking the e-mail one last time before I shut off the lights.

Third hurrah of the day. A short message, "Wonderful! Correct day jumper on the way...IF we can shovel out of this damn Yankee weather. Thanks for nothing. Send back the date jumper."

During the late news, I saw what he was complaining about. It's selfish to say, but better there than here.

I decided to completely assemble the chronograph, even without the day jumper. That way I could check everything, and in this watch there was a lot of everything to check. Even if the storm delayed the day jumper, I'd get plenty of running time on the watch.

I now had a number of chronographs running and had to remember to frequently stop the chrono units, check the "0" return, and then restart the stopwatch sections.

A brainstorm: I could simply set an alarm clock to go off every three hours as a reminder.

That was a great idea but for one tiny problem. The watchmaker, he who "keeps the world on time" did not own an alarm clock. I had watches spanning the time from before the Civil War until last week, but I didn't have an alarm clock. With a laugh, I realized I didn't have one at home either...there I used my TV's built-in alarms for the purpose.

I received a scary phone call. My customer was thrilled with the performance and appearance of the Golay Repeater. He said if he got further repeaters he'd be sure to send them to me! All I could reply was a weak thank you.

Finally! The long-awaited correct day jumper arrived. I steeled myself for the fitting of this critical part as I gently placed the jumper right into its place. The part just nestled into its post holes and waited for me to screw it down. No struggle, no wiggling...just drop it in place and secure it. A miracle. I placed the day disc in place with just the slightest pressure on the jumper, screwed down the day disc, and…done! I pushed a tiny screwdriver against the day disc advance actuator, and the disc jumped ahead a single day. Triumph… the day now lined up perfectly with the corresponding opening in the dial. Since the watch had been completely checked, I replaced the dial followed by the six hands, and with a sigh of relief re-cased the movement.

Now this deserved a cup of coffee (black, no sugar) and an e-mail to my customer.

Just to be on the safe side, I'd run it for another couple of days then back it would go. Sure enough, the watch was fine, and the day was changing as it should. The world applauded.

A new box was dropped off. As I scanned the contents I found a very unusual thing: I had six watches to repair, and every single one was a man's mechanical watch. A couple of "wind-'em-ups" and four self-winding models, two with calendar units. This was truly "back to the past" for me. I wrote the six watches up, and there weren't any surprises, only six really good watches that needed some attention.

The six mechanical *dinosaurs* were stripped, cleaned, assembled, oiled, and cased, and this single sentence is all that they deserved. Some watches take a couple of pages of description, and these *six* only required that I go for a cup of coffee (black, no sugar).

To steal a line from someone else…"I am shocked! Shocked, I tell you." As I occasionally do, I scrolled to the beginning of this tale, still checking spelling and typos. Which I'm sad to say, I still find. Anyhow, a short way in, I found an actual beginning date for this great work of literature. I began to compile a few short stories at the behest of my daughters that might be of interest to their kids…memories for an old watchmaker, Papa Barry.

Most watches that come in to me are just that...a machine that happens to tell time. However, now and then, often enough to make me laugh...to make me wonder...to make me envious...and, yes, to make me aware of my emotions...a watch with a story comes in. I truly believe that someday, and may that day be far, far away, I will sit somewhere and talk about watch repair with Dad, Uncle Abe, Marty, Morty and all the watchmakers from over the years. Even he who didn't speak a word of English. Will I have stories to tell them.

I started this in 2008, almost a year and a half ago and ninety something pages. A year to jot down sixty-five years of watch repair. Sixty-five years of watches and the people who used and abused them. Now I add the people who collect them. I find this difficult to believe. Although I thought many times that I had typed the last entry, I know I am not finished...yet. Watches continue to arrive and I continue to service and care for them. With God's help, I will continue.

Today, something improbable and utterly mysterious found its way to beautiful downtown Milford: an Armand Nicolet chronograph delivered from western Massachusetts. My curiosity was aroused as the watch looked new; in fact, brand new. I sat with a cup of coffee (black, no sugar) as I read the long note attached. The watch was truly new, just sold and returned after only four days. Apparently the day and date unit had a problem. My eyes were drawn to the watch and...wow! This watch had seven hands! A moon/sun disc and windows that showed the *day* and the *month*. Oh no. I was in for it now.

Top to bottom in the center were the chronograph sweep second hand, the minute hand and hour hand, and a red-tipped date indicator hand. At the "9" was a double...a "running second hand" and a twenty-four-hour indicator showing military time. At the "12" was a "minute minder" hand while at the "6" was an "hour indicator" hand.

At the "10" and the "2" level, near the middle, were two windows, the day on the right and the month to the left.

Last but not least, at the "6" was a larger opening that showed the daily position of the sun and moon. On the left ("9") side of the case were openings for push buttons to advance and adjust "something" that I had to figure out later.

What was the matter with this very expensive new watch? This was as dumb a thing as I'd ever read. The customer claimed that the *date* changed precisely at midnight, as it should, but the *day* didn't advance until more or less eight o'clock in the morning. This was not only stupid but, I think impossible. The only thing it could be was that somehow this new watch was assembled with two wheels out of synch.

I pulled out the stem halfway and advanced the date, which worked perfectly, even to the month advancing as the date hand went from "31" to "1," a new month. When I operated the pusher on the side, the day disc advanced easily and accurately. Now I pulled the crown out to the time-setting position and advanced the minute and hour hands round and round until I neared 11:30 p.m. I slowed the advancement, and sure enough, at exactly midnight the date hand jumped to the next number. With care, I continued to advance the time, waiting for the first sign that the *day* disc was engaged and doing its slow turn. Normally I'd expect the day to jump into its new position around 2:30 a.m. or so, of course with some leeway. The owner wouldn't know, because at that time he/she would be asleep.

Something was truly wrong as the watch was now at 4:00 a.m. and nothing was happening. I continued to advance the time, until finally the day disc began to jump. Eventually the day changed, and sure enough, it made the final jump at 7:50 a.m. Puzzled, I turned the crown around and around until the calendar unit duplicated the change sequence. Something was truly wrong, so here we go.

Just as I loosened the back of the case, I was interrupted by the phone, and it was the owner of the store who had sent me this watch. Trouble. Two more of these watches had been returned. Yesterday he had his staff wind and set the two additional watches in his show case that were waiting to be sold. Each and every one had advanced the *day* in the same wrong way. Cautiously I told him I was returning the one I had and he should send everything back to the factory. This wasn't a simple misadjusted new watch...this was something else, something I shouldn't touch. I'd have a cup of coffee (black, no sugar) and then box up the defective watch.

As I was relaxing, my brain thought back a number of years ago to a man from Fall River who was sent to me in serious trouble. He was facing the dreaded "*R*" word...REFUND. Today's store owner was a man with three indignant purchasers of very expensive watches, and I knew I had to help. I called him back and told him to hold all the watches in his store until I possibly found the problem. I had smiled at a possible assembly error in a single chronograph, but the smile vanished at the prospect of three very costly but defective watches. Something serious was wrong...serious indeed. I disagreed with myself...something, as Uncle Abe would say, stupid was going on.

I took the movement out, removed the hands and dial, and carefully visually checked everything. I was disappointed to find nothing wrong. Each part looked perfect, each part had the perfect amount of free play, and now what? I could see nothing wrong, bent, damaged, or out of place.

Once again I pulled the stem to the setting position, put the date hand onto its wheel, and set the time forward. Of course it did not matter where I set the hand; just so I could see it freely jump to the next date, a distance of six degrees on a circle. Twice I advanced time to carefully check the day/date setting sequence, and twice the date jumped forward while the day disc sat truly motionless for about six to eight hours before advancing, doing so five to seven hours late. Deep sigh. Each part seemed perfect. There was a central wheel that, in turn, advanced the date hand and then the day disc.

A light bulb clicked on and I understood the problem. The entire problem lay in the day/date advancing wheel. Nothing to do but take the entire dial side of the watch apart—really not a difficult task, just a very careful one. I carefully lifted out the drive wheel and examined a single part composed of a geared wheel, a cam, a spacer, a spring with a small projection, and a circular cap with a long triangular arm projecting out ninety degrees. This triangle did the actual advancing of the date wheel, and the small spring with the little projection advanced the day disc. The problem now showed itself.

The day/date advancing gear was similar to many older day/date mechanical watches going back to the 1960s, and its operation was no mystery given the number I'd repaired for many, many years. Memory of the old solved the problem of the new. The date wheel and the day disc were on either side of the advancing gear. Thus the two metallic projections were on approximately opposing sides, adjusted so the date jumped ahead about two to three hours before the day disc jumped. On this modern gear the projections were one above the other so the rotation of the gear advanced the date wheel and then had to wait for enough time to pass until the other projection jumped the day disc. This had actually been made and assembled that way. But now what?

There were no photos or part diagrams for this watch, which would have been a great assistance. If this part had been assembled wrong, the solution was to order a new one and take the easy way out. However, being me, I just had to find a solution myself. If this had been put together wrong, could I pry everything apart and put it back together again? Good heavens, I was reciting Humpty Dumpty and hoping the king's men could help. I carefully checked the position of the date arm and tried to calculate the proper positioning for the little day projection.

Oh so gently I inserted the red-tipped screwdriver and slowly twisted the blade to create a prying up force. I held the assembly on a piece of pith wood with a brass pin through the center. That way, if things suddenly jumped upward, nothing would fly away. Due to my precaution, the upper cap slowly slid upward, releasing the parts for (toes crossed) realignment. I rotated the upper arm what I hoped was the right amount and re-staked the assembly. However, the entire under dial sections had to be in assembled condition to check the day/date advancement. I was not surprised to find that my "put together" was off by two hours of turning time, so everything had to come apart once again. The new alignment was better, but not acceptable yet. If only I had a sample, or a drawing, I could closely approximate the spacing of the two parts. We were closer, but not quite there yet. Again everything came apart so I could spend a simple minute making another adjustment. Finally the advancement sequence was acceptable.

Now I'd just keep it wound and properly set under a plastic cover. This way I could both see what was happening and, if needed, get into the watch quickly. I thought, with a feeling of triumph, that I had it correct, finally. I started the test with the hands set at 11:30 p.m. to let the date change at midnight and then watch for the day change. I grinned as I watched the day disc advance at 2:25 a.m., well within limits. The actual time was early afternoon, but what mattered was my being in the shop to witness whatever happened. I set it right and let it run at a normal rate.

Time for a happy cup of coffee (black, no sugar). I had spent much time solving this puzzle, but it *was* solved. It was now late Friday afternoon, and I was ready to flee for the weekend. I had the promise of great weather for a large project on my boat. Being a true do-it-yourselfer, each weekend on the boat was a joy.

Just before I left, I manually wound the Nicolet and assure myself that every hand was set to the "nth" degree of accuracy. It was 5:30 p.m. on Friday, and I'd be back early Monday morning to check on this. As positive as I might well be, I would still keep an eye on the watch until at least Wednesday. Bye for now, little disaster.

Sunday morning (the forecast didn't pan out), I returned to the scene of the crime, turned on the lights, and even before I removed my coat I went to my bench to check on the Nicolet. I turned on the bench light, and averting my eyes, I uncovered the bench top and...everything was perfect, the hands were correct, the day/date/month and a.m./p.m. indicators were right on, and this surprised me, the watch had, since Friday, gained a total of sixteen seconds. I smiled to myself in joy. What a great way to start the week! Time for coffee (black, no sugar).

On Monday, I was scheduled to begin work on an Omega Seamaster Automatic Chronograph, so on Sunday, when I really didn't plan to do a specific amount of repairs, I took my next project from the safe and...and greatly restrained myself from throwing the Omega out of the window. This beautifully magnificent Omega had the very same movement as the Nicolet.

In the modern Swiss watchmaking world, only a limited number of companies make mechanical movements. In the past there were literally dozens of manufacturers, even though their movements were sold under hundreds of different brand names. I don't have the knowledge of the legal organization of the Swiss watch industry today, but it is akin to if all US automakers continued to make their own cars but marketed them all under a unified trade name.

I was furious at myself, not justified, but steamed anyway. I pulled the stem and advanced the hands, needing to check the action of the day/date hands. I grew really angry because the day/date change was perfect...perfect. Now I knew the truth...while I was cursing the lack of data on the Val 7751 in any of my books so I could match the positioning of the two advancing levers, and all during my puzzling over the problem, during my many sessions of taking a complicated mechanism apart for the second, then third, then fourth time until I got the setting right...all during that time, in my safe, eight feet from my bench, was a watch that contained a perfectly aligned unit. All I had had to do was reassemble the bad unit to look just like the good one. Nuts.

It was also obvious that the problem lay with a limited run of parts. Monday I'd e-mail the store owner to send all of his Nicolets to Milford for a quick though costly fix. At least I'd prevented a few refunds. Then I changed my mind...I would advise him to return the unsold watches for a free-of-charge repair from the factory.

The Omega was in for a complete overhaul. As the kids say, "I have a clue now," so the overhaul should go smoothly. I decided to take an extreme close-up of the day/date advancing wheel so I'd have a vastly enlarged picture of how it should be.

I opened a small box from my favorite customer, and among the group of watches, I found a smaller than normal size pocket watch. It was in tissue, preventing me from seeing a...wow! This thin dress pocket watch was a Longines special. The bezel appeared to be—yes—completely diamond set, and the numbers on the dial were also completely formed by diamonds. This time I was impressed. I thought I had seen everything, but I was looking at dial numbers composed of small, round, rectangular, and a couple of marquis-shaped diamonds. As I looked inside the case, I saw that the case back was neatly impressed with the normal company name, serials, style, and the words "10% Iridium Platinum." This was certainly beyond the ordinary.

After enough admiring of the case, I examined the movement. Of course the basic quality of the Longines was apparent. Nothing seemed to be broken. I tried to spin the movement back and forth and...I had a problem. What should have moved easily appeared to be paralyzed. Even the balance wheel would not move.

Gently I pressed a tweezer against the balance arm, and it would not move. The balance staff was not broken, but the balance was frozen into place. I tried, but I could not get the center wheel or anything to budge. My last try was winding or unwinding the mainspring...no, nothing would move. Everything was totally frozen in place, yet there was not a sign of rust.

Something was tapping me on the top of my head, and I heard Uncle Abe saying, "Barry, something stupid is wrong here. Think." Time for a quick cup of coffee (black, no sugar). What could be wrong? The whole watch was as if glued together...That's it! The watch was glued together. I'd seen this once before...back in 1959, I think. This beautiful watch had sat unused for about forty or fifty years, and the oil had not only dried up, it had solidified. The watch was truly glued together.

Well, that diagnosis was easy. I pulled the hands and dial and simply dunked the fully assembled watch into the first cup of the ultrasonic cleaner. Perhaps this would begin to soften the solidified oil. Four minutes in the cleaning solution, four minutes in the first rinse, topped off with four minutes in a second rinse and a final dipping in the third rinsing cup. Holding my breath, I put the watch into the spin drier and sat with another cup of coffee (black, no sugar).

After my coffee break and enough paperwork time to enable the watch to cool, I took the Longines to the bench and took a careful look. I looked but could not believe what I saw: the watch was not only running, but the balance was oscillating as though I had just completed a full overhaul. Now I was in a playful mood, so I put the Longines onto the timing machine and...this thing was running in perfect beat, showing a gain of twelve seconds per day with a clean record. No oil...nothing done...nothing adjusted, and this thing was perfect. Someone, including me, was extremely lucky. Now it could be put aside for a full, take-apart overhaul in a few days.

With an increasing number of mechanical, self-winding watches coming once again into the shop, I had been growing concerned about obtaining a better Auto watch winder. I had a couple, and they were a headache. Vastly overpriced as they had been made for proud display on the bedroom dresser of someone who owned a Rolex or other truly costly luxury watch. With the use of an auto winder, the watch would self-wind and continue to run, even if not worn for days or weeks. Of the four I owned, three held the watches so flat that some of the automatics with very light alloy weights would not wind.

Here it was the year 2010 and I was struggling with the problem I had solved in the 1960s with the Bulova 11ANACD. No, to be honest, I had discovered the problem, but Bulova, ignoring me, solved it a year later by coming out with the 11AOACD with a heavy alloy oscillating weight.

Earlier in this tale, I told you about the automatic watch winder that I made in the early 1950s for our own use. Not only did it work better as the watches were held vertical, thus enabling even a light alloy weight to function, the best part of our winder was that it had been a fraction of the cost of a "Look What I Own" watch winder. So instead of staying mad at the winders I had acquired over the years, I decided to just make my own...again.

Problem of the day: where could I find an electric motor with a shaft rotation of as little as five rpm so I could make a new one? I contacted a few companies that sold electric motors, and none could believe I wanted an electric motor that turned that slowly. These were industrial firms, so I realized I'd contacted the wrong people.

On that Friday morning, I went about my usual rounds, and in one of my stops I found the answer...much to my chagrin. Right in front of my eyes was a tall, large-diameter jewelry display, majestically revolving at about five rpm. I almost hit myself in the head as I stared at the solution to my dilemma...a display motor. How could I have forgotten about the rotating display that was the organ donor for my first winder? Such a motor had to have both the torque to carry a good deal of weight and a low shaft speed. All I needed was a unit I could adapt to mount on a wall. Cheers and hurrahs.

Back in the shop, I sat with a cup of coffee (black, no sugar) and a phone book and looked up the listings under *displays*. None had a unit I could use or adapt or alter. At least they spent time with me on the phone, coming up with ideas and suggestions. It wasn't often these days to find really good customer service, and although these companies didn't have what I needed, they didn't dismiss me out of hand. Oh well, back to the bench; watches needed my precious time. (Sorry about that.)

At 3:00 p.m. the shop phone rang, and to my surprise I was speaking to a very nice young lady from one of the display companies. She was rather excited as she described searching through a listing of companies around the country that did have many variations of motors made for display units, but possibly adaptable to my needs. I was given the name, address, and phone number of one company she highly recommended, as well as the name of the contact.

Naturally, with my luck, he was out for the day. Would I call the following day? Better yet, if I gave them my number, he'd call me the next morning. Done. "Oh," she said, "his name is Rich, and he knows what he's doing."

The following morning I stared at the phone, willing it to ring, which it did, promptly at 10:00 a.m. It was a happy-sounding Rich, telling me he had what he thought was the perfect unit for my need. He had a heavy-duty wall-mounted, slow-shaft-speed motor that included a very sturdy aluminum y-shaped arm that even had a center-drilled and tapped shaft hole. The hole was a one-quarter by twenty thread, one of the most common and one for which a vast array of screws and bolts were available. And to top everything off, it sold for $65 complete.

Needless to say, I was ready to order on the spot, but Rich couldn't help me with that. To place an order, I'd have to speak to Monica, and today she had the day off, call tomorrow. Rich told me that he wasn't allowed to take orders as he always messed something up. He also gave me the website address and the actual model/style number of the motor he suggested, but said I should look through the entire line, just in case.

As we hung up, I typed in the website address and clicked through to the motor number I'd just gotten from Rich. In truth, I could hardly believe how exactly perfect the unit was. Even the base had a flange that had four holes for mounting the unit directly to a vertical or horizontal surface. Oy, this was a find.

Early the next morning I was on the phone to Monica, ordering the unit. She was helpful, efficient, knowledgeable of the product, and had a friendly manner and voice. After the order was written, I commented that it was nice that the company kept Rich on as his personality over the phone sort of made up for his ineptness. That brought gales of laughter, enough that I thought Monica would drop the phone. She told a coworker what she was hysterical about and I heard lots more laughter. What had I said?

"Richard...inept?" She giggled. "Mr. Marcus, Rich is the *owner* of the company and my boss. His writing is so bad that not a single person here can read or make out what an order should be. He can't even write the two-letter code for a state that is legible, so we made him stop writing orders and leave that to us. Inept? He's a genius, he just can't write legibly. He'll love that you said we're being charitable toward him. If we let Rich write the address label on your motor to go to Massachusetts (MA) it will end up in Missouri (MO) or Mississippi (MI), or even Maryland (MD), but I'll tell him what you said."

Three days later, my new about-to-be-automatic watch winder was delivered, and it was perfect. My project could proceed.

For the unasked information of whoever reads this in 2110, this afternoon I took the Omega chronograph apart, concentrating under the dial. Sure enough, the day/date advancing assembly was the same as the one on the Nicolet Chronograph. Even before I removed the part, I could see what I would have seen had I known this particular watch was in my safe.

Tomorrow I would take another digital close-up of the assembly for my now growing "trouble scrapbook."

The phone rang. My caller was from Chicago.

"Mr. Marcus, Stan from Walpole Jewelers in town suggested I call you. We have a fifty-two-year-old Patek that has been to my watchmaker four times. He says it's perfect, but the watch isn't running and the customer is furious. My friend insisted you could help. The watch is very precious, actually despite its value. His late wife gave it to him as a wedding present fifty-two years ago. Beautiful eighteen carat ultrathin case, always cared for and never abused. You may be my last hope."

I asked, "Where is the customer...in the store staring at you?"

"No, he's not staring, he's glaring at me. Really I can't blame him; the repair was costly, and the darn watch only runs—"

I rudely interrupted, "Only six or seven hours then stops, no matter what. If you take a look at the poor guy's hands, you will see arthritis in his fingers. The problem, I bet, is your watchmaker is kind of young compared to my seventy-five years. My uncle Abe and my father told me to look for this problem. The crown on the watch is right for the watch, but way too small for tired, arthritic fingers. Have your man try a crown a half millimeter larger in diameter and a little thicker. That may or may not do the trick, but if not, just go up another half millimeter in diameter at a time. That's the problem. Hope it helps."

An incredulous voice asked, "You're seventy-five and your uncle and father just told you the problem with a Patek one thousand miles away? What in the hell are you talking about?"

"No, they did not just tell me about your problem. They taught me about sixty years ago that many problems with a watch can only be solved by looking at the watch's owner.

"The tip-off here was your telling me he received the watch fifty-two years ago. I did the most likely arithmetic and knew a wind-me-up-daily watch wasn't getting wound. Same old watch and the same old guy, but something changed. Not his eyes; he can still see what time it is. Not his politics, that wouldn't matter. Thus his fingers have another fifty thousand miles on them and they are worn out. Easy. Also I figured your watchmaker was off-site and didn't know how old the owner is and couldn't look at his fingers. All your man knew was that the Patek was exactly as the Patek factory wanted. It was just too bad that those specifications were not good anymore for the Patek owner."

He thanked me, we bid each other farewell, and I hung up. I deserved a coffee break (black, no sugar) and relaxed for a few minutes and lost a game of solitaire on the computer. Just as I gave up the phone rang.

"Mr. Marcus," Chicago calling back, "I'm calling to tell you how astonished I am by your thousand-mile out-of-sight diagnosis. I took a man's windup Hamilton from our repair box, one with a larger crown that measured two millimeters larger than that on the Patek. I gave it to the Patek owner and asked him to wind it and then give me the watch. He did have to wind it for a good while, but said it was easy. He handed me a fully wound watch. I explained what you said and promised to have a larger crown put on his Patek. He left very happy. Now, sir, how much do I owe you for your time?"

"Nothing, as this goes down as an ego boost. I'm writing for my grandkids, not memoirs, but rather a long, long remembrance of my adventures with broken, sick, and ailing watches and the people who owned them. As I told you, I learned many of these lessons when I was a (never really) little kid of ten. My grandkids will think I'm so smart. This was my pleasure."

There are, in theory, two things that are inevitable...death and taxes. To deal with reality, I add a third in my world...Rolex.

A "vintage" Rolex had darkened my door. Not placed in my hands for tender loving care. Not in for an overhaul. This had darkened my door. Old and beat-up, broken balance staff, lower hole and cap jewels broken, the self-wind unit had something rattling around inside, and a crown unlike anything I'd ever seen before, even in a Rolex. Someone was mad at me, I thought. There was *no* chance of finding either the staff or the winding parts. The jewels were not a problem, because hole and cap jewels are merely required to have the right pivot hole and the right diameter. The difficulty lay in finding the right jewel and then installing it exactly at the right height. Same with the cap jewel, just easier.

First I had to take apart the entire watch to make a list of what was broken and in need of replacing. My door was slightly less darkened as I found two tiny but completely loose screws in the self-contained automatic unit. Nothing else was needed except the most critical part of all...the balance staff. Where was I going to find a balance staff for an old Rolex? Hope springs eternal...I read that somewhere.

The Rolex, reduced to little pieces, was placed into the cleaning machine, along with an Omega chronograph. While waiting, I decided to waste some time searching the obscure material boxes, shelves, and cabinets that might contain Rolex parts for this watch. While I "wasted time" I also sipped a cup of coffee (black, no sugar). Occasionally things happen that are beyond explanation, and this was one of those times.

In a never before seen (by me) envelope in a cabinet given to me by a retired watchmaker, I found seven balance staffs, three stems, a couple of mainsprings, and some automatic parts, which of course I didn't need.

Someday I must really sort and catalog everything here. I won't, of course, because watch parts are totally useless until that split second when they are needed.

In reality, I had to admit that it wasn't worth the time cataloging watch parts I hadn't needed for the last forty-five years. It was when I needed them that the pieces became worth anything. The status would remain quo.

While the Rolex and its companions went through the ultrasonic cleaner, I grabbed the small repair box and took out a circa 1937 gent's Hamilton. This watch was something that should require me to delete the preceding paragraph and get busy cataloging parts. On with the search. Cancel the search as I grabbed my oldest GS Flexo crystal catalog and turned to the MX pages. In about ten seconds I found the crystal, and a short march to the crystal cabinet revealed five of them, which prompted a question. Who in the world had five crystals like this? Oh, I did. This cabinet was in my dad's store when he opened for business in 1944. In 1944, this particular watch was a very well regarded Hamilton, and the softer plastic unbreakable crystals were a frequent casualty of wearer abuse. Certain watches were popular enough that it actually paid to stock parts, thus avoiding the wasting of time ordering what we knew would soon be needed. A minimum of filing and the crystal fit as if it was made for this watch...as it was. Now I was down to four. Thank goodness something today went smoothly. Time for a coffee break (black, no sugar).

The USA has a new but tiny satellite in orbit. It consists of the mainspring barrel, barrel arbor, and mainspring of a "vintage" Tavannes wristwatch. As I opened the barrel cap, the lights suddenly blew out, startling me enough that I looked up, shifting my grip on the barrel, and...everything let go, and I heard the parts hit the ceiling above and to the right. Now I had to take the entire shop apart to find these very obscure watch parts. I wondered what else I might find…something I lost five or six years ago and never bothered to look for as I had a replacement right at hand. Good hunting to me.

I was, of course, in deep trouble. The missing parts for the Tavannes were still missing. The brand name was an obscure company from England, and the watch was originally purchased there during World War II. The movement was an early "shock proof" model in a rectangular case secured by four screws, of which there were none left. Also the rectangular crystal was scratched as well as cracked, and I didn't know where I was going to find a new "flange-sided" crystal for this watch. The customer was aware that he might receive the watch back repaired but with the bad crystal. I was going to have to make screws for this, but first I'd have to find stainless steel casing screws and spend a lot of time at the lathe.

Meanwhile there was the little matter of a missing mainspring barrel and barrel arbor. They had hit the ceiling above my head and I had been searching every square millimeter of the area, on hands and knees assisted by a flashlight and a pair of tweezers. I found a minute hand from a Seiko that had been missing for about seven years and a loose stem from who knows what, where, and when, but nothing I was looking for.

My knees were going to sue me, so I skittered around to help myself up by gripping the long desk beside my chair. I didn't turn off the flashlight, but moved it along the floor, and as I faced away from the bench, the flashlight beam illuminated the area under the safe. Something reflected the light, and like a year-old baby, I crawled to the safe and reached under. I found—a staple that stuck into my finger. Just what I needed. Reaching in a couple more inches, I pulled out—a mainspring barrel. I got myself up and limped to the bench (darn knees), and a miracle on Main Street occurred as the barrel fit the movement perfectly. Now to find the arbor. Maybe it flew behind me also…please, please.

I carefully washed out my staple stab, and to give my knees a break, I went back to the office to relax a couple of minutes and have some coffee (black, no sugar). I plopped into the chair and just savored the momentary triumph of finding the barrel, but wondering about the barrel arbor. I leaned back, resting against the desk, and thought out a search plan, starting with a further look under the safe and branching out. For a couple of minutes I thought while I gazed at the little battery-powered vacuum cleaner used to clean up the shop. It was used by the woman who took care of the shop a couple of times a month. She'd been in yesterday and—whoa—she had vacuumed the entire shop. Could it possibly be...possible? Could I be that lucky? Back on my hands and (unhappy) knees, I vacuumed around and under the safe.

I unfolded and stretched out a trash bag and carefully opened the dust catcher onto it. The dust bunny was big enough to call "Bugs." I started at one end with a tweezer and after twenty minutes had just gotten started. An idea emerged, and I went to the repair toolbox and took out a large screwdriver and magnetized it heavily.

Pushing it into the dust pile several times, I did indeed rescue several pieces of broken and discarded watch parts. Another stab and I pulled out another staple and a mainspring barrel arbor. Virtue had triumphed once again. Very careful not to drop the arbor, I walked to my bench and...it fit. I allowed myself a deep sigh of relief and enjoyed it. No coffee break; I'd wasted too much time for the search and rescue.

I finished assembling the movement, very carefully installing the new mainspring into the barrel, fitting in the arbor, and capping the barrel. Done. I timed out the watch, attached the dial, and quickly replacing the faded luminescence material, I was done with the movement. Without much hope, I measured out the dimensions for the rectangular "flange" crystal and dug out my oldest GS crystal book. Nothing. Just in case, I checked the next newer catalog and then the next until...I found a crystal that just might work. That is, I found it in the catalog and I had to search the cabinets again.

As usual, I found my needed crystal and three spares. This from a time when we ordered crystals by the quarter dozen. Ten minutes of very careful work with a file and I actually had a new crystal for this watch. Now to the screws...four were needed. I located my special "case back screw" cabinet and after a bit of time found the screws needed. Most critical, of course, were the threads. All that was left was the time-consuming job of cutting down the heads on my lathe and then filing the screws short to fit the case.

My lathe. It sat on the spare bench permanently mounted on a handmade wooden base. It had come down to me, Barry J. Marcus, now in the year 2010, having been obtained, I believe, in 1910 by my grandfather, Hyman Marcus, shortly after he arrived in Worcester. There was no way to ascertain the date of manufacture, but this lathe had been at the service of a Marcus for one hundred years. Traditionally a watchmaker's lathe was fastened permanently to his bench, but Grandpa Marcus found it got in his way, so he made the base, mounting the lathe in front and the motor aligned on the back. Since, I guess, the lathe was not in constant use, my grandfather preferred his bench cleared of the space-taking tool. To this day, a hundred years later, the lathe, while still operating as new, was kept off of my bench and given its place of honor at the spare, which had been for years my own father's watch bench.

In a sense, a century had passed and things had remained the same. Time passes (forgive me that) and the world of Marcus remains as it was. One at a time, I turned down the screw heads until they fit snugly in the recesses in the bezel, securing the back of the case against the underside of the crystal gasket. Then a little work with a file to shorten the extra-long threads and there we go.

Done at last...and I was quite pleased, if I may say so. Let's say I was quite pleased with the great bit of luck finding the airborne watch parts. The watch, now with its new crystal and re-done hands, looked almost new.

Does anyone know or can anyone recommend a good watchmaker? I really need to get in touch with one. On this day, April 11, 2010, I, Barry J. Marcus, noted watchmaker, became as my customers have always been...a watch abuser.

I spent a glorious weekend working on the preparations of my sail-boat for another painting. Saturday I used a roll of towels and a quart of acetone to hand wash the hull, removing the residue of last week's extensive sanding. When done the hull was as smooth as glass. Sunday promised to be another good day.

Promise kept, and I got ready to do some prep paint touching up. I had almost a quart of Interlux Fire Red paint left from my last full hull painting, and I intended to use it to touch up all the rough spots in the upper hull. There were several places where the removal of the boat's name letters caused paint to lift, leaving a visible "dent" in the paint. These I intended to fill in, with color to match. Later there would be a coat of gray primer to be followed by a new coat of "Fire Red" poly. A good deal of extensive work, requiring a number of breaks, but naturally well worth the effort.

At 1:12 p.m., as I stood on my folding ladder, reaching up to finish my work on the port (left) upper bow, three men came rushing toward me in a near panic. All pointed at my left arm, frantic in their shouts, "Barry, look...you've opened up your arm and you're bleeding all over yourself and the ladder! Down from there—now!"

Wasting no time, I jumped down, and my arm was grabbed as my friends frantically tried to locate what seemed to be a truly serious wound. One of the guys suddenly bent down and sniffed my "blood" and laughed. "He's covered with that red paint!" I'd been so careful watching the paint go on just right that I had not noticed excess paint running down my hand and arm. This was more than embarrassing.

A few bouncy steps to the back of my station wagon and I grabbed a quart of paint thinner and a used towel and started to clean my arm off. Finally getting most off my hand, I moved up and discovered that *my* Valjoux 7750 high-tech self-winding chronograph day/date watch with minute and hour recording was 90 percent covered in "Fire Red" Interlux paint! I had just committed the deed that had launched a thousand lectures to my customers. I just couldn't believe this.

There was paint inside both push button assemblies, the rotating bezel was already sticking, and every link of the band was covered with red paint. Even dipping the watch into the paint thinner wasn't help-ing. *Oy!* Wait until I give myself the estimate on this one.

I knew that by the time I got to the shop in the morning, the paint would be long dried. I might actually have to wear a different watch for a while. This would be funny if I thought it was a laughing matter, which I didn't. My "friends," those who had rushed to my rescue, now solemnly told me of good watchmakers where they lived, then laughed at their humor. Very funny. It looked as if I'd be stopping by the shop on the way home to start triage on my watch.

April 14, 2010...a date that proved that nothing really changes. A vaguely familiar customer brought her watch to me for a new battery. We chatted while I put a new power cell into the yellow Movado, and she mentioned casually her sadness that the man's automatic Bulova I'd repaired a year ago for her husband wasn't running properly any-more. My ears perked at that news. Now what? I thought.

Naturally I couldn't remember her name, but as usual I remem-bered her husband's watch. Two-tone automatic day/date Bulova, but with a Speidel band I'd sold a long time ago. My question as to the problem was answered by a deep sigh.

"Since his stroke poor Vincent has great trouble walking more than a couple of steps. His time is spent watching TV or often reading favorite books. But his watch won't keep running, and he misses the first part of his TV shows. He finds that very upsetting and is disap-pointed that the watch repair didn't last longer."

Once again, my mind's ear (sort of like the mind's eye) heard Dad and Uncle Abe saying, "Barry, always remember, more than the watch, you are taking care of the people who own and use them. Especially those who depend on them."

Gently I said, "The problem, sadly, is not the Bulova. The watch is a self-winding model that requires constant daily wearing and motion to wind itself and run. I'm afraid that your husband's current condition is the problem. Due to his confinement, the watch doesn't get the mo-tion to wind. I want you to bring in the watch for me to check, but sad to say, I've seen this many times over many years. If his hands are not affected, he could manually wind it a couple of times a day and then depend on the watch until there is a recovery."

A sad shake of her head confirmed that there would be no recovery.

"I might suggest the purchase of a battery-powered watch. They'll run whether worn or not for a couple of years. When you bring in the Bulova, I'll show you what size and style of watch to get for Vincent, and we can use the Speidel band on the new watch. The Speidel will not only fit comfortably, but he can get it on and off easily."

She thanked me and left, and I went for a cup of coffee (black, no sugar). As I sipped, I thought of my lessons as a kid watchmaker. Trained by skilled watchmakers to look at the entire world of a given watch, I was able to save a customer the price of a costly repair on a watch that was in truth suffering only the ills of its owner. How often had the "problem" with a watch been solved with the asking of one or two simple questions regarding the owner? A stroke, a crippling accident, the onset of arthritis, even a healthy retirement that radically altered the lifestyle of the owner…all events that had nothing to do with the watch but meant it no longer worked properly.

This afternoon, May 17, 2010, the ringing of the phone enabled me to put down a very stubborn and tired Waltham pocket watch. A pleasant-sounding female voice with a mid-western accent greeted me. "Mr. Marcus, my jeweler here in Chicago suggested I call you for help with a watch question. He admitted to not knowing, but said there is a watchmaker in Massachusetts to whom he sends high-quality watches for repair. Do you have a few minutes for me? It's rather important."

This is a moment for ego building…a call for help all the way from Chicagoland. "Of course," I replied, "anything I can help with. To paraphrase an old saying, my knowledge is your knowledge."

"Oh, thank you. Here's my problem…I'm trying to finish a cross-word puzzle, and I can't figure the clue 'code letters for an early digital watch.' It must be three letters only."

Okay, which of my daughters was playing with me? This "call for help" was something screwy enough for me to do, but the voice was not one of my girls. I'd play along.

"Really it's easy...the answer depending on the words that cross it is either LED or LCD. LED stands for light emitting diode while LCD stands for liquid crystal diode."

She replied happily, "That's it. LCD fits perfectly. Mr. Marcus, I can't thank you enough. Frank said you could save the day."

The call had to be for real...none of mine would have known the name of the store owner. This was as strange a call as I'd ever received...from Chicago, no less. As she said good-bye, my laughter started. This I had to tell the troops. The girls laughed themselves silly, and I called Cousin Bobby, who thought I was kidding.

A crossword puzzle? That's a new one...I couldn't stop chuckling to myself. Time for a coffee break (black, no sugar).

I went back to the recalcitrant Waltham, which had decided to behave while I was on the phone. The motion and rate settled down, and I put on the dial and hands and set it under a glass cover to watch it overnight.

The watch movement manufacturers are again producing mechanical watches. These are normally beautifully designed watch movements that truly mirror the epitome of the watchmaker's art. Then, of course, it is made more and more and more complicated, just to spite Barry Marcus.

An example is my favorite, the Valjoux 7750, known today in the industry as the ETA 7750. This is the movement in the watch I wear, the automatic chronograph that I first repaired with the use of several hand drawn index cards. Now the high-tech Barry has an album of digital photographs, printed up to 8 x 10 size for reference.

This fine watch is, of course, an automatic chronograph, which, with added parts and a few bridge alterations, is also either a date watch or a day and date watch. Of course, there are the chronograph hands, consisting of the central sweep second hand, the minute recording hand, which records elapsed minutes to thirty minutes total, then the hour-recording hand, which totals to twelve hours, with thirty-minute divisions. Last and least is the traditional small second hand, which just shows the passing seconds as long as the watch is running.

Is that enough? Indeed not, because on my bench at the moment was an ETA 7750A2C, which is truly a treasure with a dial that has more hands than an overgrown octopus. This watch had a minute hand, hour hand, small second hand, sweep second hand, minute-recorder hand, hour-recorder hand, day disc, month disc, a large central hand that indicated today's date, a twenty-four-hour hand that showed the hour according to a.m. or p.m. in military style, followed by a dial opening in the lower dial that showed the position of the sun and the moon.

The beauty of this great watch was the fact that its basic watch parts were all the same, and the variations were added to accommodate only special features. Once the watchmaker became familiar with the basic movement, understanding the add-ons was rather simple.

Naturally, since this watch was my job to overhaul, there had to be a surprise. Sure enough, and what a surprise. The hairspring was broken off at the stud, something I had never seen before because it wasn't possible. A watch hairspring can be bent, folded, and mutilated as well as rusted, but I'd never seen a broken one before. This was a disaster because the hairspring was now shorter than it should be, which would make the watch gain time. An old-fashioned balance wheel with many timing screws could be adjusted by adding minuscule timing washers to make the balance heavier. Modern watches had very precise screwless balance wheels that couldn't be adjusted.

I was going to have to purchase a very expensive complete balance for the 7750, but nothing else was going to work.

As I secured the movement into the holder, the light reflected into the stud, and I saw a tiny hole with some blue goop inside, but no broken piece of hairspring. Oy. A light bulb went off, and I realized that the modern watches had hairsprings that were not pinned by a smaller-than-tiny taper pin. Today's hairsprings were secured by a glue of some kind...like an epoxy. Could it possibly be??? Donning my extra-strong double loupe, I tenderly inserted the loose end of the hairspring into the hole in the stud.

Using a tiny flashlight, I held the balance wheel secure and looked into the heart of the pallet fork and roller jewel. I couldn't believe my eyes, but the watch appeared to be in perfect beat, meaning the hairspring was loose, not suffering a fracture.

The question was how to secure the hairspring in place. For a change, I already knew the answer to the question. For years now I'd been using a five-minute epoxy to secure loose roller jewels, loving the three entire minutes the epoxy gave me to ensure the accuracy of the jewel's positioning. It would work with the hairspring, I was sure.

I mixed a really tiny batch of resin and hardener onto an old watch crystal, mixed it up really well, and picked up my tiniest paddle oiler. Taking a very deep breath, I transferred a minuscule dab of epoxy into the stud hole, being careful not to dislodge the hairspring. I quickly checked the apparent "beat" position and used the remaining minute to gently adjust the level of the hairspring, then put the watch down to "set." And that was enough for one day, I decided. I covered everything and left, my fingers crossed.

The next morning, May 25, I sat before my latest patient and happily saw that the hairspring was firmly in place, secure in the stud, and as true in the flat and round as one could hope for. I used a puff of air to oscillate the balance, and it moved back and forth with vim and vigor, even as I changed positions. This meant altering the movement from the "dial up" to the "dial down" positions, putting the weight of the balance on both the upper and lower pivots. Then the watch is held vertically, moving the stem's position from "crown up" to "crown down" and then crown "left and right."

Wonderful...never a hesitation or missed beat. Now to assemble the watch.

Oddly, the assembly of the "time-telling" part of the watch, even an extra complicated watch such as this, was quite simple. With a final securing of the ratchet wheel screw, I wound the watch manually and watched the show. For a couple of minutes I just sat and stared at the balance wheel, almost trying to count the beats and oscillations of a watch that times at 25,000 beats per hour.

I carefully put the movement into the timing machine microphone and set the timing buttons and, holding my breath again, pushed the "run" button. I stared at the tape as it scrolled from the printer and could not accept what I saw. This super-high-tech watch, precision balance held together by something that I think would give the factory a fit, was not only in perfect "beat" but seemed to be running a mere four seconds per day slow. I very gently tweaked the regulator, and the watch settled into a gain of possibly a single second per day, and in all positions.

Now late on Tuesday night, the completely assembled watch, auto unit, chronograph unit, and multicalendar units functioning, was running on my bench, under a plastic cover, waiting for me to check on it in the morning.

Wednesday morning and now to see if I had pulled off a minor miracle. First, a cup of coffee (black, no sugar) then carefully lift the cover from the bench top. I looked, but first with one eye and…the watch was right on the mark, maybe five or ten seconds fast. Fantastic. Another boost to personal pride. I decided to run the watch for a couple more days under cover, just to be sure. I called my customer to pass on the good news.

I am becoming…no, I have become totally disgusted with the idiotic designs and engineering in many of today's watches and their watchbands. Watches are made in a way that makes case opening a major headache. The companies' defense is that there is a "special knowledge required" to repair their watches. This despite the fact that watches sold under six or seven brand names may contain the same generic movement. A high-tech, modern, well-designed, well-made, and high-quality watch movement manufactured by a single Swiss watch factory, but the case and band are a disgrace.

A man brought in a rather costly watch today, May 27. Mechanical, self-winding, with the now normal multidial calendar unit, but the problem was the band. It had been shortened, a single link removed. The customer now needed the reinsertion of that one link. The difficulty was that the customer had lost the screw that held the links together. One sad look and I knew this was a "design disaster." I took the repair in and promised to do my best.

I had two multi-vial cabinets of screws made for watchband repair. Long, short, tapered, pointed, in multiple sizes. Only by removing one of the screws still in the watchband did I realize that there was no chance of my replacing the lost one. The missing screw was unlike anything I'd ever seen. As usual, a screwball designer made something that would force the customer to go through the trouble of returning a watch to the factory service center for a simple band screw.

So there was a problem after all. The watch's owner called to check on progress and I had to tell him he had a "factory only" job. His reaction both surprised and disappointed me. He had already sent the watch to the company and had been informed that the watch was "discontinued" and parts, links, and screws were no long available. The watch had been an anniversary present and was important to him, and could I do anything at all?

After informing the customer of my deep loathing of modern watch companies, I told him the only thing I could do was to "cheat" the repair. In plain English, my (his) only hope was my ability to find something of the right length and diameter to be literally forced by hammer blows into the holes on either side of the band. The hole through the center section was larger, so the band links would still pivot as normal. With a much more cheery tone of voice, I was directed to do whatever would work.

In this modern time, I was forced to have a complete drawer filled with varying types of watchband parts, of varying lengths, varying diameters, and varying methods of securing them. Even the more costly watches today were held together with pins that were just pushed into the links, meaning they also had the ability to slide back out. Someday I'll find that designer and put him out of my misery. After 4 tries, I found a "stamped" pin that was the right diameter, but too long. I cut it to length, finished the visible end, and carefully tapped the pin tightly into the band. Thus I finished a not too difficult task, but one only required by a poorly thought out design.

In the second week of May 2010, a "vintage" Rolex came back. This watch, overhauled in July 2009, had been returned for "adjustment" twice before, and the sight of the watch back again saddened me. The original repair had gone quite easy. Receiving it back had been a problem; either time I couldn't find anything wrong with the watch. Putting the watch on the auto winder for several days revealed nothing, as the watch ran well enough to make me proud of my work. Winding it manually, just in case, also revealed nothing, and the watch continued to perform as a Rolex should. Now I had it again, and I was getting nowhere, as I could find nothing out of the norm.

A voice from the long ago past worked its way into my head. "Barry, something is screwy here. Think." Thus spoke both Dad and Uncle Abe to a young kid learning a trade. I did as directed and retreated to a cup of coffee (black, no sugar). This Rolex had been sent by my leading watch collector and dealer and was truly a high-quality, vintage…

Uh-oh…I may have found a skunk at the garden party. This watch might truly be of vintage origin, but maybe not one recently sold to a new, younger owner. It was possible that the owner of today might well be a now quite elderly original owner. Time for an emergency e-mail to my customer.

I got a quick reply…the customer was quite upset. The watch just would not continue to run, and there was great difficulty and inconvenience in getting the watch owner and his wheelchair into the car to bring the watch back again. The watch, sad to say, was perfect; it was, unfortunately, once again necessary to look not to the watch but the owner. My customers are professionals, but do not know the basics of the life of a watch.

I e-mailed a politely worded "lecture" to my customer about the facts of watch life and said I would mail the watch back in a day or two. Simply put, an automatic watch, often called a self-winding watch, *requires* the day-long wearing and active movement of the owner in order to wind and run properly. I wasn't making excuses; there had to be steady activity to provide the power behind the running of any automatic watch. I wouldn't see this watch again, but I sensed the need to question more closely the ownership of these vintage timepieces.

It is 9:32 p.m. on June 16, 2010, and I, Barry J. Marcus, watchmaker, am sitting at the computer in a state of complete awe and shock. Some time ago, as an experiment, I installed a Renata 346 battery as a substitute for a Renata 44 lithium battery. I'd explained that the 346, which sold for $10 as opposed to the 44 at $145, would not last as long but would result in the saving of a great deal of money. I had explained to the customer that I really wanted to know how long my "brainstorm idea" would run the watch. I had been quite saddened in that the watch was never returned as the customer agreed.

At 4:00 p.m. this afternoon, my phone rang. "Hello, watch repair." A very happy voice responded, "The lady with the watch you put that substitute battery in just came into the store. She was tied up yesterday and couldn't come in, but she said the watch finally stopped running on Monday afternoon. As she agreed, she brought the watch back the first chance she had. You can pick up the watch on your rounds Friday."

I spent the next two hours working on a rusty 218 Accutron while I tried to remember just when I installed that Renata 346 battery. It was important that I figure the battery's working life. I just couldn't remember. Finally I realized I could scroll back in my "remembrances" and find the original entry. Who would have thought that the "Tales of Papa Barry" would have another purpose?

It took fifteen minutes to locate the original writing about this watch, and I just sat in a state of shock for about ten minutes staring at the monitor. I had originally installed that battery on June 16, 2009, exactly one full year ago. It couldn't be, but it was…it really was. It was two days shy of a year, but who was counting? I was, at the time, hoping for a few months. I admit I didn't know how long the original 44 lithium battery was supposed to last, but everyone was proud and delighted at the $10 battery lasting a full year. I decided to call in the morning to get the latest quote on the 44 lithium battery.

Next morning's call was one I should not have made. Before I was given the latest quote, my supplier asked if I "really wanted one of those." I did not; I was fishing for information only. Friday I would pick up the watch and check it carefully. I was most anxious to measure the voltage that was now not enough to run the watch. Also I'd put in a new battery, but there would once again be no charge. This was indeed a good idea.

An extremely elderly gentleman entered the shop today, June 21, 2010. Frankly, I was surprised at the bounce in his step, because after a weekend on my boat, my knees were mad at me and I was walking "elderly." As I approached, he put a watch with a strange, wide metal band on the counter. I held up a very old Swiss-made Incabloc-equipped waterproof watch with a faded but real radium dial and hands.

I commented, "This band is a GI-made watchband from World War Two. Lots of these were made from strips cut from crashed airplane wings. Was this a Wildcat or Hellcat?"

He stood a little straighter. "I cut it from the wing of a crashed Zero on the Canal. I took it back to the *Vincennes* and in some free time made the band. It's held up damn well too."

"Oh my God," I thought to myself. I put the watch on the counter and said, "You and this watch went down with the *Vincennes* that night off Savo Island. It's an honor to meet you." We shook hands, warmly.

He stood straighter still. "If you know the name *Vincennes* and the name of Savo, you're also an old sailor, but you're just a kid, so probably from Korea." I had just been called a kid.

He continued, "I made it off as she went down and floated around and was rescued. This watch never missed a tick or a tock. We went to another cruiser, then when they needed a gunner's mate on a carrier I ended up on the *Franklin* at Okinawa, but that time we—"

"Saved one of the worst damaged ships in navy history. One of you, either the watch or you, is blessed many times over," I interrupted. "It'll be an honor to put this back into the condition it deserves."

He sighed and said, "Many times people have been unable to understand why I refuse to accept or even consider a new watch. I took it into a fancy mall store that quickly pointed out how I was wasting my hard-earned money fixing up such a piece of beat-up junk. I picked it up and walked out without saying a single word. Idiots."

"No," I said, "too many young people don't understand much of anything. This watch, a good one, by the way, is a special memory and companion to you. A special piece of your own history."

"I'm glad you understand, but I have other souvenirs to remember the past. I still have pieces of the *Franklin* in here." He tapped the right side of his chest. Whew.

I made out the ticket and told him the price and that it would take about three weeks as I was behind in the work as usual. When he questioned the low price for the "restoration," I just looked at him. He stood straighter than I could, reached to shake hands, and left.

I looked at the old, beat-up watch in my hand, a watch that had lived more history than all of the fancy, dolled-up timepieces other people wore. Wait a darn minute…He was a little under twenty when the *Vincennes* went down? I mentally did the math and came up with… Wow. No wonder to him I was a kid.

I knew the movement was an A. Schild, but I couldn't remember what model number. With my screwy memory, I remembered seeing one of these last in the early 1960s, and the number would come to me before I took the watch apart. We used to see these quite often, but of course most had vanished from use. This watch I would be proud to restore.

You would think that after over sixty-five years at the watch-maker's bench, I'd seen almost everything. Cancel that, because every time I think that…I'm proven wrong. A man brought in three watches for repair…not for estimates, but for repair and restoration.

Leading the group was an 18K yellow gold Accutron 218 complete with 18K gold mesh band. Next was another 18K gold dress watch, this one a wind-up mechanical Hamilton from the early 1960s. The third watch was the surprise. I gazed on another 18K yellow gold Hamilton complete with an 18K gold mesh band, this model a Hamilton "ThinLine," also from sometime in the '60s. As they came in together, I had the three in a single grouping of six. The first two I stripped down and put the little pieces into the ultra-sonic basket, numbers one and three of six.

When I opened the third watch, everything fell apart. The original Hamilton movement had been removed and a much too small, poor quality quartz movement had been sloppily put into the case. There was an attempt to hold the movement in place by badly crimp-ing inward the built-in movement ring. The ring could not be brought in enough, so the idiot who repaired it had filled the case with some kind of putty. The putty was still putty, and some of it lifted up with the movement and made a mess. Today, we have a two-part epoxy that hardens into a hard plastic movement form that can be filed and carved. Sadly, the dial legs had been cut off and the original dial actually glued directly onto the movement. With no dial legs to worry about, I was just able to pry them apart without damaging the dial.

Time to think, which meant into the office for a cup of coffee (black, no sugar) and a few minutes of staring at nothing. I knew that the proper repair for a watch of this quality was to restore it to a me-chanical status, but the ThinLine movement had been long since dis-continued by the factory and would not be available anywhere. I also had to find a way to properly secure the movement without that silly putty goop. Think.

Back to work on an older Bulova, an 11AN, the wind-it-up version of a past triumph of mine. I finished the assembly and checked the timing rate on the timing machine, happy that it checked out without much adjusting. Then into the case, newly polished and bright as new, except that the movement slipped back and forth in the round case opening. No big deal; using a small plier to slightly crimp the interior of the case and...and...

My brain was mush. The built-in movement-retaining ring on the ThinLine Hamilton had been foolishly crimped to secure a movement that was not only way too small but was lousy quality. The thing to do was reform the butchered movement ring into its original circular shape and measure to see what ligne movement was required. First I'd finish the Bulova then…first I'd put the Bulova aside while I tackled the Hamilton.

With the use of both the small, sharp-nosed plier and an eighty-year-old burnisher, I was able to re-form the retaining ring into a perfect circle. Judging by eye, this case appeared to require an 11.5 ligne movement. The word *ligne* is a European word of measurement I'd used all my life. I did not know what a single ligne measured, whether in inches or millimeters or anything else, yet it was a term I'd grown up with. Also I didn't care what a single ligne was; I'd never seen any watch that tiny.

Out of my vast supply of useless and dead quartz movements I took a box of 11.5 ligne movements, and to my relief, the fit was just perfect. It pressed into the case securely, but when I checked the fit in the flat, this movement was too thick. No, this version had the alignment ridge for a day/date unit. Into another box for a basic ESA 955 that had no extra features, and this one was perfect. When I properly taped on the dial, I was able to fit a water-resistant crystal, and the result was perfection. Now all I had to do was secure a properly running movement and fabricate a special split stem to fit this one-piece case.

It was a job for another day, and at the moment I was satisfied with the day's work. The 11AN Bulova was due in a couple of days, so that had to be finished up. All in all, an hour well spent.

I decided to repair another Hamilton, but a quickie. This was a 14/0 seventeen-jewel that was really fine save for a broken set bridge. Oh no, none in the material cabinet, so I went to the large drawer that held who knew how many Hamilton movements in various stages of having parts taken. Halfway in was a box labeled 14/0 with about twelve movements. Now this I couldn't believe: next to the 14/0 box was a Hamilton "ThinLine" 676 mechanical movement, or rather most of one. This was an original movement for that gold Hamilton case that was butchered so badly.

The 14/0 was rapidly fixed and put into the checking drawer, and I turned my attention back to the ThinLine 676. Sure enough, it fit perfectly into the now reshaped movement ring. The now legless dial, when checked, proved to be made for this model. I could use modern dial tape. It was hard to believe my luck. Even the parts needed made up a short list…set bridge, split stem, and a new mainspring. The new crystal was just a normal round one.

I called the watch's owner and told him of my find and asked if he'd be happy to have his very costly watch restored to its original mechanical state. The answer: "Do you really have to ask? Just let me know when it's done." Back to the computer, and the parts were ordered within ten minutes.

Suddenly my heart jumped. In the background, the radio was airing a newscast and word had arrived that another Massachusetts serviceman had been killed in Afghanistan. I stood perfectly still, holding my breath, wait for the name…then thankful it was not my young marine "twerp." One prayerful thought for the fallen and his family; another for my young marine. I thought, "Come home, my young friend, I'm waiting to engrave that watch case, and I've got the correct spelling down pat."

On June 28, a present from the past: an 18K yellow gold Patek Philippe quartz watch, overhauled in December '09 was back… not working. A little alarm bell was quietly ringing in my head, getting slowly louder. The customer envelope, for a change, listed the original repair number, so it took only a moment to look—oh rats. Only two watches in my repair log rated a special "what the heck?" note, and this Patek was one of them. This watch of worldwide prestige was my personal idea of a design that should have been shredded before the pilot model was made. The connection bridge between the circuit portion and the coil assembly was made with the strength of a plastic sandwich bag. During the original overhaul, I was afraid of the weakness and flexibility of this piece. The impossibly thin coil wires were lacquered onto the flexible bridge, and the flexing had led me to believe the wire would eventually break.

I set the Renotest to "circuit test," made contact and...nothing. The coil was open, and just as I thought, it would break. No green indicator light...open coil. After a ten-minute search for a microscope not used for several years, I could see the break in the left hand coil wire. No coil, no completed circuit, no running watch.

Think...But I could not even think about obtaining a new assembly from Patek, even if I was willing to pay the cost. This broken coil was original, not installed by me during the overhaul, and not under any guarantee. I had another Rolex waiting on the bench, and this Patek required some thinking.

I made a cup of coffee (black, no sugar) and stared out the window while I tried to figure this out. Any other watch, I would have already used the special coil repair liquid, a conductive tan liquid that, when dried, carried the current to complete a circuit and was also quite strong, protecting the circuit against further shock damage. If this was anything but a Patek, I would not have hesitated with my fix and had the watch already repaired and timed. Wait a minute. This was not a new watch. I would restore its running, and if desired, the owner could return the watch to Patek International Service Center for an authentic Patek coil. My goal was to return a properly running watch.

It took a drop of special coil repair liquid and ten minutes, and the highly prestigious Patek Philippe was stepping every five seconds as it should, the time had been properly set, and the watch movement, minus the case, was under glass for the night. I walked away with a smile on my lips and my fingers crossed for luck.

Next morning, I walked to the bench even before I took off my hat and changed glasses I had to see how the Patek was doing. I admit with one eye closed I carefully lifted off the bench cover and...

yes! The Patek was right on time...to the second. Now it was time to make a cup of coffee (black, no sugar) and check the computer for whatever had come in during the night. As usual, the normal stuff...e-mail and ads for things I didn't really want or need. Time to hit the bench.

I carefully folded the bench cover (really a thirteen-gallon trash bag carefully draped) and uncovered the Patek and...it had stopped. It had really stopped, about fifteen minutes after I'd checked it on arrival. What in hell? Too angry to touch it, I turned to open the safe and get set for the day. I managed to waste ten minutes before, with a sigh, I resigned myself to going back to the Patek. One glance told me the watch had started up once again, all by itself, which really couldn't happen, because an open coil and/or dead circuit did not self-repair.

Gently I took both probes from my Renotest checker and put one on each coil terminal. Under normal circumstances, the alternating pulse should momentarily illuminate each tiny indicator light in unison. I looked for a pulsating light every five seconds knowing the watch was not run—whoa...it was running. Every five seconds a light blinked, which prompted me to turn the watch over...and the hands had truly advanced about seven minutes since I saw it was dead...seven minutes ago.

I gently placed the movement on the quartz timer and counted seconds for a couple of minutes...a blink every five seconds and the LCD read-out indicated a gain of .13 seconds per day. Perfect for the moment.

I had a very tired Rolex crying for attention, so I carefully set the Patek, covered it, and scowled at the Rolex. This one had about a quarter million miles on it and really needed some TLC, and I was the doctor. After a careful exam, I took a minute for an irreverent thought...if I was the doctor, a second-year med student could diagnose this Rolex. I was dealing with the one weakness in older, high-grade mechanical watches.

The Rolex, in its tight case, had been kept nice and clean, allowing it to run and keep running long after the oil had failed and the watch should have received a good overhaul. As a result, the constant pressure and torque forced onto the barrel arbor by the automatic unit had worn the arbor bushing egg-shaped enough that the upper extreme edge of the mainspring barrel was dragging on the underside of the barrel bridge. Almost all of the older Swiss automatic watches had this potential problem, a problem caused by the highly protective water-resistant cases of the day. My favorite older watch, the Bulova twenty-three jewel automatics, had bearing jewels for the upper and lower parts of the barrel arbors.

I stripped the rest of the Rolex and put the pieces into the ultrasonic basket and went to the next watches in the set of six. Into the cleaning machine they went, and I went back to the unhappy Patek. I'd left it running, covered, on the quartz timer, and I read the rate. There was still a slight gain, but now it was .15 seconds per day. A tiny variation such as .30 or even .10 second per day was normal, so I guess the watch was settling down. I uncovered the movement and...it was seven minutes slow. Not possible, but really happening.

It was almost time to get mad, but first it was time for a cup of coffee (black, no sugar). I'd set the watch again and then...oops. My fingers sensed the total lack of normal friction from a canon pinion. In a mechanical watch, a badly loosened canon pinion lets the watch run, but the hands are not carried along by the center wheel post. This Patek did not have a canon pinion; rather, it was a direct drive...I think. Coffee time.

Six watches were cleaned, oiled, assembled, adjusted, and re-cased, and now I was back to the Patek. A sad finish for the day, one that had started with such promise. The design of the watch allowed me to take out the train wheels without touching the circuitry at all, so in a few minutes a bridge and two train wheels and the rotor were on my parts mirror. The rotor was fine, as were the second and third wheels, and truly there was no canon pinion.

To misquote the bard, "There is something *stupid* in Denmark." There was positively something wrong despite the appearance that nothing was wrong. I gently gripped the second wheel pinion in a number three tweezer and just as gently put pressure on the wheel itself, and was not at all surprised to find...nothing wrong at all. Mumbling, I gripped the third wheel pinion and pressured the third wheel and was stunned when the wheel turned freely. The wheel was actually loose on the pinion.

I put down the wheel and sat back to sulk. I had to find a way to re-stake the wheel onto the pinion securely, but gently. This only took a couple of minutes; before I had a sudden thought...was it remotely possible that this pinion was really designed to work as a canon pinion? It would have enough friction to carry the hands, yet be free enough to spin free when the hands were to be set. I switched to a double loupe, two lenses that doubled the magnification, which enabled me to see that the tiny pinion was *actually* part of a very miniature canon pinion. Gently I separated the two pieces in preparation of a simple and normal tightening. I quickly glanced at the clock on the bench glass and...oh no...I was out of here. The Patek could wait for me. In reality, my leaving was not because of the hour; rather, I was aggravated by the discovery of the less than miniature canon pinion. Not a thing to work on when in a bad mood.

After a good night's sleep and in a better mood, I decided it was time to tackle the Patek. To tighten a canon pinion, I always used a small precision cutting plier. The sharp edge dimpled the sides of the hollow tube, increasing the grip on the center wheel post. It must be tight enough to carry the friction of the dial train, yet loose enough that the hands could be easily set. Once, years ago, I asked Dad how tight and how loose was right. His answer, "Enough. Just listen to your fingers." My fingers talk?

As the years went by, I realized that my fingers did indeed talk, or did the watches talk and my fingers listened? They told me when a crown was too small, a water-resistant crown had a badly worn gasket, or the wind and set gears were rusted, or even the canon pinion in a fancy Patek was so loose the hands wouldn't turn.

I had a tiny oiler whose end I clipped off and slipped into the Patek canon pinion. Did that sixty years ago after I'd cut a canon pinion neatly in half. The tapered oiler pushed through the hollow tube, preventing a repeat. A gently squeeze and I put the adjusted piece back on its post. Carefully securing the pinion part, I gripped the wheel between two fingers, turned it, and...perfect. The moment of pride. I easily replaced the train wheels, secured the train bridge, turned the movement over, and turned the crown so as to set the hands. Triumph as everything was "enough."

Time out for the Fourth of July weekend. Off to the boat for a long weekend since the Fourth was on Sunday this year and the holiday was "celebrated" on the fifth. A whole extra day off.

I was at the bench on Monday, having been driven from the boat by a really hot turn in the weather. Extreme heat was something I no longer handled well. Luckily the shop had a good air conditioner.

Good, the Patek was running beautifully at long last. It would go out on Tuesday, along with a couple of Rolex automatics. Maybe three Rolexes, if a back-ordered crystal showed up on time. (On time...a joke...a bad joke. Maybe the heat did get to me.)

I had cleaned and oiled the Hamilton I was restoring to mechanical status, and it was running fine without a dial and manually wound from the ratchet. Parts had come in before the Fourth, and I spent some time completing the assembly. Everything fit as if made for the watch, which, of course, they were. I spent about five minutes locating proper hands and fit the crystal, and I was done. Into the safe for running and watching for a couple of days, and I relaxed for a few minutes, quite satisfied.

Despite it being an official holiday, I was content to spend the day in the shop. Far too few people are that happy with their work. I consider myself blessed to be doing what I love to do.

Fifty-eight years ago, a seventeen-year-old watchmaker fell in love with a beautiful young woman who lived as a photo in the back of an antique pocket watch. I only knew the young woman as *her*. This very morning, July 5, 2010, for a moment I really believed I was to meet *her* again. What I thought was the *same* pocket watch was carried into the shop in search of a good watchmaker. Once again I couldn't catch my breath and could feel my heartbeat increase. Truly I was running with a bent balance staff. Fifty-eight years ago *she* was too old for me, a teenage watchmaker. Today I'd be too old for *her*.

I realized that Waltham made thousands of these watches, vast numbers of which were surely still running. With bated breath, I carefully opened the case back to see…a normal Waltham watch with no engraving to a departing love and naturally no *her*. (If I close my eyes, I can still see *her*.)

Anyhow, the watch was left for repair, and an elderly watchmaker was left with some strange memories.

Next I assembled the old veteran's watch. Carefully I oiled and adjusted a watch that had gone through what most people cannot imagine. As I wound the mainspring, the balance began its oscillations as though it was five years old. Onto the timing machine, and I leaned back, amazed at the accuracy of the watch as it ran without any adjustment from me. No, I could not charge for the repair of this. Decision made. I changed the interior case gasket, put on a new crystal and crown, and into the safe it went for a few days of running.

I had been procrastinating regarding a watch sent in by the collector. It was a LeCoultre alarm watch, old, high quality, and a special watch. When set and "alarmed," at the appointed minute, the mechanism caused a vibration that would startle the proverbial granite statue. This watch was in dire need of two pounds of tender loving care, as it was to be "prepped for sale." Obviously the crowns had to go, the crystal was really bad, and it appeared the time mainspring was broken. By mere coincidence, I needed a heavy man's watch to balance a set of six, so the LeCoultre became number one of six.

Carefully, as thousands of times before, I took apart a complicated watch bit by little bit. A quick inspection and each part was put into the ultrasonic basket for cleaning.

I opened the time mainspring barrel to pull out and discard the broken mainspring. Time for a large oy vay as the mainspring was not broken; in fact, it was a modern "unbreakable" type, and I was in some kind of trouble. The mainspring would not wind, yet it was fine. The real culprit was a broken "time spring click spring." This brought forth a deep sigh.

All mechanical watches utilize a click spring, which keeps a locking "click" engaged with the ratchet wheel, thus preventing the mainspring from unwinding. Just one percent of mechanical watches were insanely designed with a specially made click spring that was held into a slot by a special screw. Every watchmaker in the world had a box of hundreds of assorted springs, just in case. The LeCoultre, a "prestige" watch, used and required a spring specially made, so off to the phone to order, or try to order one.

Four phone calls later, I took time for a cup of coffee (black, no sugar) and stared at the wall. Four calls and four men telling me not to bother trying to locate a new spring. One hadn't seen one in about twenty-five years, and the others were less optimistic. Now what?

Time for me to go hunting in my own movement drawers; there was, after all, over seventy years' accumulation of whatever came our way. What was used in the normal course of watch repair was carefully sorted, recorded, and stored, but something like this was not worth the time required to be that careful—*until* the moment a part was needed. Happy hunting.

The fifth drawer down in my largest movement cabinet did indeed have a gent's LeCoultre that actually looked right. Naturally it only *looked* right; it was a single mainspring wind-me-up that was just a look-alike. Astonished, I saw the click spring was of the exact same design, and with a song in my fingers, I loosened the retaining screw and slid out the clock spring. Oh boy...it was much too long... about 2.5 mm. The only good thing was that the actual "click" end was perfect. I decided to think about recutting this piece to fit the smaller watch. It would be worth the attempt. The movement I'd be "borrowing" this from was a broken-beyond-belief very-high-grade piece of junk now.

Three ladies' wind-ups, an old Illinois classic, and a gent's Hamilton made up the six watches, and all went into the ultrasonic machine while I went into the office to sulk about the LeCoultre. My mood was interrupted by the ringing of the phone.

Oh good, it was Cousin Bobby from Holden, probably with a watch problem for the "master" to solve. Often when he was in trouble he called for help. Of course, I often reminded him that I knew what to do only because I'd gotten myself "up the creek without a paddle" numerous times over the years. I'd accumulated lots of knowledge on how to salvage one's personally created "troubles." This time, it was merely to have me send him a mainspring from my vast supply. Then time to kibitz.

When I mentioned my disaster with the LeCoultre alarm watch click spring, the phone was dead quiet for a couple of moments. Then… "Barry, what movement is the LeCoultre watch?"

I told him to wait a second while I went to the ultrasonic machine, picked up the dripping plate, and came back to the phone.

"Bob, it's a LeCoultre K841 and it's okay except for the broken time click spring. Four of the big material suppliers told me not to waste my—"

"Barry, you may not believe this, but yesterday I bought an 18K LeCoultre case for the gold scrap and it's an alarm watch. The crystal, hands, stem, and crown are gone, and the dial has a big ding scratched into it. I took the movement out of the case and tossed it in my old move-ment drawer because even the staff and hairspring are wrecked, but I'm going to check, and I'll call you back in a few minutes." (Dial tone.)

I sat like a statue for five minutes until I heard the joyous chorus of the ringing phone. "Bobby, what's going on?" I asked, fingers crossed.

"Barry, even I don't believe this, but mine is the same model. I pulled it apart and the time click is perfect. The movement is now garbage, so I'll have the spring in the mail when I leave the store tonight. Talk about perfect timing. Might be a good night to play your numbers on the lot-tery. Gotta run. Maybe you'll have the spring in the morning." Click…a dial tone…and Bob was gone. Whew. I could not believe my luck.

A day later, Bob called. "Barry, I was so busy I never got to the post office to send the time click spring. I just mailed it out, and you'll have it on Monday morning for sure. Remember to call if anything else turns out no good. Take care."

Well, I really could not believe my luck. It seemed as good a time as any to call it a day and head off to the boat for the weekend. Maybe I would stop in Rhode Island and buy a lottery ticket.

Monday morning, after a relaxing weekend on the boat, I was in the shop bright and early. I checked to see if any mail wandered in Saturday morning and...an envelope from Bobby. Even before I got coffee, I checked and saw a beautiful LeCoultre time click spring. After required coffee (black, no sugar) and computer time, I sat with the LeCoultre. The click spring fit perfectly, naturally, and I was amazed at the ease with which the watch was assembled. Even the alarm mechanism and setting went easily. The time and alarm adjustments were perfect on the first attempt. Now all I had left was a day under glass while I made the case presentable.

I killed a couple of minutes at the computer and checked e-mail. I couldn't believe it, but one of the parts guys who had advised me not to even bother looking for the LeCoultre time click spring was now telling me he had found one. To top it off, I couldn't believe the quoted price...it was so low that I was surprised. I didn't need it, but I did see this model prestige LeCoultre, so I e-mailed back to send the part to Milford. Bobby's movement was really dead, but I'd offer him the spring if he decided to salvage his wreck.

During the afternoon, I was just finishing re-staffing an 18S Waltham pocket watch, vintage 1864. The last adjustment was to re-level the offside of the hairspring, which was down too close to the arm of the balance. Foolishly ignoring the fact that the three o'clock news was just starting, I gripped the hairspring in my especially sharp tweezers and gently bent the hairspring when the LeCoultre alarm went off three inches from my ear. Now the hairspring was up against the underside of the balance bridge, the LeCoultre was buzzing away, and I just sat back in disgust. This was again the time to retreat with some dignity and pause for coffee (black, no sugar). At least I had evidence that the LeCoultre would be okay.

Getting back to the Waltham, I "re-trued" the hairspring without any difficulty, timed it out, and set it in turn under glass to run overnight. At the same time I gave the LeCoultre a really dirty look. I'd check them both in the morning.

The next morning, again before doing anything beyond turning on the lights, I checked the two watches from yesterday...perfectly perfect. I decided to let them run until they ran down while I worked on the cases.

A couple of days had uneventfully gone by and the LeCoultre was running...like a LeCoultre. It was cased up, polished, and fitted with a new crystal, but without either of the crowns replaced. This watch was to be put up for sale, and it would be a good deal more valuable with original crowns. I had e-mailed my customer to stress the potential vulnerability of the watch to water damage. The watch was running and was guaranteed for everything except being water resistant. At the buyer's option, I, of course, would change both crowns.

I was looking forward to tomorrow, when my elderly navy friend would come in for his souvenir from hell. I was determined that there would be *no* charge...none. He wouldn't argue...I was a lot bigger.

The phone rang and it was Bobby, and he was busting up proud and excited. A man didn't want to pay the price for repairing a very badly scratched, dented, abused, and wrecked Valjoux 7750, one of the newer models. (My own chronograph is an original version 7750, put together from the wrecks of several L. L. Bean chronographs.) Bobby had spent the time and effort on the Valjoux as a personal learning experience, and it had turned out so well he felt a need to tell his "teacher" all about it. Of course he had no case for it, but it was worth the effort, if just for the learning lessons in repairing the "assault and battery" on this poor movement.

"Bob, nice job," I said. "What about the case?"

"This one is really gone, beyond any hope. But the dial is so good looking I'd actually put this on and make it my *official* watch for the whole world to see. You were right; people often look to see what the watchmaker is wearing."

"Bob, without exaggeration, I have at least a dozen Hamilton cases for the 7750. All apart, but if you want, I'll take the best of the parts and bezels and make you up a case for the watch. I have a good supply of double O ring crowns to keep it really water resist. How does that sound?"

"I can't believe it, Barry. No kidding, do you have any real idea of what's buried in that shop of yours? Of course, it's a hundred-year-old accumulation."

Now I had another project to "play with." It was fitting that a watchmaker like Bob cobble together his own personal timepiece from old wrecks. Anyone can go out and spend money. There is more pride and satisfaction in this.

The following morning, an old guy slowly walked into the shop, and the first thing I noticed was the baseball-type hat with an embroidered destroyer above the brim. I looked closely and saw a typical "tin can," three twin turrets of 5"/38s, a large number of 40 mm AA mounts, and a large scattering of 20 mm gun. I sadly noted that today my old sailor was walking stiffly and in some pain as I went to the safe to retrieve his "good as new" watch. I approached him, winding and setting the watch and...

"What watch is that one?" he asked. "I'm bringing one in to be fixed."

Uh-oh. My famous memory had fooled me again. It was the destroyer hat that did it, but my elderly customer was a cruiser sailor. I apologized and explained my confusion as I was expecting a crew member of the *Vincennes* and *Franklin*.

That explanation drew a really incredulous expression. "You mean to tell me one guy survived *both* of those ships?" The watch was left, and he departed, shaking his head, as I had, that one young sailor could be so lucky.

I awaited the visit of my "old shipmate."

A man stopped into the shop with a really large pocket watch. At first sight I could tell it was a "coin silver" hunting case pocket watch of American make. I carried it to the bench for exam, all the while admiring the heft and workmanship. Nothing like this these days. I adjusted my loupe and pushed the lid release and—oy. This watch was an 18S Seth Thomas, made by the famous clock people (which I won't fix) in Thomaston, Connecticut. The watch was dried out and sort of dirty, but nothing unusual. I flipped my hand and watched carefully while the balance oscillated back and forth. Good, the balance was okay. A little alarm rang inside my head, reminding me that this company had been out of business for one hundred years, and any parts were going to be a nightmare to get. I gave the customer the price, but cautioned him about the potential problem if any parts were needed.

To my surprise, he knew of the problem. The watch hadn't run in about thirty-five years, and several watchmakers where he used to live refused the watch for that very reason. They each claimed the ability to repair the watch but refused to chance being stuck unable to obtain parts after putting much time into the watch, thus losing both time and money. I explained that I would do the absolute minimum work, actually only enough to determine what parts might be needed. I'd do no cleaning, oiling, or repair but would merely study and think about it. And of course there would be no charge for studying and thinking, done, I admit, while drinking coffee (black, no sugar).

He thanked me for at least being willing to attempt the saving of this family heirloom. He left, and the Seth Thomas went into the "to do" box while I crossed my fingers.

This afternoon (no date this time) two women and a man came into the shop, each one unhappier than the other two. I hoped it was nothing I had done. A very new and expensive-looking watch was placed on the counter by the man (midforties by my guess). The women were somewhat younger, but just as mad about something.

I picked up the watch, a modern variation of my own 7750, but in addition to the automatic, chronograph, day/date features, it also had a twenty-four-hour dial and a sun/moon dial. I think this model sold for around $1,500...very nice.

Sad to say, as I idly turned the watch over in my hands, I read the engraving on the back of the case and...oh good Lord! My brain exploded and I knew exactly what the problem was going to be.

From the age of ten, I had been in a jewelry store, repairing the watches of those who came in as well as selling articles to fill needs and wishes. Whether an article of jewelry or a watch, whether it was to be for a birthday, wedding, graduation, or even "getting released from jail," the jewelry store helped in the choice of the correct item for the gift. Today, however, I often found circumstances of such stupidity and ignorance that I was now basically ashamed of my industry. There was a world of people out there trained carefully to work high-tech cash registers but all the while possessing a total ignorance of the industry in which they worked.

"We purchased this for our father six months ago, and it's been back to the company three times already. It just won't run, yet they insist it's fine and runs fine. Could you possibly look inside and help us?" the man said. "My sisters and I wanted this to be very, very special for—"

I held up my hand. "Your parents' fiftieth anniversary party," I interrupted him, "and the watch has been a problem from the first day, but your mother's watch is fine."

"H-How could you possibly know that?" the younger sister demanded. "You're correct, but how do you know that?"

"Experience," I said gently, and again I read the engraving on the back:

To Dad with Love
On your 50th Anniversary

"All I really did was guess that your dad probably married in his mid-twenties. Add to that fifty years, and I came up with he's in his middle to upper seventies today. A problem with a brand-new self-winding watch of this quality translates to, I'm sorry to say, a debilitating health problem. Experience tells me that your dad suffers a health problem that severely limits his mobility. The lack of movement during the day prevents the watch from winding itself. Oh, and your mother's watch, probably of a similar but smaller design, is battery powered and runs all by itself. I hate to ask, but am I right?"

"How can this be?" the older girl asked. "We told the store about Dad's difficulty and told them of the fiftieth anniversary when we gave them the engraving. They even knew that he had to use a *walker* to get around, even in the house."

"Many sales people in the fancy mall stores know nothing," I again interrupted, "except how to write up the sales slip. Any properly trained person in my sales field would have known that this was the absolute *wrong* watch for your dad. This is an old and basic problem with all self-winding watches when, through age or temporary circumstances, the wearer has lost most of his mobility. You've been mad at this poor watch, but you really should be upset with the store that sold it to you. This watch should *never* have been sold to you for your dad."

"I'm sorry to say," I continued, "that if I called my three daughters right now and described the watch and cause for the purchase, each would jump right in and ask if the watch was a mechanical self-winding model. They've learned that merely by growing up in their daddy's jewelry store and listening to me as I, let's say, interviewed customers."

"What can we do if the watch is really okay and the problem is Dad's health? We've spent all this money and Dad still doesn't have a working watch."

"To be frank, selling you this watch isn't a criminal act, but as far as I'm concerned this is truly criminally stupid. I wish I could do something for you, but the watch is really fine," I said.

"Mr. Marcus," asked the brother, the oldest, "would you be maybe willing to put what you've said in writing if it would help us? We do have a family lawyer I'd like to talk to about this. You have no idea how mad I am since you've taught us something."

Oh boy, lawyer talk, but as a kid I was taught that my job was to repair watches, but even more important was to help the one who owned the watch. That had been my life. "Sure, whatever you need. Thank you for coming in." They left, but I was afraid I hadn't heard the end of this.

NOTE: For whatever it is worth, later in the day I really did call my three daughters, and Carol caught the problem the instant I said the presentation watch was a self-winding mechanical watch. Julie jumped on both the problem and the reason as soon as I said "fiftieth anniversary" without mentioning the self-winding feature. Amy, my youngest, cut me off when I mentioned the oldest child. The son was more or less in his midforties, and she did some quick addition to come up with the father's age. Three daughters, living from Milford to Maine, never having seen the watch or heard the entire story, had instinctively known and understood the cause of this difficulty. None were watchmakers, but all three grew up working in the world of watches. I was very proud of them and disgusted with those who had replaced them in my watch world.

Time passed and I found nothing wrong with the Seth Thomas pocket watch. So far, I'd only determined that it would not wind properly. Weird, but when I turned the crown forward, it wound as it should, but when the crown was turned back to reset the finger grip, the hands reset....technically impossible, but this was what was going on. A swiveling plate held three wheels, the center one connecting to the crown and the left one having the task of moving the hands, while the right one connected to the ratchet wheel to wind the watch. The difficulty was that they wouldn't stay where they belonged. More study and thought was needed.

A box arrived from one of my favorite customers. Even before I opened it I sensed it was quite a bit heavier than normal. Either a couple of 18S American pocket watches or several mechanical watches. I wanted to see how smart my hands were, even when they couldn't "see." I was right and wrong at the same time, as I saw a single very large Waltham 18S pocket watch and five mechanical automatic watches. Time to make six estimates and e-mail for customer approval or rejection. Five mechanical estimates didn't take too long, as what was needed was truly obvious, then on to the pocket watch.

This was a very large gold-filled case, thus the weight, holding an 18S seventeen-jewel movement. This 18S movement was of 1870s manufacture, having lived about 140 years. I wondered if anything manufactured today would last 140 months, let alone 140 years. Probably just a couple of high-grade mechanicals, but definitely nothing electronic. Anyhow, this watch was in great condition but for one little bitty problem.

Some idiot had pulled out the hairspring and twisted the balance wheel until it looked like a highway map. Who would do such a thing? This would be big trouble for me. Oh well, with what the estimate had to be, I was confident that the watch would not be approved for repair.

I e-mailed the estimates and returned to the bench to finish the assembly of a very basic Swiss Army watch. Happily, a Harley movement went together almost by itself, and, of course, I had a new crystal for the watch in the cabinet. Next I reached…

The door opened, and my "old shipmate" came in for his watch. In his hand he had the "ready" card I'd mailed and some $20 bills.

"Mr. Marcus, what is this on the card showing NO CHARGE for the repair? I cannot accept that…no way. And why? Just because I survived Savo? That in itself is all the reward I need. Now take the money."

I didn't quite know how to respond, so, "No, I'm showing respect for what that watch has been through, stuck with you. Now put the money away, and don't try to argue with me."

He backed up a step, stood tall and challenged. "What if I put the money on the counter and just walk out? You wouldn't tear it up, I know that."

Easy answer: "No, I have your address on the watch record, and I'd mail it to your wife with a note. Put the bills in your wallet already. As a matter of fact, why don't you use the money to take her out to dinner? Look, you took your turn, making sure I had a country to grow up in. Later I took my turn in another war, even though I was not in danger. That's the way we do it."

I pretended not to see his eyes brimming as he extended his hand. He then turned and left quietly. I stood there for a minute and pondered the history that man had both seen and made, he and that watch. That watch…like so many others.

Into the office for a cup of coffee (black, no sugar). Just a few minutes to think and then the phone broke the quiet. Oh good…some estimates approved…I'd be busy next week. Four approvals, a "return not done," and, oy, the 18S Waltham not only was to be repaired, but must be "restored to old glory." It was to be presented to a young man, the sixth generation of the family of the original owner. Just by chance, the soon-to-be-owner of the watch was the youngster who, fifteen years ago, opened the watch and tried to get it to run. The beginning and ending of his watch repair career. (If he knows what is good for him.)

On August 12, 2010, I, Barry J. Marcus, admitted defeat at the hands of a watch. My head was bowed, my ego punctured, my shoulders slumped in defeat. What, the world wonders, could have done the undoable? A special chronograph? A handmade classic? A rusted automatic? No…I had been brought down by a two-year-old Citizen. This was given to me last week by a trade account. I just needed to set the watch after a battery change. I knew at once it would require the owner's manual to set. The customer would mail the directions directly to me. This would surely be fun.

The booklet arrived on Tuesday morning, and it was not a booklet. What I received was just slightly shorter than Tolstoy's *War and Peace*. I beheld 117 pages of descriptions and directions on the setting up and adjusting of the craziest watch I'd ever seen. Naturally it told the hour and minute and running second; added to the mix was a complete chronograph unit of four more hands. Just inside the four o'clock position was a multi-LCD unit that showed a "chosen" city, hour, minute, second, a.m. or p.m., and whether or not it was daylight savings time.

Push a button and the LCD showed the day, date, month, and year in your choice of twelve-hour or twenty-four-hour digits. You could also set the watch to indicate daylight savings time in only selected cities, as not all countries reset the hour from season to season.

After forty minutes, my eyes fell out of my head, and I quit. I put the watch into its envelope, set, I think, to the time and date on the second moon of Jupiter. I quit.

I admit it. Any driver who tried to read the data on this watch would be off the road into a ditch before he took it all in.

Tomorrow I would recover by working on a mechanical self-winding day/date/month chronograph complete with sweep second, minute minder, hour minder, and a sun/moon disc to indicate day or night. It would be easier than setting the Citizen. Hopefully my pride would be restored to me.

I now had about twenty minutes of actual time invested in the Seth Thomas pocket watch, and I was getting nowhere slowly. Thank goodness the owner was not in a rush for the watch. It was taking a lot of coffee and thinking, but I had a lot more to go.

In the middle of August 2010, I was deeply saddened by the depths in which my happy profession had become mired. I received a package from a trade account that included the normal collection of very high-grade vintage timepieces. The only thing not normal was the single envelope written entirely in red. What the hell?

Inside was a ladies' Baume & Mercier, stainless steel case with a gold bezel rim set with smallish diamonds. Visible problems were a very badly scratched mineral glass crystal and a missing screw-down crown, a tiny one. Peeking inside the case tube, I could see that the stem had also been broken out. The request was for an estimate of complete overhaul and a new crystal, stem, and crown. There was even a note that the use of a *generic* crown would be okay. Baume & Mercier was one of those companies that believed an independent watchmaker could not possibly be talented and skillful enough to screw a crown onto a stem. Imagine the arrogance.

Strangely, I received the okay to proceed with the Baume overhaul in ten minutes.

That was quite unusual, and I sensed something was wrong somewhere. The e-mail included a request for all haste within my personal demand for enough time to do a quality job. I checked several catalogs and ordered what I thought would be the crown for the watch and planned to start the actual overhaul the following day.

Despite Baume's delusions of grandeur, the movement inside the watch was a normal ESA 955 model. This movement, of beautiful design, great engineering, and wonderful ease of repair, could only be classified as a generic movement. The word "generic" in today's world denotes a copy, a rip-off, a no-name product. What a shame. Maybe I should come up with a new word to join "necktie watch" and "who cares watch."

The stripping, cleaning, oiling, reassembly, and adjusting of the Baume movement was as easy as expected, and I set it aside complete with dial and hands to test run. I just had to await the crown.

A few days of the type that pass as "normal" later, the package containing the Baume crown arrived. This crown was not a genuine Baume part, but it matched all measurements, gasket size, and stem threads of the original. All it lacked was the logo of the original manufacturer. I sorted out the order over a cup of coffee (black, no sugar) and sat to finish and case the Baume watch. This was a very well-made, high-quality crown that had one drawback...it wouldn't fit the case tube. The post was 3/10 mm too thick, so that was the end of that.

Four phone calls later, I was forced to admit that there wasn't a crown made that was going to fit the case tube. The tube post was thinner than any other watch and seemingly not used by anyone but Baume & Mercier. Knowing the pressures and abuse that watch crowns suffered, I wondered if that was the basic problem. I had to do something, figure something out. I'd already repaired the watch, and without the crown, my time was a total loss. I hated having to e-mail bad news.

Two days later I received a reply and information I hadn't known. The watch had originally been sent to Baume & Mercier for the stem, crown, and crystal. The estimate had come back with a notice that the company would not do any repair without doing a complete overhaul. The estimate from the company made the customer "freak out" it was so high. The watch was demanded returned without repair of any kind, thus ending up in Milford. My instructions now, "The customer *begs* you to do anything you have to do to make the watch, her wedding present, usable again." They had confidence in me and "knew I could save the watch."

Out of curiosity, I e-mailed my customer inquiring if they had any idea what the "freaking out" price from Baume had been. I promised not to raise my own price if they told me. In the past I'd been told of some "impossible" factory estimates.

With dedication and great skill, I took the time to carefully punch out the undersized case tube, find a proper tube to fit the hole at the three o'clock position, swage it in, and find a Tap 10, 3.5 mm crown in white to match the case body. I then e-mailed an account of my success, but notified them that all the extra time, parts, and special skills I was required to use in order to save this expensive watch had forced me to raise my original estimate by $17.50. More than fair, and I was a hero. Right? By the way, it should have been $20 additional, but the $17.50 was a bit of "sticking it" to B & M.

The preceding is a fine example of a ridiculous situation in the watch world of today. A "prestigious" company adopts a "service" policy that "freaks out" an owner of their product, which is then serviced by a local service person for a very fair price. In the end the company has created a consumer who will miss no chance ever to heap bad publicity on them. Not only will the watch owner bad-mouth that company, but she will recommend to all her friends my customer in Boston, thus me, a simple watchmaker in a small town. Several times now I have mentioned this same problem involving other watch companies. The old-timers in my "world of watches" would turn over in their graves at the lack of true customer service.

I had to do some more work on that "murdered" Waltham pocket watch. I'd found that the damage was much more extensive than met my eye. Both upper and lower balance hole jewels were gone, broken into little pieces. The lower balance cap jewel was cracked. So far I had found a good balance wheel, with a broken staff, a very good hairspring, and I had to find a roller jewel. Once I found a good 18S long-shoulder balance staff, I'd have to find 18S balance hole jewels to fit the pivots. Waltham had balance staffs with pivots of varying sizes. Personally I think this was due to the limitations of machine precision in the 1860s. I'd tried, but couldn't find anyone who worked at Waltham back then to confirm my hypothesis.

One thing I knew would be a tough job. Once I'd re-staffed the balance wheel and fitted the roller table, I had to cope with the hairspring taken from another dead watch. The variations in individual watches meant that no matter how good the repaired balance was, extensive regulating would be required to match the balance weight and the hairspring. Only once did I have to do this, back in the 1950s. It wasn't fun. I was almost ready to tackle it again.

At noon sharp I wound and set the Waltham movement to the precise time and set it aside under cover to let the watch do its thing for twenty-four hours. Then I could determine the rate of gain or loss and do my thing. The "covers" I used were a clear plastic cover that enabled me to see the progress of the watch without bothering with anything. There was even a recessed bottom that would hold the watch case and band so my bench was kept "just this side of chaos." Here's a secret...my professional watch covers are in fact a set of plastic "dessert cups" I found at Walmart.

This afternoon I received an e-mail from the account that sent me the Baume & Mercier. Anything I write here that is truthful will not be believed, so let me just say that the estimate would have cost the owner of the watch money beyond reason. There are some things that are beyond reason, logic, or ethics. In the meantime, tomorrow would be the day for me to case up the ladies' watch. Maybe I should raise my prices a little, or more than a little. I'd think about it.

I was growing discouraged regarding the Seth Thomas. No ideas had come to me. But I'd keep thinking and drinking coffee (black, no sugar). If only I had technical manuals or material notebooks from that era. I once had a watch parts book from the late-1890s. I lost the book when it was destroyed along with everything else in a fire that took our house and my in-home shop in August 1970.

Middle of the afternoon and in walked FedEx with a package. I couldn't wait to see today's patients...an 18K/platinum Tiffany pocket watch and an Omega Flightmaster, another watch with as many hands as an octopus. I quickly checked both watches and was surprised to recognize the Tiffany movement as a Longines movement. Superb quality, but I wished the staff wasn't broken. Well, that was why it was sent to me. I picked up the Omega to apply the spanner for the opening of the case and read an engraved date...3/21/71. In the back of my mind an alarm started to beep...something about the year 1971 was unsettling. I took the spanner and turned the back halfway around. A quick reset and another half turn. Only a half turn because my fingers got in their own way. A third halfway turn and...and...the fingers holding the case were turning black...that's what 1971 meant. Oh no!

Omega watches, in my opinion, offered the best of the high-grade watches and the best value for the customer's money. In the long ago 1970s, I'd run into a series of Omegas that had a peculiar problem. The case gaskets, made of (I think) rubber, frequently came in melted. Something (I think petroleum products) caused the gaskets, both case back and crown, to form a tarry goo. The water resistance was not compromised, and years could pass without a problem until it came time to open the case. Half of the gasket goo stayed in the bezel groove and half stuck to the case back. When the back was unscrewed and lifted off, the goop stretched until individual strands broke and snapped down onto the movement. A true disaster until I discovered that soaking the case, front and back, and if needed the movement (minus dial and hands), in a jar of acetone actually did melt the gasket material and the watch could be repaired.

I managed to get the movement out of harm's way, with just a little of the black goo on the extreme edge of the dial...no problem. I checked the inside of the front of the case and saw deep, deep trouble.

There was a lot of gasket goo oozing down from under the crystal, and it was then that I noticed an internal rotating ring that indicated each five-minute increment. This was part of the flight calculator. I had been unable to turn the extra crown to rotate the ring, and now I saw that it was virtually glued in place. With great difficulty I mounted the case into a press and forced out the domed mineral crystal, and by the time I lifted off the crystal, I had to wash my hands in acetone. The word mess didn't fit the situation. My hands stung from the acetone, so I took a coffee (black, no sugar) break while I sulked in the back room and wondered where in the world I could get a new crystal gasket. The back gasket wasn't a problem...it was just a normal O ring.

That was something to worry about another day. I had some watches to assemble. One thing was sure: Omega would not furnish a peasant watchmaker like me a gasket.

At noon *sharp* the following day, I gently put aside a man's Omega to check the Waltham. It had lost seventy-two minutes in exactly twenty-four hours. Under visual inspection I could see that the balance was still oscillating with very good motion. I stopped the balance with a feather touch of my finger, and on release the balance instantly began to run. What I had was simply a balance wheel that was too heavy. I would remove the two smallest balance screws and try to get a readable record from the timing machine. Even a poor rate, but at least readable, would make my job much easier and faster.

On September 3, 2010, while the world waited for Hurricane Earl to finally reach New England, Papa Barry laughed himself silly for about fifteen joyful minutes. For a number of years I'd realized that certain self-winding watches had their own problems. These problems had been made more critical with the introduction of those fancy "auto winders" that I saw advertised frequently. The difficulties were technical in nature, not too complicated, but I personally believed they had been worsened by the auto winders.

Many of the early self-winding watches had what I believed was a functioning weakness. Very early Rolex, LeCoultre, A. Schild, and many brands that used generic movements were wound by oscillating weights that rotated back and forth, attached gears turning wheels that would wind the mainspring. The weights rotated more or less 270 degrees, each swing ending at a coil spring. I often saw a problem in that the weight wound while rotating in only one direction, swinging free on the return.

I'd always noticed that there were often problems when these "one-way" winders were worn on the right wrist of a left-handed person. Not to mention when the watch was worn by an older, more infirm person, who did not give the watch enough activity to perform its winding function. Sadly, but all too often, a "comeback" involving an automatic watch turned out, as I described in prior pages, to be a problem with the wearer of the watch.

By the 1950s, virtually all of the automatics were wound by oscillating weights that spun a full 360 degrees and wound the watch while turning in both directions, clockwise and counterclockwise. Problems were greatly reduced, but occasionally there was still the difficulty with the individual who just could not impart enough activity to keep the watch fully wound.

Several years ago, watch winders were introduced as many more mechanical watches were finding their way into the market. The watch winders were to keep the higher-priced mechanicals running while the owners wore their everyday quartz models. I came to believe that certain of the *best* new automatic watches had a peculiar problem that showed up only when the watch was on the auto winder.

Then one day, I popped to attention when I suddenly remembered my personal triumph involving that Bulova automatic watch, the 11ANAC/D, the one with the all too light oscillating weight. Here we go again. Some of the newest, and best, mechanical automatics had very lightweight oscillating winders, and some of the auto winders held the watch almost flat as it turned round and round, so gently that, in my opinion, the watch did not get enough energy to wind itself.

Today I received a brochure from one of the leading material suppliers that featured a whole page of new winders. The first thing I noticed was a group that could be self-programmed to rotate clockwise, counterclockwise, or alternating in both directions. Additionally the watches were held much more vertical, and even the lighter weights rotated with the unit to wind the watch. It seemed I was right. After a laugh session I called Bob and explained the new brochure.

"But you've been saying that for years now. This means you were right all along. I've run into those difficulties, and I always remember what you've said. How are you coming on with that new auto winder you're making for your own use?" Bob asked.

I had to admit I'd not done anything with it for quite a while. Thankfully I'd been too busy.

To really make me wonder how things work out, thirty minutes later I received an e-mail about a vintage Rolex I'd repaired. The very elderly owner had brought back his very vintage Rolex once more. Even when he kept it on his auto winder it wouldn't run more than twenty-four hours. Naturally this was a one-way winder. I'd check it out, but sad to say I already knew the problem, the solution, and the reasons. Often it was really no fun to be deemed "correct all along."

I still had the Omega bezel gasket to worry about. Having little to lose except another phone call, I turned to the Internet and typed in the name of a company I knew about but had never dealt with. I checked the website and decided to call the 800 number, which was answered by a very friendly guy. He was actually familiar with the gasket I needed, but he didn't think one was available. However, if I would furnish my phone number, he would search the place for this vintage 1971 part, but without a lot of confidence.

I put new batteries into half a dozen watches while I waited for a return call, and just as I opened the seventh, the phone rang and...

They had it! They had the gasket! Actually they had three. Instantly I put in an order and used the time to set up an account. Whoever was on the phone was so helpful and truly happy he could save my day that I decided that this was a company to do business with. I also discovered that a computerized material system that I'd purchased on CD in 1998, but had been "discontinued," was now their property and had been brought right up to date. Truly a lucky decision to check these people out online.

The more things change, the more they stay the same. A very good customer from the building came in yesterday with a problem affecting another new, high-grade automatic, day/date watch. It seemed that this six-month-old mechanical treasure had a little problem...the date ran fast. To be blunt, the date gained about ten or twelve days a week. To be more blunt, I told my friend he was nuts. He took his left hand from his pocket to unstrap the band so I could examine the watch. I caught the pocket stretching over the crown as it emerged from the pocket. Another watch problem that had nothing whatsoever to do with the watch. Time for a little fun.

"All you have to do to cure the watch is to change your pants," I said. That got the exact response I expected. He looked at me as if I was crazy. "Are you nuts?"

The watch, of a modern *very* large design, had a crown that matched the oversized case it stuck out of. It might have had a modern design, but it was a foolish design. When the left hand that wore the watch was put into or taken from the pants pocket, the protruding crown could readily catch on the outer edge of the pocket. When the cloth snagged, it actually snagged between the rim of the case and the inner part of the crown, pulling it out partway. Thus the crown was now in the "change the day and date" position. Then, as the crown rubbed on a coat or shirt sleeve, or against something, it turned and advanced the date disc. As my friend habitually stood or walked with his left hand in his pocket, the watch "gained" many days per week."

As I explained, a wry smile grew, and he nodded with understanding. Then he informed me that I'd solved the mystery of the same problem he had with another watch, just one not too frequently worn.

He turned and left as I heard both Dad and Uncle Abe repeat, "Often the problem with the watch has nothing to do with the watch. Remember that!"

The following day he returned, carrying a medium coffee (black, no sugar) in payment for the "watch repair." He also admitted the store he got the watch from had sent it back to the factory twice for the problem I'd solved. Each time the watch came back with the explanation that nothing wrong was found. I was forced to "modestly" explain that it was my training from Uncle Abe and Dad along with many, many years at the bench that allowed me to see the "real world" things that could make a perfectly good watch seem broken.

October 2, 2010, an idyllic New England Saturday down at the marina. It was cool but still nice, just a degree or so above what I call "cold." It was chilly enough for me to head over to the 7-11 for a thermos of coffee (black, no sugar). While I was in line to pay, I overheard the younger man behind me complain to a friend, "Eight hundred dollars and I can't pull out the crown to change the date to the second. This dumb thing is stuck on the first. Now Monday I have to take it back to the mall. What a waste of money."

I half turned and asked, "How long have you had that watch?"

"Why do you care? I got it two months ago, early August, and it's been fine until—"

"August has thirty-one days, so it went automatically from thirty-one to one and you had to do nothing. Now September has only thirty days and you have to change the date yourself, but the crown won't come out. You bought the watch at a prestige store from a salesperson who was only trained to write up your receipt, not trained well enough to show you how to set your new watch."

He replied, "But—"

I interrupted, "You didn't read the owner's manual. If you had you'd know that the watch has a 'locking crown' that screws down for

240

extra water security. Take it off and carefully turn the crown back-ward, which will unscrew it. The crown will pop out to a neutral 'run' position, then you very gently pull the crown out to its second position. Then turn the crown forward, and the date will jump to today's date. Then push the crown back in and screw it in 'forward' until it locks in place. The days are not a problem…always in perfect sequence, but the dates need changing every couple of months. Trust me; I'm a watch-maker. Have a good day."

It was my turn to pay for my thermos of coffee (black, no sugar) while the young man followed my directions and set the date on his $800 watch correctly. Suddenly someone was holding my arm while a hand reached around me and put a couple of bills on the counter. "Coffee is on me", my newest *customer* insisted. "What are the chances that a real watchmaker would be in line with me?" We shook hands and I left. That coffee tasted wonderful.

October 6, 2010, began quite early with the phone in the shop interrupting my morning routine. It was, of course, a watch problem. The tough part was that the watch had been in the shop since July while I tried to obtain a new screw-down crown for this "prestige" timepiece. So far, I'd had no luck whatsoever. The lady described the watch and why I had it, and before she had a chance to tell me her name, I was able to interrupt…

"That's the two-tone TAG watch with date, with a two-tone band that I can't find a crown for. I'm sorry I don't remember your name, or any name frankly, but I know the watch without checking the record. I just can't obtain the TAG crown as they refuse to allow peasant watch-makers like me to get replacement parts. I'm afraid you'll have to send it to TAG itself for this repair."

Her voice cracked a little. "No, no, please, there must be something you can do for me. Please. The watch was sent to TAG, but even though it was running perfectly, they wouldn't replace the crown without a com-plete overhaul for a huge amount of money. The watch was an expensive wedding gift and…and…well, he died…and the watch is precious to me. I can't afford such an impossible repair price. Can't you help me?"

I heard Dad and Uncle Abe in unison, "Barry, remember we fix a watch and take care of its owner." Once again I was in a position of being unable to criticize the design or quality of a watch but found myself with a burning hatred of the companies that cared not a whit for those who bought their product.

I took a deep breath. "I am truly sorry for your loss, but I can promise you one thing. If you don't mind the watch no longer having that screw-down crown, I can make your watch perfectly functioning once again. It will still be water-resistant. Your watch is really a fine one. It's too bad the company's customer service is really a disgrace. Should I go ahead and do my thing?"

I heard a quiet voice: "Thank you more than I can say. Let me know when the watch is done. Thank you so much."

I sat quietly sipping a lukewarm coffee (black, no sugar), brooding. I knew which would be the first watch of the day. It was a cold, rainy day, and this would make someone happy. The watch was in a plastic case awaiting the new crown, so the preliminaries were already done. Punching a large broach into the threaded case tube, I twisted the tube back and forth as I worked it out of the case.

It took "only" fifteen minutes for me to locate my leatherette cabinet of forty-eight different sizes of case tubes. Not using it often caused it to sink to the bottom of whatever drawer I put it in. Locating the crown cabinet was easier, but it took checking twenty-eight crowns before I found the perfect fit. Doing it my way, I pressed the tube into the crown and then carefully used a press to force the new case tube into the case. The crown acted as a limiter in inserting the post. I fitted a new stem, changed the battery for the heck of it, and sealed the case. Into the pressure tester, and of course the watch was water tight. Time to make someone happy.

The phone was answered on the fourth ring, "Hi, this is Barry Marcus. Just called to let you know your watch is done and you can pick it up at your convenience. Oh, I put in a fresh battery while I had the case open." Then I told her the total price and heard tears over the phone.

"But that's only half the price you originally quoted. Why?" she asked.

"I didn't mean to upset you, but the original estimate included an overpriced genuine crown from TAG. This is the normal price for the work I did. I only did it so quickly because you were obviously upset about the watch," I replied.

She said she would be in to get the watch as soon as possible.

Just as I secured the sweep hand on a gent's Rolex Datejust, the door opened. I glanced up and saw a very familiar face. "Hi, good morning. I'll be right with you."

I added, "I sure hope that Bulova of yours is not all busted up like it was in 2000. They worried about Y2K, but the only casualty I know about was your watch. Then again, I could use the money. Be right with you...just a minute."

I took his watch to examine and returned to the counter to write it up. Of course, first I asked the name, and he backed up three steps.

"Mr. Marcus, at a glance you recognized who I was. You remember the brand of my watch. You spoke about the damage I'd done to it and even remembered that I did it New Year's Eve 2000. But in the name of heaven, you can't remember my name?"

What could I say? Somehow the part of my brain that held the name memory circuits either had a short or a bent balance staff. I just never could keep a person's name firmly in my memory. It was just me, I guess.

Today, November 5, 2010, my professional career reached a new extreme. I—as a watchmaker who had repaired timepieces ranging from antique American pocket watches through the age of the self-winding day and date models, experienced in ultra complicated chronographs and repeaters (okay, just the one) continuing to the all-electronic quartz movements of today—was in the process of overhauling a genuine mid-1930s Mickey Mouse watch. I'd been at the bench slightly less than sixty-five years; this was a watch I had never seen before. Back in the day, a Mickey Mouse watch would not have been accepted for repair by a "real" watchmaker but would've been sent back to the factory.

The irony is that today, the value of this *genuine* vintage Mickey Mouse watch equaled some of the high-grade watches I've written about. I could only guess that the combination of its very early production date and its rarity had increased the sale price. This watch was being serviced "for sale." In 2010, my repair price would be many times the original sale price. Cost of living and all…

Also on my bench, sharing space and time with "the Mouse," was a special Corum "coin watch," made, I believe, either from a US gold coin or a beautiful copy of one. I'd only heard of them in the past and wanted to find out just what the truth was. The pride of this grouping was an automatic twenty-three jewel Vacheron Constantin 18K gold waterproof watch. Both movement and case were what one would expect of a Vacheron, but the poor case was in rough shape and would require a good deal of skillful cosmetic care. The Mickey should feel proud to be in such distinguished company.

Next week's projects included two clocks. I didn't do clocks, but these were taken originally from World War II war birds, one of ours and one, my first, from a Japanese fighter. Really, these clocks were just large watches, so I could stand by my "I don't do clocks" policy. If you're waiting for a really interesting war story, you're going to be disappointed. Both of the clocks had been taken from airplanes that were being scrapped. There was no personal connection between a serviceman and the timepieces. The repairs ended up just being easy overhauls.

In the interim, on November 17, 2010, I turned seventy-six. Now I was over sixty-five years at the bench. Last week I worked on my very first original Mickey Mouse watch, and today, November 19, I accepted my very first Timex ladies' watch.

A couple entered the shop, having driven from near the Massachusetts border. The woman had a watch from her grandmother, a treasured memory that the factory was now unable to service or repair. I reached for the watch to examine it and discovered that it was a 1950s Timex. Timex...the original "throw it out, the repair is too costly" watch. The case seemed in good condition, but my fingers "told" me the movement was rusted tight.

Sitting at the bench, I opened the case, paused, and met the eyes of the customer who peered through the bench glass. "Sorry, this is beyond any hope at all," I said.

It took no special insight to read her crestfallen look. I could see the deep sadness in her eyes, but I was helpless with this one.

She sadly told me, "Each morning I remembered Nanny carefully winding that watch. She was so careful of it, never wearing it around any water, taking it off while doing household chores. She always said it would be mine someday, and it would always be there to tell me when to get a move on."

I don't care who believes me or who doesn't, but I heard Uncle Abe remind me that "while it is the watch we repair, it is the people we take care of." Another voice, my father's, added, "Don't ever lose sight of that." Enough already.

I spoke softly. "In all honesty, the Timex movement is beyond hope. But if you look closely, the case and the band are in extremely good condition for their age. Knowing how precious this is to you, I have an idea. I can discard the dead movement and convert this with a twenty-one jewel ladies' Bulova movement...a wind-it-up mechanical watch. You'd have to carefully adopt your nanny's morning ritual of winding your watch and avoiding water."

"H-How can you do that?" she asked.

"The shape and size of the Timex movement is really a foundation shape and size for millions of ladies' watches, from Timex to the most prestigious ever made. It's called a six and three-quarters by eight ligne. Any watch of that size and shape will fit that case, and I can utilize the original dial and hand style. The watch will visually be what your grandmother looked at and cherished for all those years. My hands were hidden from you, so you didn't see me take a watch movement from the drawer next to my bench. See, I already have it in the case back to show you."

I opened my hand, and she drew a deep breath as she saw what I had just explained was a twenty-one jewel Bulova 6¾ x 8 ligne watch. I wasn't surprised to see tears on her cheeks.

"I'll give the watch a complete overhaul to return it to pristine condition and put a better crown on to make winding easy, and this watch will be ready for another forty years."

I was afraid I'd said the wrong thing, because I saw more tears. "You're telling me that this watch could someday go to my granddaughter?"

"Of course," was the easy answer, "these mechanical movements were really made and meant to last for one generation to the next. That's where heirlooms come from. You live too far away to pop over here to Milford to check on the watch, so I'll mail you a 'ready card' next week when the watch is all set."

They left, and I retreated for a cup of coffee, (black, no sugar). A sudden thought made me laugh, then grab a towel to wipe the coffee from my shirt front. I tended to not keep track of dates. If it wasn't boating season, I knew I'd be in the shop tomorrow. I just realized that next week I'd be in Maine for Thanksgiving. One of my longest "vacations" of the year.

So the next, next week I would be overhauling, in the same group of six, the Bulova/Timex movement and the movement from a diamond-and-sapphire-set platinum watch case. The Bulova/Timex was a timepiece, cared for and cherished for generations, while the diamond/sapphire "work of art" was sold for *scrap* because it meant nothing to the owner. I think this meant that "value" was merely a relative word. A nice lesson for Thanksgiving.

More than ever I proudly admitted to feeling blessed that I had a life's work that I had enjoyed after sixty-five years as much as when I was an oddity in Uncle Abe's store. Of course, this did not include certain "Watches I have Known." Yet the aspect of my work that most awed me still was the long history of *people* firmly attached to watches that accompanied them on a journey.

A laughing female voice was on the phone. In fact, she couldn't stop laughing. This was the customer for whom I had resurrected the Mickey Mouse antique. What was so funny?

"Mr. Marcus, one of the girls in my store just opened the box containing the Mickey watch. When she slid the watch from the envelope, she let out a yell and jumped back two paces. She was pointing and said that someone put a little square of cheese into the envelope with the Mickey Mouse watch. It even had little bites out of it. Even customers came to look and laughed their heads off. Funniest thing in a long time. I just had to tell you that this made the day. Thanks." I'm glad they had a sense of humor; it made life better.

Another year was drawing to a close and the watches continued to come for help. To finish November 2010 in a blaze of glory, a man brought in a very large AWW hunting case pocket watch. AWW stands, of course, for American Waltham Watch, one of the parade of names that finally became Waltham Watch Company of Waltham, Massachusetts. Without thinking, I pressed the crown to see the dial, and it was a beauty, in pristine condition.

Just a normal and very common large hunting case pocket watch, but there was a slide on one side that I fiddled with as I carried it to the bench. Just as I sat, I heard a *ding, ding* then a lower note *dong*. Good heavens, this Waltham watch was something I'd never even heard of, let alone ever saw or held. The design and engineering was positively Waltham, and I just gaped at the movement. When did Waltham make a repeater? I'd have to investigate, but sure enough, around the movement I could see the two circular "gong rods" that did the chiming. This was an American-made repeater, made to chime the time for its owners in the years before night-lights and radium dials.

I'd always known of the European chimers, but I had never seen or heard of the existence of American models. Of course, I was repairing watches brought into small family stores in Worcester and Milford, and I admit to being in my forties before I ever saw my first Rolex. No matter how busy we were, certain watches just did not exist in our world. Until now.

I e-mailed my customer, who specialized in these vintage timepieces. I was the one who knew how to repair them, and he knew *of* them. Within minutes, the phone rang. This watch was (quote) "Very, very, very rare and very, very, very valuable, and was the watch, by any chance, for sale?" Of course it isn't and wasn't. This was a personal family treasure. I did promise to give the repeater's owner my customer's business card.

Naturally I was nervous about this watch. I remembered my last repeater very well, which was, after all, my very first one. As Adam would say, "I'm batting one thousand."

The phone again. "Mr. Marcus, we saw your ad in the *Uxbridge Times* and wonder if you'll be there later in the afternoon. We have a watch that needs looking at and a lot of repairing. It's an older Seiko that winds itself and has the day and date."

Naturally I'd be here all day (where else would I be), and they said they'd be here in a couple of hours. A couple of hours...where were they driving from, I wondered.

Meanwhile there was a box of watches needing batteries...too many to do at random. I sorted them by ease of getting the case open, as it was truly a difficult job just getting to the interior of some of the modern watches. It had reached the point where I had actually doubled the price of installing batteries in those not-user-friendly cases.

Yesterday I told a man I'd give him the battery at *no charge*, but it would cost him $20 for me to install it. Why not? There were eight screws holding on the case back. Talk about over engineering…just stupid.

Just before 5:00 p.m., a couple came in, well dressed but looking stressed. For no reason at all, I had a sense of something that should not be.

After my "May I help you?" the man handed me an envelope obviously containing a watch. He said, "We saw your ad while visiting a friend in Douglas, and he told us he'd seen the same ad in the *Uxbridge Times* and had taken his watch to you. To be frank, he insisted that you were the man to repair my son's watch. We'd given up hope of getting it repaired." Oy, given up hope? Something was going on.

I sat at my bench and opened the envelope and…my mind started racing, trying to think of something that was just out of reach. I did not need to be told what happened to this watch. I held an early-1970s Seiko automatic/day/date steel watch. Typical for the time, it had a bright-orange dial but no crystal, no hands, something dark red on the "12" end of the case and a really twisted multilink band with a broken buckle. The dial had two thin gouges near the "O." Instinctively I already knew the answer, but of course I had to ask, "What happened to this watch?"

I truly believe that some things never change. The answer came, "My father bought this watch in Saigon, before he came home and retired from the army. He gave it to me, and I carried it when I went to Kuwait in the First Gulf War. It's been a really reliable watch ever since, so I gave it to my son when he shipped to Afghanistan. Now…" He paused and looked at his wife, and she nodded for him to continue.

"He was seriously wounded and is now at Walter Reed in Washington, where, thank God, he will fully recover. He may even be able to stay in the army. It's corny when people say that doctors can do wonders today, but believe me, it's true. Anyhow, he's quite upset that he has ruined his father's watch and keeps asking about it. Can you do anything? To be honest, the cost doesn't matter…no matter what, the watch must be repaired for my son. Can you help?"

I asked them to wait a few minutes, and I carried the watch to the drawers beside my bench. The human mind must react in odd ways now and then. I was looking for a Seiko movement I knew I had, so starting at the bottom drawer, I opened one labeled Bulova and found nothing. Then up one to Hamilton…no luck. Next one indicated it was full of Longines/Wittnauer movements. The next one happened to be have a couple of Seiko movements, and I found exactly what I was looking for. I held up, in victory, a plastic box and suddenly realized what had unsettled me.

I had flashed back mentally to a badly damaged Seiko that had been returned to a grieving father "with his son's effects" so many years ago. I was not a thinker of great thoughts…just a watchmaker in a little New England town, and the world was really aggravating me more and more often. Did this ever end?

"I knew it…I have what's left of a duplicate watch I've been taking parts from for thirty years now. The best part is we still have the original hands that come with this watch. I'll be able to completely restore your boy's watch, even down to the original hands. Of course the band is beyond any hope, but if you'd like, a similarly styled link bracelet can be ordered. I hope that will be okay."

"Mr. Marcus, I can't believe how lucky we are. Our son will be as new, and now his watch, which is so important to him. How much for the repair?"

There was not an instant of thinking. "The watch will be completely restored to new condition and the new band furnished. There will be no charge, and there will be *no* discussion of that. Is that satisfactory with you?"

I could not meet the father's eyes, so I turned to his wife and again asked for her approval. All she said was a quiet, "You overwhelm us with your kindness. Bless you."

What could I say but, "No, ma'am, doing this for your son is *my honor.*"

She stepped around the counter and reached up for my shirt collar to pull me down. Quietly she kissed my cheek, I shook hands with her husband, and after telling them I'd send a "ready card," they left.

What better time to retire to the back office for a cup of coffee (black, no sugar)?

I sat quietly for quite a while just looking out the window. I didn't know how to think about it, but I saw with a sense of deep humility. I was just a typical watchmaker, yet in my now sixty-five years at the bench I'd had the responsibility of the repair of watches that had served in every war, on every front, and in most of the major battles of my country from the Little Round Top to Cuba, France, Africa, Europe, Italy, Germany, the Pacific, Korea, Vietnam, Kuwait, Iraq, and now Afghanistan. And some were timepieces that served even the enemy of those wars and battles.

Some time ago an elderly man walked slowly and with apparent difficulty into the shop. As I approached, he, with some difficulty, removed what I could tell was a Rolex watch. He fumbled with the clasp of the band and then, gingerly holding the watch in both hands, carefully put the watch on the counter. It was sadly obvious that his hands were a great problem, and I felt great sympathy, gently rubbing my own watchmaker's fingers.

I picked up his Rolex Datejust, noticing that both the actual time and the date were way off, even though the second hand was circling the dial. A moment's general greeting and I asked how I could help him. I could only describe his voice as slightly tremulous.

"I am no longer active enough to keep my watch wound, and it often stops. My hands don't work well, and I can't unscrew the crown to either wind the watch or to reset the time. I don't worry about the date, as my eyes aren't what they used to be. I sent the watch to Rolex, and they overhauled it, but it came back the same way. I returned the watch, and they checked it and returned it saying it was right up to their standards in all ways. Can you help *me?*"

The emphasis on the "me" told me there was something beyond the watch here.

I picked up the watch, unscrewed the crown, and wound the watch enough that I was sure the mainspring was fully wound and walked to the timing machine, my EKG for watches. Sure enough, the watch showed a beautiful record, dead-on accurate, dead-on beat, and a watch record for Rolex to be proud of. Therein, I knew, lay the problem for the gentleman.

"Sir, the watch is, unfortunately, perfect. You're right, the problem lies in your fingers and hands. It's obvious you no longer have the strength or dexterity to grip and unscrew the crown in order to either wind the movement or to set the hands. This watch is and will remain an impossibility for you, I'm sorry to say. It's the way it was made and it's no longer right for you."

Tears welled in his eyes as he asked if there was *anything* I could do to help him. This was going beyond the repair of a man's Rolex. This was about the repair/care of a person. My advantage was personally meeting, seeing, and talking to the owner.

"I can alter the construction of your watch, but with your specific request and agreement. What I would do would, I think, give Rolex a heart attack, but it will solve your particular problem. Think it over and get back to—"

"I must be able to wear this watch, you must understand that. Do what you will."

I took his name and address and other data, and he slowly walked out, having some difficulty with the doorknob. I think it was an act of kindness that I did not rush to open the door. There was something with this particular watch, but the man hadn't shared any information, and it would have been rude of me to ask just to satisfy my curiosity.

Onward and upward...when the Rolex's turn came, I opened the case and removed the movement. Utilizing a large broach, which I drove into the interior of the case tube, I managed to remove the threaded tube. In its place I managed to locate and fit a properly fitting smooth case tube. This meant there were no threads projecting beyond the edge of the case. More hunting enabled me to locate a large, water-resistant stainless crown that would safely grip the now smooth case tube. Hopefully I had just made this into a simple case tube and crown repair job. When finished, I put the Rolex into the pressure tester and pumped up the pressure until the watch was "90 feet underwater." As I expected, no bubbles, and the watch was as safely water-resistant as a Rolex should be.

I resealed the case and kept the watch running manually for three days, frequently changing the time to be sure the watch could be set easily by the owner. When sure, I called my customer to pick up the watch at his convenience. I was quietly informed that "I will leave in about ten minutes." I knew that meant about an hour or a little more before he came in. I was pretty close in that guess. He slowly walked in, and I bade him sit on one of the chairs in the front of the shop as I settled into the other.

"I'd like you to try to wind the watch several windings and then pull out the stem and then set it to the correct time, if you can. The watch is wrong on purpose for this test."

I closely watched as he indeed was able to wind the watch crown without difficulty by fingering the larger-size crown. He took a deep breath and put a thumbnail behind the crown and pulled it out to set the time. Finally the stem was pushed in and he looked up at me with tears. "I'm sorry," he said, quickly wiping his face. "I can work the watch...I can work the watch. How did you do it?"

I carefully explained my changes to the watch and pointed out that Rolex wouldn't like it at all, but that the watch now suited him.

Before he left, I gave him one of my business cards, and he held my hand in both of his in quiet thanks.

The next day the phone calls started...three calls from three children, each thankful for the "blessed service" I'd done for their father. I'd had thankful customers before, but what was going on? The oldest, a son, caught the uncertainty in my voice and chose to explain...

"In 1951, my father was reported missing in action and presumed to be dead in action in Korea. His fiancée, to become my mother, was devastated, of course, and was soon hospitalized. A telegram came that my father had been found on the battlefield, without identification and very badly wounded, but alive and thankfully expected to survive. By miracle, that news seemed to cure my mother. She was soon on the road to good health. When he returned to the States, his 'girl' had obtained that Rolex in celebration of his return from the dead." Wow, I thought.

"They married, had the three of us, and were happy until she died a couple of years ago. That Rolex became, to Dad, the symbol of his true love, and he was truly heartbroken when his hands became such that the watch wouldn't work for him. We'd overhear him speaking to the watch, calling it my mom's name. I don't think you can really understand what you've done for him. Again thank you."

No, I did indeed understand.

Several months later I received a phone call from Mr. Petit. The name meant nothing to me, and I apologized for my nonexistent memory for names. He said he was the son of the man for whom I had altered the design of a Rolex. That I remembered, of course, and...

"He died last week and insisted the Rolex, the symbol of his love, go with him. Of course we carried out his wish. Also, he asked me to once again thank the man who took care of *him*. We didn't understand what he meant by that, but the message seemed very important." After a long pause, "Again, thank you."

I was, as my nana would say, verklempt. Dad and Uncle Abe, did you hear that? Yeah, you did. How many times have I told you that you were correct? Time for coffee (black, no sugar).

Frequently there are a number of watch questions I seem to solve merely by instinct as opposed to any traditional watch repair skill. A man drove up to Milford this afternoon with a watch that had been turned away by various watchmakers for several years. It was one of the original Hamilton electric watches, and no one could help him. It required a very special battery, one not made in many, many years. That description told me it was a Hamilton 500, truly the original one. Bad news, naturally.

I opened the case and tossed out a dead battery, then put power to the watch using my Renotest as a power source. Naturally the balance began to oscillate instantly, "telling" me it was delighted to be running again.

I said to the customer, "Somebody put in a badly wrong kind of battery. You're lucky it didn't leak and kill the watch. How long has that dead battery been in the watch?"

His disgusted answer was, "Three days ago it was put into the watch. The person who put it in was quite pleased that it fit so perfectly. The battery went dead the following afternoon. I'd seen you for years around the marina (he'd seen me at the marina?), knew you had a shop in Milford, so I tracked you down for a last try. I received this watch as a college graduation present years ago and it means a lot to me. Oh, some of us have finally figured out the meaning of your boat name. You have more nerve than any of us."

I laughed. "The name fits, believe me. But as to the watch, there is no battery for this watch, nor has there been for years. They were discontinued when Hamilton changed models, and there was no other watch that utilized the same battery. It became way too costly to produce. The battery had a special insulator built in that no other watch ever needed. Now sit down for a little while and I'll make one up for your watch."

"You'll *make* a battery for my watch. What are you talking about?"

I ignored him and collected what I needed...a properly fitting battery, a new razor blade, a Band-Aid, and a "from junior high school" re-enforcer for notebook paper. This was a precut circle with a hole in the center, sticker and used by every kid I ever knew.

An incredulous voice asked, "What the hell is the Band-Aid for? This all looks crazy."

"I've done about a dozen of these over the years, and every time I manage to cut my finger, so now I know to have the Band-Aid handy. Prevents bleeding into the watch, which I've done twice before I realized the physical danger of this repair."

I carefully placed the re-enforcer on the bottom negative side of the battery and firmly pressed it into a foam pad, which secured the battery and its new "insulator." Then with a deep breath, I held the battery in my left hand and the brand-new razor blade in the other and began trimming. All I had to do was cut the diameter of the re-enforcer down to the size of the battery and we were all set. Working so closely under magnification that brought my finger, nose, battery, and razor to within an inch was careful work, but... wonder of wonders...no blood this time.

In triumph I installed the battery and secured the clamp, and we were all set. I carefully closed the screw-back case and handed the now running watch back to its owner. One of my off-the-wall solutions had worked again.

My customer held his now running Hamilton with a look of awe. He raised his eyes and met mine, and I could easily see the emotion behind them. Again, as so often before, a watch, just something that tells its wearer the time, was restored to its place of honor on the wrist of one who cherished it. And after all these many, many years, the watchmaker was really glad to have helped.

We shook hands, and he happily said he would see me on the water in just a few short months. In my opinion, they were l-o-n-g months.

I 'd been struggling with a 16S Illinois that had a broken balance staff. I had only two new staffs for a one-hundred-year-old watch whose maker went out of existence in the 1920s. The staff fit the balance wheel, both halves of the roller, and hairspring collet perfectly, but the pivots were too thick for both balance hole jewels. This was weird, leaving me with nothing to do but to lathe down the pivots.

This created a big problem with this particular watch. Normally I could lathe down the pivots and test its fit in the hole jewels, and if it seemed okay, I'd stake on the balance wheel and then use a little air blast to spin the wheel for a real free-running test. If not quite right, then back to the lathe for a little final finish. My problem was that this balance wheel was a "split balance," meaning that on opposite sides, next to the balance arm, was a slit in the wheel. This was a method of adjusting for temperature variation and the expansion of the metal of the wheel. Putting this wheel on a high-speed lathe could well warp the balance arms and kill everything. The question was how to test an unstaked wheel.

Well, the best way to think was to do something else, so I collected a half dozen watches for some small repairs. Couple of batteries, a band adjustment, and a crystal fitting on an old Hamilton gent's watch. Everything went smoothly, and I did the Hamilton last, finding and filing to fit a rectangular simple crystal. With this, the critical part of the repair consisted of running a good bead of crystal cement around the bezel to securely hold the crystal. The crystal cement also helped keep dust out of—

My head popped up and I smiled, having solved the Illinois balance problem. All I wanted to do was attach the balance wheel and test a spinning balance with its shiny new staff. Why couldn't I simply *glue* the wheel to the staff...why not indeed? It didn't have to time out, it didn't have to be poised and true, it just had to spin free. I pressed the staff into the pith wood and applied a tiny amount of crystal cement before pressing on the balance wheel. Then I finished up the small job details while the glue dried.

Ten minutes later I put the glued-up balance into the watch, secured the upper balance bridge, and gave it a puff of air. The wheel spun like an airplane prop, continuing even as I turned the movement to any possible position and/or angle. Even putting a little pressure directly down on the upper cap jewel had no effect. Success was at hand. It required only a few seconds to separate the two glued pieces and to clean off the barely dried glue. A quick dip in acetone, and I was ready to really stake together a now proven Illinois balance. Sometimes the best solution was laughingly simple. But only if it worked...

Stake the wheel, then fit both halves of the roller table and guard, and position the hairspring and put it into the watch. Since nothing really goes easy, naturally the hairspring was way out of the flat and required some very precise bending (bad word). I grabbed the tweezers I used only for hairspring work and with only two tries had a perfectly aligned hairspring. Onto the timing machine, and I smiled as the tape showed a gain in all positions of only twenty seconds per day…an easy tweak of the regulator. After the tweaking I sat for a minute, wiggling my fingers, sort of relaxing them.

I looked at my hands, hands blessed with an ability that still occasionally amazed me. I remembered the two doctors in Worcester who years and years ago told Uncle Abe that "the boy's hands belong at the operating table, caring for people."

I think that Uncle Abe and my father both would simply reply, "The boy's hands *have* truly been caring for people, just in a different way."

H APPY NEW YEAR!!! It is now 2011, and for the hell of it I wrote 2011 on a little piece of paper. Under it I wrote 1946, the year I'd started at the bench. As I learned in the third grade, I drew a careful line under the figures and did the subtraction. I stared at the result, wondering how anyone could love doing the same work for sixty-five years, and doing it at least five days per week. I stopped wondering because the simple fact was that sixty-five years had passed and I still just plain enjoyed this work. I did wonder *how* sixty-five years had gone by so quickly.

As the Patriots finished the 2010/2011 season in a blaze of glory, I was in the shop on Sunday, January 2, finishing up a couple of very high-prestige watches for shipping on Monday. I found the Pats' performance interrupting my work as every time the announcer's voice got excited my head went up to hear better. Of course I was glad they were winning, but I was not getting much done. Did they have to do so well today? (I didn't dare make that complaint to Julie or Adam.)

Finally I finished the watches. The one watch I managed to start was an old Elgin pocket watch, a model I'd not seen for years. Nothing special, so off came the hands, then the removal of the movement from the case. I decided to remove the dial and then call it a day, but as I lifted off the dial and…and…I beheld a winding/setting arrangement almost exactly like that blasted Seth Thomas I'd been "studying" since last April. This one was working beautifully, winding and setting just as it should…good heavens…there was actually a spring in the Elgin that pressed against the swiveling unit when in the winding position. When the crown was turned forward, the torque of the unit combined with the tension of the spring held the crown wheel against the ratchet wheel and the watch was wound a little bit. When the crown was reversed, the torque disconnected the wheels, but the spring acted to reset the wheels for further winding.

That had been the problem all this time; the Seth Thomas was missing a spring, and there was no indication of there ever having been a spring in place. Mystery well solved, but I still had no way to find and obtain that spring. Time to go home.

Hell no, I couldn't go; there were a few minutes left in the game. It was still close, and the Pats had only a thirty-point lead with five minutes left. Not to be superstitious, but there was no way I could leave.

With five minutes to go in the last quarter, I decided to check in some watches that arrived Friday, New Year's Eve day. Happily I wrote up three Bulovas, a Benrus, two Hamiltons, and a Longines, which would start 2011 off on a good foot. In a separate package were two more watches in for estimates to write up. Holy cats…two badly broken Rolex watches. Both had smashed sapphire crystals, with little pieces of glass stuck between the hands. One was a "normal" automatic calendar watch, but the other seemed to have, inside the broken glass pieces, an extra hand. Oh, this was a Greenwich model, with an extra hour hand that told the hour on a twenty-four-hour basis. The year 2011 was off to a great start. Tomorrow I'd e-mail out the estimates and await the replies.

It had been a great day! The Seth Thomas puzzle was solved, the Pats were walking off the field in victory, and I was outta here for the night.

Monday, January 3, 2011, the first working day of the New Year for the world, and for me, time to finish with the Seth Thomas. There was no place for a spring. Where it belonged was blocked by a broadheaded screw that held down the ratchet wheel plate and…it did not hold down the plate. Two small screws held the plate in place, and the broad screw was where a *click spring* would nest. I removed the screw and saw a threaded post, which was where the spring would be held in tension, with the screw holding it down. Problem was there was nowhere to get the spring. I sat back in defeat and brooded. Suddenly…wait a minute, this kind of spring did not mesh with anything; it just sat in place under tension and pushed against something, in this case against the swiveling plate that held three wheels.

In the large top center drawer in my handmade bench there was "supposed" to be a two-inch-square plastic box containing literally hundreds of watch springs of the type I needed. This would be a good day as it took me only thirteen minutes to find the box of springs in the drawer. Another few minutes of digging through the box and I found a spring of the correct type but wrong shape. Carefully I laid the spring in place, stared at it for a couple of minutes, and determined exactly where I would create a curve near the end.

I needed a ring-forming jewelry plier not seen for about fifteen years, so naturally that one I found in about five minutes. This place was a nuthouse. It took actually less than a minute to form the spring, and crossing my toes (the fingers were needed for the watch), I forced the spring into place and screwed down the holding screw. I picked up the special multistemmed winding tool, took a deep breath, and…wonder of wonders, the watch wound and then set as it did the week it was made.

My quest for the really old, orphaned Seth Thomas watch, begun last April, was done. The dial and hands were replaced, and I put the watch, properly set, under cover to run for a couple of days of checking. I admitted to myself that I'd spent infinitely more time just thinking about this problem watch than actually working on it. The actual cleaning and overhaul not being counted, the problem part that took all those months to puzzle out required about four minutes of hands-on time. Happy New Year to this hundred-year-old watch. This deserved a cup of coffee (black, no sugar).

It was January 8, 2011, and I had developed a case of the terminal smugness in addition to the discomfort of a swelled head.

A few weeks ago, an account had given me, among others, what was left of a ladies' Ray Weil watch. Normally I could pick up a watch to examine it, but this one I had to scoop up it was in so many pieces. What in the hell? The store owner caught my puzzled look and related a real tale of woe. The watch had somehow gone through the washing machine, in the pocket of the owner's blouse. It fell out of the pocket and then somehow worked its way under the agitator of the old top-loading machine. The watch then somehow got into a set of gears, and the watch and the machine ate each other up. I was told the washer was in worse shape than the watch. To repeat an oft-told tale, the watch must be restored to its former glory. Somebody was nuts, but as usual I agreed to take the wreckage to Milford and at least check everything out.

The movement was beyond help but not a problem as it was just a generic good Swiss model, Weil name or not. There were small white stones at the hour markers, but most of them had been knocked out of place by the pounding inside the machine. The cracked round crystal, of course, was just routine. The band, or rather the many, many pieces of the band, was pulled apart, scratched, and bouncing around loose in a plastic baggie. The pivot pins were broken. The pins were actually part of the individual links, one side pressure fitted into the other. Nope, there was nothing to be done beyond obtaining a new band from the factory. I noted the model number and called my customer for her to order, if possible, a new band. Frankly I thought this would be a very costly error. But...

Two days later the phone rang.

"Barry, I called Weil about the band, and the price is beyond reason. I contacted the owner and all she did was cry. The watch is beyond precious to her, for whatever reason, just as you've often said. Anyway, between tears she begged for you to do something to save her watch. Even if you have to mickey-mouse it!"

Don't ask why, but I replied, "No, I can't mickey-mouse a ladies watch. I'll see what I can do to minnie-mouse the damn thing." All I heard was laughter and a dial tone.

Buoyed by a cup of coffee (black, no sugar), I attempted to fix the Weil band. I spread out all the pieces of the band except the complete clasp itself. The clasp for some lucky reason had broken off cleanly as the pivot pins were snapped. No problem to reattach the clasp and adjust it, but there were no pieces made to fix the band. This was a lost cause and I was wasting precious time. I carefully put all the pieces off to the side.

I called my customer to pass on the bad news. The moment she heard my voice I was informed, "The Weil customer called three times for news on her watch. This one I can't understand. Barry, she's on the verge of hysteria. I know you called to tell me nothing can be done. I'll wait a few more days and then tell her it's all over. Bye."

I'd only managed to say hello and never had a chance to say good-bye.

There was something very wrong here. There was something tragic behind this, and it wasn't the trip through the washer. There was a connection with this watch, and the customer was not telling us anything, just crying. Still, there was nothing I could do.

I grabbed an overflowing box of small jobs, batteries, crystals, broken but fixable bands, stems and crowns, loose hands. These were all the little things that kept me busy when I didn't want to be.

To make my life easier, I segregated the watches by repair need. It was a lot easier to concentrate on a single procedure, like changing batteries. Just one set of tools, one reference book, one case opener, plastic tweezers, a compressed air can, and a handy Band-Aid, just in case.

I finished the last of a dozen battery changes and grabbed a half dozen cracked, missing, or simply broken mineral crystals. No extra problems, thankfully.

To finish a busy day, I'd take care of the broken bands. There were always many of these as the bands of today were often held in with a simple sliding friction pin. It seemed that designers didn't understand that a pin that merely slid in would slowly slide out. Band number five of the day had a broken loose safety clasp locking device. These were really sort of clever; simply put, a hollow tube of the right diameter and length slipped through the clasp and a locking bar device. Into each end of the hollow tube, a piece that looked like a rivet was friction-driven into the pivoting tube.

Suddenly a very bright bulb lit up inside my head and I sat up straight in a fit of anger. Furious, I slammed my hand down onto the center catch drawer, swore, and got up to locate where I put that Band-Aid. First, I had to extract a shard of broken mineral crystal from my hand. Ah no, there were three pieces. After using a hairspring tweezer to extract the pieces, I squeezed enough blood out to help clean the boo-boo and finished the medical treatment of the day. I was still mad at me because I should have thought of this all along, but at least I'd needed only one Band-Aid.

I took all the pieces and parts of the Weil watch and tested the diameters of the hollow friction tubes and they were, by coincidence, a perfect fit. They would act exactly as the broken originals. The friction post heads were a beautiful fit, if somewhat smaller than the originally designed ones, but the same visual style. After I had completed the surgery on my hand, it took me no more than five minutes to fix the Weil band. I couldn't do anything about the deep metal scratches from the washing machine gears, but the lady would once again have what was completely her original watch. I decided that I had to get nosy and find out the reason for the importance of this watch.

As my "teachers" would have pointed out, whatever brainstorm I'd had hadn't fixed a simple watch, it had truly "treated a person."

A bright note on a gloomy Monday. The Seth Thomas pocket watch was doing fine at long last. In the last few days I'd wound the watch, but only halfway, to test the bridge spring I'd made up. Perfect. Note: partially winding the watch made me wind it several times a day, rather than merely once. I knew the watch would run fine. Good news. A card (finally) went out to the customer.

For a long time, and in my musings, I'd been worrying about the growing lack of capable watchmakers. A town that once had at least a half dozen now had…me. Not good at all. Few and far between were jewelry stores, with cases of watches for sale yet not a single one with a capable watchmaker to care for customers' watches. I had a good idea why, but I was worried for the future. At least there was Cousin Bob to carry on the family trade. I had a thought...my grandfather, a watchmaker who eventually had six children, immigrated to America in 1908. Doing the arithmetic, there had been a Marcus repairing watches from Grandfather Marcus to Uncle Abe and my dad, Cousin Marty, me, Cousin Bob, and Cousin Alan, not to count the group of young army vets who married Marcus girls and learned our trade. That was 103 years, not counting the years my grandfather worked back in Lithuania before coming here. And I have no intention of putting down the tools as long as my hands work.

What brought this on? Early this afternoon I received an e-mail from my watch collector customer. A man from a Deep South state had e-mailed to Boston the tale of long-term trouble with a watch. The watch was a 1960s vintage Hamilton automatic/calendar watch of a thin design and hadn't worked properly in about thirty years. It had been to four watchmakers over the years but still would not run. As expected, the watch was a personal treasure to the gentleman, and would I contact him personally and possibly help him. At the time, I did not know where the man lived, but were there no capable watchmakers there? What in the hell was going on? Well, why not...I'd risk an e-mail.

I sent a quick e-mail, inviting the man to call to talk about the problem with the Hamilton, a watch that should never be a problem. Then I killed a minute for a couple of sips of coffee (black, no sugar). Time to go back to work, and just as I sat at the bench, the phone rang...good timing.

I spoke the usual, "Good afternoon, watch repair...May I help you?"

"Hello, I just got your e-mail and I hope you can help my watch."

I was stunned at the impossibly fast response. Naturally a few minutes were spent getting "phone" acquainted, then on to the Hamilton.

I asked if his watch was marked on the lower part of the dial with the word "Thin-o-matic."

"How...how could you know that from way the hell up north? That's exactly what the watch dial says, except for the name and tiny letters 'Swiss' under the six. How could you know that?"

Easy answer. "I was e-mailed that your watch was from the early 1960s. By then Hamilton was using high-grade Swiss movements for self-winding models, and yours has a date unit with a little window at the three. Also it's a very thin watch, in what is called a 'one-piece case.' If given to you for a special occasion, it could well be a four-teen carat case. I've been repairing those watches since the sixties, so my knowing the particulars is just something normal for me." More yet: "The movement itself is a Buren. Not the original Buren 1000, but most likely the Buren 1200 something, I can't remember the exact number for the moment. Sorry."

From the South: "Sorry? You seem to know more about this watch over the phone than the people down here who wasted all my time and a lot of money. They all told me there's a broken calendar drive wheel, and no one could find one. I'll send out the watch and you can let me know what you find. I'd like to know the cost, of course."

We ended our phone call with a little joint complaining about the cold, snowy weather. But, he bragged, "We have a fuel-efficient, non-polluting snow removal system, much better than you have." When I didn't believe him and asked what it was, he laughed and said, "This is the South. All we do is wait for the sun to melt everything."

We said our good-byes, and I went back to casing up the Ray Weil watch. I was still feeling great about figuring this one out. I knew the customer, overwrought about the watch, would be so happy. I was still going to...Wait a minute!

I spun the chair around and stood in front of four large cabinets with dozens of drawers of watch movements. I ran my fingers up the nameplates until...I opened the drawer labeled Bulova–Newer Models. I had suddenly remembered that Bulova used that same Buren move-ment, and the Bulova was marked, under their system, the 12EBACD.

The number/letter designation told the watchmaker that the watch was a Bulova 12EB, with a self-winding unit (A), a center-mounted sweep second hand, the C, and the date unit (D). Thus the 12EBACD.

Sure enough, I found a two-inch-square plastic box with three of these movements, two in various stages of having had parts removed. Back to the bench, and sure as heck, I had three perfect date drive wheels here. These wheels could well be the only chance in the country to repair the Hamilton. We would see.

Hey, world, I had a day off! A Wednesday off. The fact that the snow was so deep that I could not find my very large station wagon in the snowdrifts outside helped. Of course, I admit that on Tuesday I was informed by my daughter Carol that I was *not* to even think of trying to get to work on Wednesday. I knew better than to argue...I'd have the day off on Wednesday.

As usual, I got to the shop late on Friday morning. I was way behind in the work because of Wednesday's snow day. I spent a great deal of time on a couple of extra, extra complicated watches, and at least I had one tiny break...there was only one message blinking on my answering gizmo. Let it wait awhile as there were a couple of things I *must* do on Friday.

Chores taken care of, I finally checked the message to see who was looking for me. Oy, I had an uncomfortable feeling as I listened to a call from a gentleman in northern New Hampshire. He could not find anyone to trust a special watch to, and someone from New Hampshire whose watch I repaired years ago when I did all the work for L. L. Bean had recommended me very highly. Would someone tell me what the hell was going on in the country? To be truthful, I really liked getting the work, and so did my checkbook, but *why* was I getting these calls from around the country? Where the hell were the capable watchmakers?

Anyhow, this gentleman described his search for help. The watch was about five years old, fairly costly (but no specific number), ran wonderfully for about four and a half years and now stopped when the mood hit it. He also mentioned the watch was a self-winding mechanical model with day and date. Also, there was the tiny word "Swiss" just above the "6" position. In other words, nothing out of the ordinary, besides being a modern mechanical in the "age of the battery." I asked

266

about his seeking watch repair so far away, and could the shortage be that bad. He said there wasn't a good watch repair man within a hundred miles of his home.

After some interesting talk about mutual interests, I gave him my normal instructions about sending in a watch. It was imperative to carefully print his name, address, phone number, and an e-mail address. He would mail out the watch Monday morning. Note: I am really worrying about this watchmaker "shortage."

I always give the same little speech when a customer is shipping a watch to me. A few years ago, a watch was mailed into the shop with the customer's data so poorly written as to be totally illegible. The watch was in the shop for just under eight months before I received a call from a very irate customer demanding to know the status of his repair. When I replied that the watch had been ready for him for about seven months while I waited for the owner to contact me because I couldn't read a single bit of his writing, all I got was thirty seconds of silence. He promised to send a check the next morning and then dictated his vital statistics while I printed them in my own precise printing. (Printing because I'd need to read it later. Normally my cursive is unreadable, even by me.)

Because of Wednesday's "day off," I worked most of both Saturday and Sunday. I concentrated on some "spaghetti" and "octopus" watches. The "spaghetti" watch was a modern automatic, self-winding, calendar, twenty-four-hour-dial, second-time-zone chronograph. Before I took apart the "spaghetti" model, I spent twenty minutes with a double loupe tracing the "pasta bowl" collection of levers, springs, cams, wheels, and lock springs that made up *just* the chronograph part of the watch. The "octopus" watch was merely a manual wind chronograph, day/date/time zone, Greenwich Time watch. It was simpler because it lacked the automatic unit.

I started a vintage Rolex Oyster, still a good-looking automatic of the old, old style. The direction for this one was "do whatever is needed." For some reason, it struck me as ominous sounding. This model had an automatic wind unit that covered the entire movement, held in place by three screws. Of course it came off easily, and I separated the oscillating weight from the winding unit and...oy! As I lifted the weight from the unit, the corner of my vision saw...the balance staff was broken. Was there even material available for this oldie but goodie? Oh, I was in trouble now. I finished taking apart the watch, which showed no further damage...except for a badly cracked upper hole jewel. No problem as a balance jewel merely had to fit the hole in the balance bridge and have the proper pivot-sized hole. I was worried about the staff.

I called my customer, who was quite upset at the news of the broken staff. He had a potential customer for this *solid gold* model and... well, he would make a few calls on his own. Cross all our fingers, I guess. On to the next watch.

Wait a minute! I still had four drawers of watch material, each about three feet long, that contain material I hadn't even looked at... ever. Could it be hiding another treasure? Into the *Bestfit* book, the old one, to find the part number for this Rolex staff. Aha, here it is. I made a note, and off to the hunt. With faint hope I wrestled out the top drawer, the one with the lower numbers, low to about "900." I fingered my way through the large envelopes, trying to decipher my late friend's bad writing and...here was an envelope with the right number. I carefully opened it and in disbelief saw three little part envelopes, two unopened and one sliced across the top. It could not be possible, but I had twenty-four plus five for a total of twenty-nine balance staffs for this vintage Rolex. What could I say? I put the unopened part envelopes back and took the other staffs to the bench for later fitting.

For the 175th time, I promised myself to someday carefully check through whatever was buried in here. But truth be told, I wouldn't, simply because it wasn't worth the time wasted just playing "tourist" through the watch material stash. When a particular piece was truly needed, the time was well invested. After every search, I told myself I should get truly organized. I always answered myself, "yeah, right."

The mailman delivered the Hamilton automatic/calendar watch from deep in the south, the state of Georgia. Killing a minute, I manually wound the watch, and from the feel of the gears, I knew I was correct in naming this a Buren movement. I pulled the stem and set the time, eventually passing midnight, and the date did not advance. This was what the owner was unhappy about. Just to check, I went forward a couple of days, but with no results. The calendar unit was truly out of commission. I grabbed the crystal lift and was able to quickly remove the movement from the one-piece case. Two minutes and the hands and dial were removed and I was able to see the exact problem.

It took but a moment to see that the problem with the calendar unit was that there was *no* calendar unit in the watch. I saw only the minute and hour wheels and a date disc glued into place. No broken drive wheel, no date-centering lever and spring...no nothing.

I'd have to call the world to see if I could find the missing parts. To my complete surprise, this watch, while positively a Buren from the 1000 family, was a variation. The parts were not the same as in the four movements I had in the Bulova drawer. I'd have to call the owner and give him the sad facts. Oh well. Another task for tomorrow morning. Today I'd had a full day. Time to bug out.

This morning at 11:00 a.m., I received a phone call, saying hello to a man whose voice and accent sounded Eastern European. To my slightly diminished hearing, I thought I heard him say he was calling from somewhere that almost sounded like Romania.

I apologized and asked him to repeat where he was calling from. The reply really stunned me as I clearly heard a slowly spoken "Romania." Who was playing games with me? However, be polite: "How may I help you, sir?"

"Some years ago, while I was at the United Nations, I sent my watch to where I bought it in Maine...L. L. Bean. It was a self-winding Hamilton, but with the name Bean on the top of the dial. Anyhow, to save time, you were asked to mail it directly back to me in New York as I was due to return to Romania."

(Do you happen to recall that I'd mentioned being surprised at the number of Bean watches I'd received from people from behind the Iron Curtain?)

It seemed the watch had finally stopped running and he contacted L. L. Bean for the repair once again. I smiled to myself. He was informed that L. L. Bean would exchange the watch, but if he desired, they would furnish the name of the man who could repair the old mechanical model. Guess who. He already had my name and address in his file, but was surprised when my name was, after all this time, given to him. Thus we were talking over a few thousand miles.

When I explained the repair could of course be done, but not as part of L. L. Bean service, he countered that he was aware of that. But the watch was important as a reminder of his happy time in the United States. With a word of caution that the mail might be slow, the watch would go out to the USA tomorrow. I hoped the post office mule could swim. Did this mean that I was now part of international commerce? Did I have to take payment in Euros? This'd be fun.

I'd been getting in for repair some of the new Swiss-made ETA automatic watches. Here in late 2011, they were reliable proof that the mechanical watch was not dead. Well designed in the Swiss mode, they were made with variations ranging from basic self-winding movements to the additions of date units as well as day/date sections. So far I'd only seen them with a sweep unit, a feature that harked back to the "hack" watches of World War II, in that pulling out the stem to set the time pivoted a lever that actually contacted the side of the balance, stopping the watch in its track. When the *exact* time was set, the user waited until the proper second then "hack," the stem was pushed in and the watch was running and synchronized. (I'm sure you've seen it in the movies.)

A couple of these very fine watches had been a problem, but without a reason. I also had what I hate to say was a bad sense in the back of my head. I had a feeling something was not right with these watches, but in reality there was nothing wrong. What bothered me was I'd had little alarm bells rung in the past, and there turned out to be good reason. Occasionally there is no fun or victory in being right. I had a couple of pages of notes, just in case.

I was in the shop on the last Saturday in January, but not with a smile. To steal a phrase, the snow was as high as an elephant's eye. The roof over the shop was leaking, and some of the ceiling tiles had been cut down. There were a couple of large wastebaskets and a thirty-five-gallon barrel under the leaks. At least the leaking was at the rear edge of the building and at the opposite end of my office space away from the shop and the watch materials. We were having a real old-fashioned winter. This week Milford, Massachusetts, made all the radio stations in the East, because we had the high honor of having more snow in four hours than anywhere else in the East. What an honor.

FedEx had a couple of presents for me: a box of watch materials and a heavier one that contained some interesting watches: an 18K Rolex Oyster that "clunked" along with a Bulova Oceanographer, and—ooh—an Accutron day/date model in an 18K case and a "time to put on a suit and tie" Vacheron Constantin vintage classic. There were also a couple of high-value "nothing specials."

I think I should define my idea of a "high-value nothing special." It just defines a higher-grade watch that is just a basic, no extras mechanical watch. Often I find an average automatic/day/date Swiss watch of more challenge and interest than a watch of infinite value, outstanding prestige, beautiful design and yet is nothing more or less than a seventeen-jewel "wind-it-up" normal watch.

The winter of 2011 was turning out to be no fun. Beside lots of snow and snow piles taller than me, everything had a coat of ice, including my beloved station wagon. I'd lost two days to the weather this week. A steady customer wandered in, a man whose fervent hobby was collecting unusual and limited edition watches. A year or so ago, he gave me a Tissot chronograph with a broken case. The case was made of fiberglass, a one-piece design, with the movement turned so the crown and the stop/start buttons were at the twelve o'clock position.

The watch had been sent to Tissot to no avail, as the model had been discontinued and a replacement case was not available. I'd been trying to come up with an acceptable solution to save the watch.

Somehow, the watch was struck sideways at the nine o'clock position and the entire top of the watch and case sheared off. In reality when this kind of case is made of steel, it is sturdy and long lasting, but when molded of fiberglass, it is a dumb idea. The center part of the case was much, much too thin to have any strength when made of plastic. A crystal was pressed onto the case ring, securing the movement, and then an outer ring was pressed, with difficulty, down around the crystal. In theory, we had a sturdy one-piece case that was well made and water resistant. However, if hit at the right angle, the thin fiberglass ring would break from the top of the case. That extra thin center ring just did not have enough width for anything, epoxy or even any of the fiberglass repair compounds that I used on the fiberglass hull of my boat.

My boat (heavy sigh). This was the first year I'd been unable to go to the boat two or three times a month for "winter visits." The weather had been unrelenting, and the snow and ice at the marina was so dangerous that the word had been given to "Keep the Hell Away." Last night, I went to sleep dreaming of cruising Narragansett Bay. I admit that when I put up my new 2011 calendars, I sneaked a look ahead, and sure enough, at least an April, May, and a full summer season had been scheduled. In the meantime, there were still watches to keep me busy. Heavy sigh. Time for coffee (black, no sugar).

Anyhow, for well over a year I'd been replying to my customer's phone calls and questions with, "I'm thinking about how to do this, which I already told you can't be done. Even Tissot has told you to forget it."

His answer was always both a compliment and an annoyance: "I'm not asking Tissot, I'm asking you to do something."

After kibitzing and catching up, he asked about the Tissot. "Any progress?" I answered in the usual way, only to get the usual response. Today, he added a question. "What about the Longines that I left a couple of months *before* I gave you the Tissot?"

This Longines was a special diver's watch, naturally no longer made. Diver's watches have a rotating bezel on the top of the case, usually marked in five-minute increments. When the diver/ owner wished to start recording elapsed time, he or she turned the bezel until a "0" indicator aligned with the minute hand. The Longines had an internal elapsed time ring, rotated by turning an extra crown located at the "1:30" position. This watch was damaged when hit in a sideways direction, like his Tissot. Like the Tissot, the crystal was torn off and with it a tension ring that kept the timing ring pressed down to make contact with the geared wheel on the end of the setting crown. He had learned that Longines no longer had a presence in this country, and there was no way to obtain the parts missing for this special watch case. Naturally he brought it to me, and it ended up in my repair box so I could (try) to make something that didn't exist.

All that my friend could do was shrug his shoulders and ask me to keep thinking. He thought I was his last hope. I didn't think many people would take the time these watches required. Not "hands-on" time, I wasn't nuts, but the time spent thinking about the problem. I'd had more than the normally required cups of coffee (black, no sugar) and I still hadn't figured out these puzzles. Quite often when a watch problem was driving me frantic, I'd pick up one of the "specials" and brood about it for a few minutes. In the past this was when I'd gotten one of my sudden brainstorms.

Meanwhile I was finishing the casing of a Waltham automatic/ day/date watch. The movement inside was a Seiko-made watch from the 1970s in a funny convergence of models, a one-piece case, almost like the Tissot. This one was made differently, since it was really just one piece. Where the Tissot required the crystal to be put over a center case projection and then secured with an outer compression ring, this Waltham utilized only a case shoulder, built in. The shoulder received a special crystal that was compressed and then lowered into the case opening. When the crystal vise pressure was released, the crystal expanded outwardly against the case and also down onto the dial. Thus the movement was secured in place. Sort of simple when you think about it...and now I stood up, grabbed my cup of coffee (black, no sugar), and stormed into the office to be mad at myself.

For well over a year, I'd been trying to think of something to save the unique Tissot chronograph, and there was nothing that could be done. Why was I mad at me? As I was installing the new crystal into the Waltham, I realized that if I changed the *type* of crystal in the Tissot I could pull off a "Barry."

The broken case pieces of the Tissot, in effect three concentric circles, fit together and could be picked up as one piece. When in the case, unbroken, the crystal was pressed into place and the assembly was done. This was a smooth-sided crystal, just a tiny bit too big, thus secured by the outer compression ring. Once again, as it had for over sixty-five years, a puzzle months old was solved by a twenty-second insight.

I located my two tubes of epoxy chemicals and filled a discarded watch crystal with first the resin and then the hardener and thoroughly mixed them. I had five minutes to complete my bright idea. Using a special watchmaker tool, a round toothpick, I laid a coating of epoxy on the smooth top part of the case and then very carefully put the "assembled" top part of the case in place. Onto the desk next to my bench, I very gently laid a ten-pound block of stainless steel on the Tissot case. Since this was a five-minute epoxy, I set a timer for an hour and retreat into the office for a cup of coffee (black, no sugar).

The timer startled me as I was finishing the staff on a Longines, and I lifted the weight from the Tissot, and sure enough, the epoxied assembly held beautifully. I really put lateral pressure on the top of the case, trying to force things apart. They held just as I'd thought (nope, just as I'd hoped).

I installed the crystal and again tested the strength of the epoxy and was delighted when it held as though made at the factory. With extreme care, I used a scalpel-sharp Xacto knife to remove epoxy that had been squeezed from the case by the weight and was quite pleased with the visual results. The simplest thing was to put the chronograph movement back into the watch, reconnect the split stem assembly, and put on the special wedge-sided crystal. To my utter delight, everything worked, and even Tissot would be proud. E-mail time.

I e-mailed my customer the news and went back to the bench. Ten minutes later the phone rang, but I knew who it was. "How could it be fixed? It was only a couple of hours ago that you told me it couldn't be done. You were giving up a couple of hours ago. What happened?"

"Easy, an hour and a half ago I was fixing another watch and it helped me have a brainstorm and I figured out what to do," was my simple reply.

"I'll be by during the week. I can't believe this. Thank you so much."

The Tissot repair was the highlight of a full working weekend. The repair was even a bigger boost than the Super Bowl.

A man drove out from Worcester with a special watch, searching for help. Sadly the watch was, I think, beyond help. As I carried the watch to my bench I read the engraving on the back:

Rebecca to Brad

1942

A bit of arithmetic and I realized this ailing timepiece was sixty-seven years old. There was no crystal, minute, or second hand, and I couldn't quite read the dial. Just as I sat at the bench, I turned the crown, and *oy*, the hour hand started its rounds. I opened the case and beheld *most* of a Gruen Curvex movement. I typed "most" because there was no escape wheel bridge and no escape wheel in there. What in the hell?

The Gruen Curvex line was quite unique. Watch movements were flat, built up on a flat "pillar plate," with the wheels, gears, levers, and escapement and balance mounted between the flat base and a normal set of three flat upper bridges. Some gents' watches had cases curved to match the curved shape of a man's wrist, but the restricted available interior space was filled with a small ladies' watch movement. From the outside it was a man's curved case, but on the inside, a small movement ticked away.

The curved plates in the man's Gruen matched the curve of the case, thereby using the full length of the case interior. I'd never had to measure the curve, but I'd guess that if I put a Curvex movement on a flat plate, dial side up, there would be a three-millimeter rise in the center. Rather clever, I thought.

This particular watch was a disaster, with critical parts gone. I'd have to start a grand hunt for an escape wheel and its bridge and screw. Regretfully, I told the customer that we had two chances of finding these parts... a cliché of "slim and none"...but I would try.

I'd contacted every part supplier I could think of and had come up with exactly nothing. One supplier, who I'd given a good deal of business to, had even contacted someone in Canada, but without luck. Last week, the customer had driven in from Worcester to retrieve the Gruen, finally resigned to not having the watch repaired. I didn't know he was coming, and the watch was still on my bench mostly taken apart so it couldn't be picked up. We agreed that he'd be back on the twenty-third, and he sadly left. I'd spent time on the hunt, but actually only a very few minutes could be classified as "hands-on time." I felt badly having failed him, but what more could I do?

Two days later, the world turned difficult as I tried to salvage a gent's Banner, a real "nothing" watch. This brand was at one time rather common, having a fairly decent case and a good generic movement. The movement itself was frequently seen at the bench way back when, but very seldom seen these days. The few watches of this type to survive were those "important" to the individual owner, and this one truly was. The watch was another casualty of the winter of 2011 during the second of the January snowstorms. The owner was kept busy shoveling and managed to get an inch or so of snow up his sleeve. It was nice and snuggy in his sleeve, so the snow melted and became plain water, resulting in a rusty watch. Sheepishly he put the watch on the counter, promising me that he had not been swimming with it. Funny.

I searched my large cabinets of parts movements to no avail. While I did indeed find two plastic boxes properly labeled with the right designations, the parts I needed to replace the rusted wind and setting gears had already been "donated" to other watches. This movement was made during the late 1940s, and then they seemed to vanish. I hadn't seen one for over twenty years, but thought I'd had something. I did know there were still some boxes of old watches from the early days of Dad's store and even from Uncle Abe's things. I decided to check them out, even though I had not laid eyes on the boxes since I carried them from the old shop location to this one. I wasn't even sure just where the old boxes were. This time it only took about a half hour to find a couple of old boxes, sealed up with old-time masking tape.

The first box had about fifty cased-up old movements, none of any use, but I was most interested in the half sheet from the *Worcester Evening Gazette* from June 1960 stuffed in the box to prevent the watches bouncing around. Fifty years plus, these unwanted watches had been just sitting around. Someday I should catalog them, but I knew it wasn't worth the time.

The second box contained more or less the same collection of watches. Ladies' watches and men's that were too small to be the needed movement were easily cast aside. As I picked up each one I mentally recited the name on the dial. Waltham, Benrus, Helbros, (couldn't read it), Elgin, another Waltham (dial was too dirty), ooh, a Longines, a Gruen Curvex, an old Illinois, Waltham, a...what did I say? A Gruen Curvex? I had to dig through the little pile of discards, and sure enough I had a gold-filled Gruen Curvex... just about the right size. I usually don't move too quickly, but I was out of the office to my bench in a flash; no time for coffee.

Virtually holding my breath, I opened the case, even noting the watch lacked a crystal, but the dial was in beautiful condition. The movement inside was seemingly in perfect although dirty condition. The question of the day, was it the right movement?

For a panicky moment, I couldn't find my customer's watch; it wasn't in any of the drawers containing watches waiting for parts. Neither was it anywhere on the top of the bench. I type this smiling as I remembered how flustered I became. Finally I remembered that I'd put the wreckage of the Gruen back together and into the safe to be picked up on the twenty-third, and there it was. Moment of truth, was it the same?

I carefully placed my customer's movement next to my newly found treasure and...they were the same. For well over a year I had been looking for repair parts for this watch, and the needed movement was about twenty-five feet away buried in the office part of my shop. I could not believe it. Even the beautiful dial on my watch was the exact match for the mess on the customer's watch. It just wasn't possible, but there it was.

For the hell of it, I tried to wind my discovery, and it was completely unwound. To my complete surprise, the balance began to turn, not well, but freely. Just unreal, I thought.

I returned to the office, closed up the box of old watches, and sat with a cup of coffee (black, no sugar) and mentally composed an e-mail to my customer. I told him that a very workable movement had suddenly turned up and his treasured watch could after all be saved. I did not have the nerve yet to tell him that I'd found the watch not a thousand miles away, but twenty-five feet from my bench. I would tell him, though; we'd talked over the phone quite a bit. I hoped he'd understand.

It was still not worth the time and effort to catalog everything here...in both of these long lost boxes there was only a single watch worth even having...until the moment one was actually needed. They would sit there once again until, in desperation, I turned to them as an absolute *last* resort. I bid both boxes a wry "farewell" and consigned them once again to oblivion.

I sent the e-mail, and the next day I received an excited phone call. I explained that a good movement had "materialized," even having a beautiful dial, and the watch would be ready in about two weeks. I promised to send him another e-mail when it was time to pick up the Gruen. I'd make the grand location confession in person.

The actual "restoration" went almost too easy. The new parts fit perfectly, and I had a dozen new unbreakable mainsprings and a beautifully fitting crown. After some more hunting, I located the old GS Crystal Catalog and quickly located the correct "MX" crystal. With fingers crossed I went to the cabinet and took out the crystal made for this watch. Now (I couldn't believe it) I was down to five of these. At last, the case was polished and cleaned, the new crystal was fit, three new hands were found, and the watch was cased and ready for the customer. All he had to do was to locate and choose a new strap. First, I had to explain where I finally found the movement to use in restoring his fine watch. I would be happy to see him on the twenty-third.

There was always some new problem. This time, it was a lithium battery that kept falling out of the really inexpensive LCD movement. The battery that had been installed was a 2016, which translates to 20 mm in diameter and 1.6 mm thick. The diameter was critical, but the only other battery was the 2025, somewhat thicker, but still, I found, thin enough that there was nothing to hold the battery down, thus not making contact permanently.

Wait a minute, I thought, there used to be a gizmo...sort of an aspirin-sized disc of rubber with sticky goo on the bottom. This was stuck onto a battery to, in effect, double its thickness, causing the back of the watch to actually press down and keep the battery in place. I had seen some here in the shop a number of years ago. Now where in the world could they be? I thought about it and suddenly remembered seeing them years ago in my late friend Vinnie's store, in a plastic small parts cabinet. One that had been given to me shortly after his death.

Where was the cabinet now? Oh, it was out front in the tall bookcase against the left wall. I took the cabinet from its shelf and sat to hunt through the drawers for the rubber "buttons." All kinds of material and watch parts were in there, in drawers I'd never looked into. One was full of watch movements. Out of curiosity, I poked through the watch movements as I removed it completely from the cabinet. Wonder of wonders, the next drawer down held the supply of "rubber buttons" I'd been hunting for. I grabbed them and scooted to the bench to try them out. They worked perfectly, and the problem with the LCD watch was solved.

I still had to put the cabinet back in place, but first I poked through that drawer of movements. Really a bunch of nothing much except for a one-and-a-half-inch square plastic box labeled…This was *not* possible…Gruen 311. The damn plastic box was full of Gruen 311 movements…the very miserable thing I'd been searching the world for without any luck. Then one turned up in my own back room and a box of them out front in an old cabinet from Vinnie from Worcester.

Now I had a good supply of Gruen 311 movements in the Gruen drawer. I doubted I'd ever need any of them again. In fact, I'd bet a cup of coffee that I wouldn't.

A man limped into the shop, obviously in some pain. I guess I had an inquiring look, and he explained the ice under the snow got him and he did a job on his ankle and lower leg. He was afraid that he damaged his watch when he slipped and fell backward, landing hard in a spread-eagle position, the watch slamming down on the icy sidewalk. In any event, it hadn't been running properly since the fall. I wrote the watch up for a complete overhaul. The watch was one of the new ETA automatics. No matter how high-tech, modern, and handsome, a watch would lose the argument with a sidewalk every time. I admit it was an easy job, and three weeks later the customer walked into the shop, walking without a trace of a limp and a smile on his face. Of course I recited the "commercial," and he promised to bring the watch back if there were any problems. As he happily left the shop, I sensed a tiny voice trying to be heard. I wasn't sure what thought was trying to surface, but there was work to be done.

How often had I said to myself, "Now I've seen everything"? A package came in with the normal variety of "go aheads" and "estimates, please." One, marked to just proceed, had a tale of woe harkening back to the days of the sixth grade at Granite Street School in Worcester.

In disbelief I read, "Don't say a word. Just fix this watch. The owner's DOG ate the watch." Not his homework, but his Hamilton pocket watch. What a mess. The crystal was mostly gone as were the minute and hour hands. There were teeth marks in the dial. The back of the watch case was dished in, and again, there were more teeth marks. I thought maybe I should give the watch to the dentist across the hall. Then to my disgust, I realized my hand was *wet,* yuck! The dog had really eaten the watch. No way was I going to work on this watch in this condition. I dropped the entire watch into a large Folgers's coffee tub, one I'd punched drain holes into, squirted in a double load of Dawn detergent, and turned on the hot water. While my "watch washer" did its thing, I took time for a cup of coffee (black, no sugar).

Ten minutes under hot running fresh water, followed by a trip through my special dryer, and I could bring myself to touch this poor Hamilton. Oh, my "special watch case and band dryer" was born a *toaster oven.* I simply put the watch cases and bands, wet from washing, onto a broiler tray, set the heat at 250 degrees, and turned the toaster on for about ten minutes. Worked like a charm; everything came out perfectly clean and dry, with no time of mine wasted. It proved to be a great idea, but for the one time I decided to make toast for lunch. Whatever had gone through that toaster oven gave a never-to-be-forgotten taste to lunch that day. Now I had two toasters.

I loved my "watch case drier." I also laughed a little bit every time I received a brochure that included a "high-tech drier" at a special price of over $200.

The "real" one does indeed have a blower beneath it, but I enjoy my version at only $30 or so. I'd rather have the money in my bank account.

After I'd stripped the Hamilton, I was surprised at the minimal damage to the movement, so the repair was rather routine. A great deal of time was invested in restoring the cosmetic appearance of the watch. The case turned out surprisingly fine, as did the new hands and crystal, leaving only a dial that still looked like "the dog ate the watch." The owner did not want to have the dial redone…it gave the watch character.

I e-mailed my success with the Hamilton and for the hell of it asked just how big was the dog that ate the watch. The answer: "It's entered in the Kentucky Derby this spring." To be honest, I laughed, but I didn't buy it for a minute. When I returned the watch, I included in the envelope two Doggie Bone treats.

Note: I just checked the page number I'm writing on, and I can't believe that I've accumulated over 250 pages. This started as a few notes, hopefully interesting for my children and the grandkids. Preserving Marcus stories, as my girls suggested I do.

No pun intended…time goes on. Phone call this morning: "Good morning, would you be willing to attempt the repair of a 1940s man's Hamilton? The case is 14K gold and it means a lot to me. Would you look at it, please?"

I did not understand the question, but gave him directions to my shop and was told to expect him in about an hour. I wondered why he asked if I "would be willing" to repair a Hamilton? How could there be a doubt?

Sure enough, almost an hour later a man came into the shop, older than me but still walking straight and easily, but really old. I got up, saying bad things to my knees, and approached as he held out the Hamilton. The watch brought a big smile to my face as I exclaimed, "Oh, this is a good one indeed…14K heavy case with a 987 movement in it. How could you even question my willingness to repair this great watch? I'm really curious to know."

He shrugged and said, "My wife and I were in the big mall in Natick on Saturday, and I took the watch into a couple of fancy jewelry stores to see about having the watch repaired. In both stores, a clerk asked why I would want to bother with such an old and out-of-date watch…wasn't that a waste of money? This watch was given to me in celebration of my return from the service. My whole family chipped in whatever little money they had way back then, and it's a treasure to me. Would you be willing to try the repair?"

What could I say? "Look, this is one of the, in my opinion, best watches ever made. It only lacks some of the 'snob' prestige of certain

Swiss watches, but it's better. I'd be both happy and proud to make this like new. But I admit it's in almost new condition, which tells me you've always taken very good care of your treasure."

I couldn't resist adding, "The so-called jewelry people today do not understand the special meaning of a treasured old watch to the owner. The watch may be the last reminder of a beloved elder, a sorely missed wife or husband, or as in your case, the thankful reminder of returning from a bad situation. They just want to sell you a new whatever that may or may not last through the guarantee period. The watch will be fine, I promise."

I took the usual information, and we shook hands as I promised to send a card when the watch was ready to be picked up. What was it I was told so often? "Barry, we may 'only' repair watches, but never forget we are taking care of people." I could still hear the voices from the distant past and marveled at how right they were.

Business slowed up with the lousy winter weather as people were stuck inside more, but I had to admit that today's watches, even those without quality, were more rugged than those of years past. I still kept busy. February ended with a trio of boxes from different towns, but each one had an ETA watch movement inside, but with three different brand names. Again a little voice was bothering me, but I couldn't quite hear it. Was there really something not 100 percent with this very good watch? Hope not!!

As I typed this, the world was mourning with and worried about the aftermath of the horrendous Japanese earthquake and subsequent tsunami. A major concern and danger was the nuclear plants and their stability.

Hearing the news got me thinking about my first experience with radioactivity. Many years ago, many, many years ago, watch companies and watchmakers actually used *radium* as the number on watch dials and in minute and hour hands for the purpose of making it easy to tell time in the dark. It was quite normal for any watchmaker to use a wax-based radium compound to refinish the hands on a watch in the process of repair. Now, in 2011, I often had to redo the luminescence in a modern watch, but with a lumi compound that contained *no* radium and had *no* radioactivity. The new material did not glow as bright as the radium but worked well enough.

Old habits die hard. Especially really old habits. I first learned the phrase "radium hands and dial" at age ten. Out of habit, I still occasionally, and without realizing it, told customers that I'd put "new radium" into the hands of their watches. Sometime people reacted instinctively to that word, radium, and I quickly explained that it was merely the term I learned as a little kid, and it still slipped out. Most people would smile and say they understood and agreed not to worry about it. *Most* people.

The TV and newspapers had been trumpeting the "extreme peril" from the radiation escaping the facilities in Japan. The news reports brought certain words into the public conscience. On Thursday early afternoon, a young woman came to the shop to pick up her husband's watch, newly overhauled and made to look as it should. I'd changed the crown, gaskets, and crystal and redid the lumi in the minute, hour, and sweep second hands. As I always did, I carefully explained just what repairs had been done to this higher-grade Swiss watch, detailing the cleaning and oiling, the changing of important parts, the water resistance of the case, and, last, renewing the radium in the three hands. It just came out…out of habit.

"You did *what* to my husband's watch?" she yelled at me, dropping the envelope on the counter and bounding from the shop. Into the elevator, and she was gone. Nothing I could do but fold the money and put it into the envelope with the watch and put everything into the safe. To be blunt, I had no idea what set the woman off.

Later in the afternoon, a man entered the shop, a man with an unhappy expression who simply asked, "What did you say that set my wife off? She kept saying radium…radiation…over and over."

Oy! Carefully I explained just what I had done to repair his watch and then added my boyhood training and the use of the word radium when referring to the redo of the lumi in the hands, and I really apologized to him. I was quite relieved when I saw his expression change as he removed his watch from the envelope and put it on.

He truly surprised me when he grinned and said, "I thought it might be something like that. When I was little we had a Big Ben alarm clock that my dad always said had a radium dial and hands. Almost lit up a room, especially if we kids put a flashlight against its face. Anyhow, don't worry. When she calmed down, I told her we still have a clock with radium hands up in our attic." We shook hands, I gave him the receipt, and he left having reassured me that all was well.

I t was almost April and I have almost never felt so foolish as this Tuesday. Setting up the usual group of six watches for overhauls, I alternated them for the sake of balance and began. The first three came apart as normal, and it was obvious the fourth would be just as easy. Number five was a vintage Rolex with about 135,000 miles on it, but it would turn out fine. I was a little surprised at how clean number four, a day/date Seiko quartz, seemed to be. Hands, dial, day/date unit, and holding plate, then I flipped over the watch to take apart the circuit, train, and rotor…into the parts basket. There was a round plate that secured the spring and gears of the date unit that wouldn't fit into the parts basket, so I tucked it next to the disassembled movement. Holding the plate in heavier tweezers, I gave it a quick inspection, first one side then turned it over, and…I saw a "U" inscribed on one side of the plate.

This was something I did, especially on hold-down plates that had no indication of which side was "up." The "U" even looked like my writing, so I tucked the plate safely into the cleaning recess and picked up the back of the case to see when I last repaired this Seiko. What the hell?

The marking on the back of the case told me I'd completely overhauled this Seiko…last week! After I'd cased up the watch, and watched it for the required few days, I actually and stupidly put the watch back into the "to do" box rather than the "shop done" box. If I wasn't such a good boss I would dock my pay for lost time.

Into the office for a cup of coffee (black, no sugar) and a good sulk. I hoped that this was not an "elderly moment."

Watches came in, thankfully. It had been sort of slow, but signs of life (and spring) were most welcome. A man came in with an "almost too new" automatic that, on exam, was another of the ETA automatics...the new model. This one was creating a problem because the wearer, a *tax specialist*, said the watch had been recently stopping, causing him to miss a couple of appointments. He was also off schedule and this was his "impossibly busy season." I commented that the watch didn't like taxes just like most people. No reaction.

That aggravating little voice was way in the back of my head again.

I needed the weight of a man's automatic to balance a group of six, so I made this ETA the number two. First was a ladies' Longines mechanical, then the ETA, a ladies' Bulova, and then...a Bulova 11ANACD. A really good watch with an unsuspected design flaw. Suddenly that little voice was not so little. The "flaw" in the 11ANAC was the lack of mass in the oscillating weight. The following model corrected that flaw with the famous heavy alloy oscillating weight. Could that be what was sending these ETAs in for repair? Could it?

Each of the ETAs I'd had appeared to not require an overhaul but would not keep running. I knew that one began to give trouble when the owner caught something-or-other and was confined to home. After recovery he picked up the watch and went back to his normal routine...a busy one. The number two in this group of six belonged to a man now sitting at his desk doing taxes day after day, his left hand probably used to hold down papers...not getting a lot of physical motion.

These movements were much flatter than the automatics of years past. The weights were also flat and not that heavy. Before I took number two apart, I manually wound the watch and put it on the timing machine, which, as I suspected, showed a beautiful record, just a gain of about six seconds per day. I was getting paid to overhaul the watch, so I stripped it so I could give it a full thirty-hour run, not just a few seconds on the timer. I needed to call Bobby.

I called, and he answered himself. I sensed he was relieved to hear my voice, which didn't make me happy. "Barry, I think we have trouble with that ETA automatic. I'm having issues with one I just did; belongs to a local CPA, and the watch keeps stopping. It ran perfectly on the auto winder but now—"

I interrupted, "It stops and starts and it's messing up his tax season schedule. I have a couple of the same watches with the same problem. It is almost like those—"

Bob's turn, "—Bulova 11ANACs we had the same problem with. I'd really hate to see a similar fault in these watches. They are really very good, but if they are that sensitive to a lessening of motion...then there's a real problem."

"Bob," I cut in, "it's worse than a real problem. Remember I told you the worst situation is the watch that *sometimes* acts up, no rhyme or reason. When you have it, the watch is perfect, but give it back to the owner and it reverts to trouble. Even a totally dead watch is more reliable...you know it won't work. Same with a watch that is perfect... you can rely on it to work as it should. Let's keep in touch with this."

End of phone conference and back to the bench. I really hoped that Bob and I were wrong about this. It really was a good design, and—surprise—the fifth watch in this group was a ladies' version of this watch, very similar, but smaller. I hoped the problem wouldn't carry over in the ladies' movement. I had a note on my ticket that said this watch seemed to stop, but then ran great. Oy, big time.

Ten days later and I was having the "vapors" over this ladies' ETA automatic. It was a Baume & Mercier by trade name, with a date unit, but one of the ETA modern automatics. This unit was used by Baume, TAG, Omega, Movado, Breitling, and who knows who else. For some time now, Bob and I had been exchanging sad tales of trouble with this seemingly fine watch. There was something not right.

Back to the phone. I tell Bob my ETA wouldn't run past the middle of the morning, and he replied that a lot of his quit between 7:00 and 8:00 a.m. He had even been personally wearing some, knowing that he was quite active all day, and even wore the watch to bed, but to no avail.

I was positive that both of us were doing perfect clean-and-oil overhauls, so my mind went to something stupid. Honestly, as I thought of the word "stupid," my mind's eye saw Uncle Abe smiling and nodding yes.

I was almost convinced the problem was the mainspring, the basic, simple, modern, unbreakable mainspring, introduced by Elgin in 1955. How could this be?

An idea: I called a longtime material supplier, the McCaw Company, the Bestfit people, out west somewhere. I was on the East Coast and everything was out west. I got on the phone with a nice-sounding young man and related my problems with these ETA automatics in all of their configurations. Before I could describe anything further, he stopped me by saying, "You have to change every last mainspring in every last one of those watches as part of the repair."

He continued as I sat up straight, "We don't know why, but we're selling an impossible amount of mainsprings for all of the ETA self-wind models. Our longtime regular customers, the ones we know well enough to converse with, have been going nuts over these. There is something with the mainsprings, but I don't know what."

Oh joy, I was not nuts after all…this was truly something stupid. That magic word was turning out to be the problem. I asked if he knew how many different models there were of these watches, but he didn't know the total variety. A quick decision. "Send me two of each spring, now if not sooner. Thanks." We said good-bye.

Instant phone call to Bobby. "Bob, I just called McCaw, and before I got out the whole tale of woe, the guy told me I had to replace every mainspring in every model. I can't believe this. It's stupid. Just like my problem with the Bulova 11ANAC so long ago. He didn't know what the trouble is, but they are selling a ton of these springs. I ordered two of each."

"Good idea. Let me know how many different springs you get. I'll be in touch."

My curiosity aroused, I went to my bench and grabbed the ladies' Baume ETA. Taking off the auto unit as a single unit, I withdrew the mainspring barrel. Lifting off the ratchet wheel, I flipped the barrel and pressured off the barrel cap. I wanted to see the mainspring, and as I removed it, I was astounded at the weakness of the spring. Almost as weak as I'd ever run across, and in an automatic, with sweep unit and a calendar section. Now I couldn't wait to see just what spring came in for this watch.

There was now, on top of everything else, another thing I'd noticed about these watches that did not ring true. Not really wrong, but enough to make an impression. A task for tomorrow. What a day.

These pages contain many instances of me solving a perplexing puzzle. At first I was leery of sounding too proud of myself. Happily, in April of 2011, I was able to prove to myself that I too was capable of, dare I say it...being plain dumb.

I had overhauled a gent's Rolex, a Greenwich model, automatic, day/date with a twenty-four-hour hand in addition to the minute and hour hands. I received the watch back after a week, with the customer complaining about being unable to properly secure the screw-down locking crown. This Rolex had something I'd not seen before. The locking crown, smaller than any other man's crown, was tucked into what I referred to as "ears" projecting at the traditional three o'clock position. I admit that I too found it awkward to secure the crown. I spoke to the customer, who had left the watch with one of my retail customers, and after a series of questions, he reluctantly admitted that he had very little finger dexterity. He worked construction of a very heavy nature as a foreman, but was a menace to himself with a small hand tool. We ended on good terms, he realizing that it was the combination of *his* fingers and that particular watch that gave him a problem.

I'd opened the watch case of the Rolex in order to check the alignment of the movement to the case opening for the stem and crown.

It was fine, but I decided to run the watch for three days on the auto winder, "just to be really sure." Opening and closing the case of a Rolex was a difficult job, due to the extra designing of the case to ensure water security. To properly open or close the case required the removal of the heavy link band, so for the checking I merely hand turned the case back and put the watch onto the winder. I confess this was the very first time I'd ever put a "hand-sealed" watch on the watch winder. Naturally the Rolex ran perfectly, and I returned it to the store the following Friday. I received a call late in the afternoon... the watch was picked up and the customer was quite happy with the quick service.

Tuesday, a really furious Rolex owner called me directly to bitterly state that the perfect Rolex had fallen apart and the case back was loose in his hand. Of course this was not remotely possible, and I had to really talk the owner into bringing the watch back for me to return the Rolex to the way it should have been. I hung up totally puzzled as to what went wrong with this watch. For two days I mentally reviewed my handling of the watch, and suddenly, on Thursday, while hand starting the case back of a Wittnauer, I suddenly realized what had gone so wrong with the Rolex. Idiot that I can be, I'd hand tightened the screw-back Rolex case to check the running, but had actually forgotten to properly tighten the case. A slight turning of the case and the back fell off into the owner's hand.

With a sense of shame, I decided to confess all to the customer when he met me on Friday to leave the watch once again. Thankfully there had been no damage to the movement, and the owner said he understood how such an oversight could occur. Said he too had experienced such a "senior moment" (heavy sigh).

A very long winter has slowly given up, and I was able to get a start, albeit a late start, on the boat. As always, watches continued to need my help. More trouble with one of the newer ETA automatics meant many calls back and forth, to and from Bob. This we'd have to puzzle out. I was more convinced than ever that something really stupid was going on with the ETAs. One, a small gent's watch that held an even smaller ladies-sized movement, ran perfectly when manually wound, but wouldn't go through the night on the watch winder. With an abundance of frustration, I put a piece of wood under the back side of the auto winder to tilt the unit more vertical. I was quite saddened to discover the watch began to run beautifully, now being fully wound by a *vertical* watch winder. More calls with Bob, and more certainty that we were on to something, but we just couldn't figure it out. Rats.

Almost the end of April 2011, and a younger (than me) man came into the shop. Usual greetings, and he handed me a gent's Rolex, asking if I remembered the watch. Uh-oh, I thought, when did I do this? I just didn't remember it, and I was the one who could remember a watch, just not its owner. Oh well, nothing to do but ask the problem.

"No problem, the watch is running like new, which it really is." What in the hell?

"I see you don't remember the watch or me. In February I was in with this thing full of water. I'd taken a bad fall on the ice, and I landed backward, busting the crystal, packing a lot of snow into the watch. It melted and seeped under the dial. Anyhow, that afternoon I brought the watch in to show you. I was bothered that you got excited and said that it had to be pulled apart 'right now' and put into your solutions to stop any rust and save the movement."

Okay, now I was remembering the incident, but not the guy, and I did remember that he didn't leave the watch.

He continued, "I thought you were trying to scare me and build up a big deal on my costly Rolex, so I asked if you were an authorized Rolex service guy. You said no, so I took the watch back and decided to send it to Rolex. I have to admit, I sort of bad-mouthed you over the rush, rush push on the repair. Anyhow, the next day, a Friday, I mailed the watch to Rolex, and everything went downhill from there. The watch was in the mail over the weekend, and Monday was President's Day and there was no delivery. Rolex didn't get the watch until Tuesday afternoon. I got an estimate saying the movement was beyond any repair and needed replacement. It was virtually rusted beyond help. It cost me a hefty bundle for a new movement and crystal and all that, just because I didn't believe you were telling the truth. I'm in here to apologize. Also to tell you I told the friends I bad-mouthed you to that you were right all along. I'm sorry," he finished.

My turn: "I don't blame you at all. You show your multi-thousand-dollar watch to a guy you never saw before and he gets all excited and insists the watch has to be worked on right this second...I'd be leery too. The real problem is you didn't know me. Wait a second."

I walked around to my bench and came back with a half taken apart Omega Constellation and its case with the repair tag attached.

"See the date on this. I took it in two hours ago. The crystal was completely broken off, and water was running out of the case, even worse than yours. I've known the owner for about thirty years, and I've overhauled the watch a few times over that stretch. When I said the watch needed starting that minute, he just nodded, gave me his name, which I never, ever remember, and left. I'll call him when the watch is ready and the new crystal comes in and is installed. The only part needed will be the crystal, and that's only because the watch was here within the hour of the accidental swim. And that's only because he's had all those years to build confidence in me. It's too bad, but not really your fault."

We shook hands and he left, saying, "I'll be seeing you again, but I hope not for quite a while. Thanks and good luck." Back to my bench and the Omega.

The first ten days of May 2011 were, in a word, screwy. Four prestige watches came into the shop; two walk-ins and two from trade accounts. Four watches that had nothing wrong with them yet wouldn't run. After those ten days, I was totally disheartened at the world of watches I lived in. Actually, I realized that I was unhappy at the people who populated my world of watches.

First, the FedEx man brought in a "present," a Cartier that had been overhauled and then returned three times to the store. My task was to determine the cause of the problem and report along with the estimate. I didn't do the original overhaul, but the watch made the trip from Illinois for me to figure the puzzle. The envelope told of the repair history and the importance of the Cartier for this—holy cats—eighty-two-year-old gentleman. I bet myself a cup of coffee (black, no sugar) this was nothing but a worn smooth genuine crown. I should have bet more, because it took fifteen seconds to feel my own fingers slipping over the crown, with no winding occurring at all. I sent a sarcastic e-mail to the store and placed the watch into the small job "to do" box. Then I sent an e-mail of apology, explaining how angry I'd become with "watchmakers" not familiar with such a basic problem.

Tuesday's "victim" was worn in by a customer of Dad's store from many years ago. Here my screwed-up memory was on display. I didn't give him time to remove his watch before saying, "When I fixed that Longines about five years ago, I told you the crown was going to need replacing before long or you wouldn't be able to wind the watch. I'm surprised it lasted this long."

He removed his watch, passed it across the counter, and in less time than required to type this, I'd found my answer. A new crown would be put on, but I pointed out the obvious dust and dirt under the crystal of this dress watch and brought out a ticket to write up the overhaul and crown repair. When I asked his name he just laughed out loud.

"You remembered my Longines, remembered how long ago you fixed it, and reminded me that you warned me about the crown, and you can't remember my name? You are something. I'll wait for the card you send when the watch is ready. I still live on Highland Street, and you'll remember my name on your own one of these days. See you later." With that he slowly walked from the shop, no name written on the tag. I hoped he was correct...that before the watch was repaired, the name would come to me. I was glad we didn't bet coffee on it.

Wednesday afternoon, it continued. An elderly lady (about my age, so I could label her elderly) came in and presented a vintage Omega in what was probably a 14K gold case. She had difficulty removing the watch, as she struggled to manipulate the fold-over clasp, and I just knew what the problem was. True enough, the watch had been repaired elsewhere and wouldn't run through the night, even though it had been sent back to the repair center twice. Once again I had to explain that the problem was not the watch but fingers that were no longer what they once were. I gently explained that the crown size that was correct years ago was now too small and she couldn't grip the crown to wind it. She'd be back on Monday, and I'd give her a completely run-down watch that she'd be able to wind.

Friday I picked up watches for repair and delivered those I'd finished during the week. A group of five was rubber banded together and a sixth was handed to me by itself. The singled-out watch had been repaired through a store not too far away and was not running properly, having been returned three times with the same complaint. Sadly, I again just knew what was wrong as I accepted…wait a second… this was the same model Cartier from Monday, but with a different dial. Same 18K case, with four side-inserted casing screws and the same too damn small crown, one worn smooth, no less.

Before my customer could say anything, I said, "The problem is the crown is worn smooth, especially if the owner is, let's say, the original owner. I'll take care of it, but this won't need any additional repairing."

Four newly "repaired" watches, each with the same unsuspected problem. I checked all four carefully, and as I expected, all four had very fine records on the timing machine. All were carefully cleaned and the cases given a cosmetic going over, carefully timed, and then returned with a fatal flaw that wasn't the watch's fault. There was not a single thing I could criticize about the repairs, but four different watchmakers didn't know enough about the fact that people own and wear watches, and many of these people were truly the "problem" with their watches.

Once again, actually four times again, I played my little "game" with my daughters. Each, brought up in the jewelry store listening to their daddy speak to his customers as he spoke about their watches, had absorbed lessons that professional watchmakers didn't get. Of course I wondered if they'd even been taught those lessons.

I laugh, but sadly, as I write that at the first mention of "extra thin, extra high-grade watches," each of the girls diagnosed the problem as "crown trouble, I bet." Any time I mentioned a problem with an automatic wind watch, they asked for the age and general health of the wearer.

I, with no memory for names, did remember when I first learned the lesson. The sad young man who, in 1947, spoke to Uncle Abe about his inability to find a watch that would run a full day. Uncle Abe shook his head sadly and explained the problem was his hand, never fully recovered from injuries suffered someplace in Europe. He wore the watch on his left hand, and the right hand couldn't grip the crown, even the larger ones of the day, to wind the watch. The right hand could only close about 90 percent, so doing small things were beyond his ability, and winding a watch was one thing he couldn't do. Of course the problem was solved by Uncle Abe using a larger and thicker crown.

Uncle Abe suggested he consider the purchase of an automatic wind watch, a new feature becoming more widespread in moderate-priced watches. A good trade-in was offered, but the young man declined, saying he'd taken the watch from a "German who had no further use for it." He wanted it as a reminder that he had made it home and in one piece. Then he added, "Believe me, the hand is nothing that I can't happily live with...because I am living." I saw the watch again in 1951, when I overhauled it. I was quite proud that the customer remembered me.

On Friday, I'd returned that second Cartier on my rounds and asked the store owner to check the different feel of the new crown. One touch and her eyes lit up. I stopped her from winding the watch and suggested she call the owner, and when he came in for the watch, give it to him unwound and have him "test" the crown.

On Monday, the shop phone rang at eleven o'clock, and sure enough, the customer had come in for the Cartier. She laughed as she reminded me that her eyes lit up and that was how she described the gentleman as he held the watch to wind it. I was glad the customer left the store happy.

I was quickly corrected.

"No, he left *furious* with the other store. We are the heroes to him, having solved the problem so easily. I think you made a loyal customer for me. Thanks."

The phone rang just as I momentarily squeezed the trigger on an air can. I wanted to check the spin and freedom of a Waltham staff I'd just fitted. Good. It was free as a bird and spinning like a propeller.

"Good afternoon, watch repair. How may I help you?"

"Years ago, there was a Marcus Jeweler on what was then Front Street in Worcester. There was an older guy, the owner, and a real, real big teenager that I think was learning to be a watchmaker. The older man cannot still be alive, but are you maybe the really big kid? I've been looking for that kid for weeks now."

What the heck, I thought. "Yes, that was me, the kid. The older guy was my uncle Abe, my prime watch repair teacher. His store was on Lower Front Street before the city of Worcester tore it down and demolished a vibrant business area to build the Galleria. I bet they wish that old Front Street was still there. Anyway, how can I help you?"

"In the late forties, maybe 1949, my father brought a watch to you for repair. He said that before you looked inside, you noticed the back was engraved in Jewish printing. He told you where and how he ob—"

The caller was still talking, but my mind was spinning. "Dear Lord," I thought, "it is not possible...not after all these years...can't be..." I didn't want to see that watch again. I didn't want to service it again. How could I get out of this?

When I was a kid, I didn't really understand what that watch and its history represented. Now I truly understood the horror behind that watch. My mind screamed at me, "NEVER AGAIN!" I focused back on the caller...

"I learned of this watch last week. After sixty years of silence, my father told me he was given the watch in Germany but wouldn't say anymore. I don't understand, but my father says the 'owner' still visits him at times and that he shows him that the watch is still safe and cherished. I couldn't get any other details, but Dad was crying as he spoke to me. Do *you* know what he won't tell Mom or me?"

My reply: "Yes, I know."

"Dad is going...he doesn't have too much time left. He directed me to look for the 'huge kid' and to have the watch cleaned a last time. Dad has led a good life, and he says he knows where he's going, so he wants the watch in perfect condition, as it's going with him. He is determined to find, once again, the man who gave him the watch and to return it to him, with gratitude and love. We're short of time and I'd like to bring the watch to Milford on Tuesday morning because you'll be closed Monday for the holiday. Is that okay? Oh, can you tell me the cost of the overhaul?"

"Listen carefully, I said (through my own tears), "the watch repair was *paid in full* about sixty-two years ago by your dad and his buddies."

"But—"

"Don't even say a word. Bring the watch Tuesday, anytime at all."

"Thank you, Mr. Marcus. What's your first name? Dad said he never knew it, just knew that you were, as a kid, bigger than any of the men in his company."

Now he knew my name...naturally I couldn't remember his. If I ever really knew it. Maybe it was better that I never forgot that watch. Possibly, someday, as far from now as allowed, I'd get to greet the man who would once again wear that *blessed* watch. I hoped so.

Tuesday, after a long weekend, I got to the shop, and there was someone, seemingly waiting for me, sitting in a chair outside of the elevator. Sad looking, he stood outside the door while I "safed" the alarm system and set up for the day, then waved him in.

"Good morning, Mr. Marcus. I called last week about my dad's watch...the one given to him during what he called his 'visit to hell.'"

"I remember him and the watch quite well," I replied.

"Well, Dad passed away over the weekend. To the end, he remained worried about this watch. He was confident he'd find the man who presented him the watch and he wanted it just right...had me promise to have it taken care of...by you. The problem is the funeral is tomorrow and I must ask if there is anything you can do for him?"

I put my hand out for the watch, and it was handed to me in a rectangular old-fashioned jewelry box. Good Lord...as I lifted the cardboard cover I read,

A. Marcus, Jeweler
Front Street
Worcester, Massachusetts

This was the box I'd put the watch into when I repaired it in 1949. Can I admit to my tears? I don't care...I admit to them.

I reverently took apart the watch for cleaning and put it into a cleaning basket by itself. This watch was to be treated as something sacred...which it was. I changed the solution in the cleaning machines and talked quietly with the veteran's grieving son.

Quietly I told him some of what his father had refused to tell his mother and added a little to what was told to him. As I moved the watch to the next cleaning tank, he declared, "I have a sense there are things you are not telling me. Why?"

I turned to him. "Your dad understood *why* and also *what*."

"How could he tell you? You were just a kid."

I had to use a very soft voice. "Do the math yourself. Your father was just a kid, not that much older than I was. That war was won with a lot of 'just a kid' soldiers who weren't old enough to legally drink. What he was telling me was about the watch, how he got it and why. Over the years, many men have told me, in telling about their particular watches, things they never told their families. Some were really funny, some were scary, and a couple choked you up. A few, like your dad's story, just took your breath away."

I pulled the watch from the cleaning tank, carefully put the watch back together, wound the watch, and put it on the timing machine, thus having to regulate to compensate for a half-minute loss.

"You are regulating a watch that will be buried with my father tomorrow morning. I'm sorry, but I have to ask, why?"

"Your father was given this watch under conditions that the mind has difficulty accepting. I think he has regarded this as only on loan, and I'm sure he would want it in perfect condition when he returns it. Bluntly, this is an extremely high-grade European watch of quite a high value. I'm humbled at being given the honor to return it to new for the return. I put my mark into the case in 1949, and I just entered today's date and ticket number in the case back. For all time, I will be proud to be part of this watch, and for that I thank you. I want your father to know that I also put in a little Hebrew letter. The symbol for *chai*, which stands for *life*. To me it is a single-word prayer."

I gently put the watch into a plastic envelope and placed it into the cotton batting in Uncle Abe's box. The plastic was to keep lint out of the watch.

Our eyes met and we shook hands for a long time. He said not a word; rather, he nodded, turned, and left. I stood there and watched as he entered the elevator and didn't move until the door closed. I sighed and went into the office for a cup of coffee (black, no sugar).

W ow, three boxes of watches mailed out. Not a lot of watches, but going to three places...two stores and a watch owner. This one was special, a pocket watch cased chronograph with wires factory soldered to the case at the "12" and "6" positions. This made the watch a *wrist* watch and was an innovation for the First World War. Up to then, watches were carried in a front-of-the-hip watch pocket. If you were lying in the trenches and needed the time, you had to pick yourself up enough to remove the watch from the pocket and....you were killed by a sniper. A watch bound somehow to the wrist could be read just by turning the wrist to the right position.

Both this watch, engraved with the name and number of a British artillery regiment, and the special timing features were invaluable for artillery usage. Another piece of history still functioning as it had on the day it was made (hey) *almost* a hundred years ago. My head picked up suddenly as I realized…this was May 2011. The First World War began in August 1914. I picked up the watch and asked, "What did you see and where did you see it?" I remembered asking the same questions of a clock from a Messerschmitt 109E. Neither time did I get an answer.

A gentleman several years my senior slowly walked into the shop. Because of his short sleeve shirt, I could easily see the 1940s-era watch that sort of looked like a Hamilton, which I think of as the best of the time.

I was a little puzzled as he hesitated three or four times before finally taking off the watch and handing it to me. Even as I took the watch, he kept a loose hold until I removed the watch from his reach. Naturally I thought, "What the heck?"

As I walked to my bench, I turned the watch over to get a quick look at the condition of the case, and just as naturally there was engraving…

My love,
Never "goodbye"
Always, "see you soon"
1946

I checked the movement and noted that it seemed the watch hadn't seen any service for years. As I walked back, I commented, "Yes, I can restore this to 'new.' Very sincere engraving on the back. This must mean a lot to you."

I instinctively knew his reply.

He said, "You are very aware, aren't you? I was one of the marines virtually blown up in the battle for Sugar Loaf Hill on Okinawa in 1945. Medics and buddies got me to the beach, and a boat got me to the hospital ship, even though I knew I was as good as dead. The last thing I remembered, even to this day, was saying good-bye to my fiancée back home. Obviously I survived, beat up but alive. Eventually the hospital ship reached the States. My second day in the stateside hospital, I awoke to find my girl sitting beside my bed, gently holding my bandaged hand. I never saw anyone so beautiful."

He sighed and continued, "I could only say, 'Honey, I had to say good-bye to you.'

"She jumped to her feet and yelled at me like a marine corporal, 'You SOB, you *never* say *good-bye* to me again, you hear me? You say 'see you soon.' Got that through your head?' Believe me, I sure did.

"This watch was her wedding present to me. In all these years I've only taken it off when there was a danger of it getting wet. I worked at a desk, so I wore it to work. She died eight years ago, and since then, except for the water danger, I haven't removed this watch from my wrist, even when it stopped running five years ago. I tell time with a cell phone. Now I think it's time to have it serviced. How much longer do I have, and I want the watch to go with me in running condition. I'm just upset at having to be parted from her words while you fix the Hamilton."

I have been trying without success to understand why I did what I did next.

I asked him to sit for a few minutes while I checked something in his watch. He sat, and I went back to my bench, wondering if I was doing right. I took a chance.

I returned to him, sat down, and strapped his watch back onto his wrist. I waved him off as he started to ask...

I interrupted, "I think you should wear the watch as you have for so many years. I've taken out the movement and used Scotch Tape to fasten the dial back into the case. There are no hands, but the watch hasn't been running for years anyhow. The case belongs with you, and I understand that. In the meantime I'll service and time the movement, and I don't need the dial for that. When I'm set, I'll call you, and you come in planning to spend some time as I redial and re-case the movement. Okay?"

Silently he nodded agreement and wiped his eyes. As he left, he hesitated, turned, and asked, "Why?"

I replied, "I understand."

He straightened as much as possible and gave me that "mock salute" old-timers will give each other and left as I returned it. Time for coffee (black, no sugar).

The Hamilton movement was third in the next group I serviced. The old marine was called and came right to the shop, arriving a couple of hours later. This time he brought two coffees and sat while I redialed the watch, put on the hands, cleaned the case, and returned the symbol of a young couple's love to his wrist. We shook hands, and as he asked the cost of the repair, I informed him he had paid for it sixty-six years ago.

He seemed stunned, but again straightened, and we exchanged salutes.

Time passes in the watchmaker's domain (no pun intended), and the normal selection of ailing and injured watches takes my time. On a very quiet morning, as I concentrated deeply on an Accutron 218 that was in trouble, the chime indicating the door opening bonged its thing. I called out, "Please be patient for a few minutes...I really can't let go of this poor watch."

In reply I heard, "Good morning, sir. Take the time you need, sir. I'll just sit over here and wait, sir."

I thought, "What the hell is with the three sirs? Three sirs! Good God, *he's back!*" Forgetting the Accutron, I jumped up and bounded around the shop and front case—and my heart fell to the floor. It was my *twerp*, who had become a marine private on his way to Afghanistan. I beheld a man tired of body and spirit. One arm in a sling and his other shoulder showing bandages under his tee shirt. He rose from the chair slowly, like me an old man, and limped to the counter, hand outstretched in greeting.

"Sir, I would be honored if you would engrave my family pocket watch. Do you remember telling me you would double check the correct spelling? My dad sort of bet that you'd forgotten, sir."

"You tell your dad, not for a moment. Between us, every time I heard of another casualty from Massachusetts, my heart stopped for an instant. As far as honor, believe me, young man, the honor is mine, all mine. This is how I say thank you. I have to ask…will you be…?"

"Thank God, I will be more than fine. My injuries were many, but not of a permanent nature, and for that I'm truly grateful. Too many weren't as lucky, but that's the way it's always been, I guess, sir."

I bade him sit next to me while I engraved the old-fashioned pocket watch. I reviewed each line and had the thought that this watch was a history course in itself. From San Juan Hill in the late 1890s to Afghanistan in 2010 2011, I think it would take an entire year to read up on and study the wars and battles "seen" by this American classic. Am I allowed to say I felt and feel privileged to have been able to service this watch?

I handed him the watch, open so he could read this latest entry, and he sighed deeply. "There's no more room for engraving. Let's hope that means there will be no more need for engraving. This is enough. Thank you, sir." He turned to leave and turned back. "Oh sir, my buddies never quite understood how it was a watchmaker in the States was buying the beer, but they said to say thank you. Semper fi, sir." Again, that informal salute, and he walked out to his life.

My only thought: "Bless you, marine." I had to retreat to the office for a few quiet moments. Time for coffee (black, no sugar) and three quick phone calls to my girls to let them know my *twerp* was home.

August 2011, and I turned from the computer to answer the phone with my usual greeting, and, "Good morning, sir, I'm calling from Topeka."

In the sixth grade, I'd learned Topeka was in Kansas…This I remembered!

"Good day, how may I help you?"

"I've been advised to consult you regarding an Accutron watch that I'm having trouble with. A couple of men out here haven't been able to get it to run. There is a famous watch dealer in Boston near you, and he gave me your name and number."

We talked for a few minutes, and he would be mailing out the watch that afternoon. Another watch from another state. I guess I was still "keeping the world on time." We visited for a few more minutes, and then he warned me about the heat. I didn't understand.

"It's already hot here. What are you suggesting? I know heat here comes from out west; even my brother-in-law in Illinois warns me, but Kansas?" Uh, maybe I just flunked geography.

"It's 104 outside my store. I seriously wonder if the Accutron is getting shut down by the extreme heat. Anything is possible. You let me know…okay?"

The watch arrived, and so did the unbearable heat.

Tuesday, a man came into the shop with a vintage Rolex. He didn't smile when I gave him a friendly "Can I help you?" It was obvious to me that something was wrong and that I needed to fix it. We had a quick discussion on the day's weather. He asked me if I was willing to check out and repair his Rolex. What was this with the "was I *willing*" to look at a watch? This was how I made my living.

"Of course I'll be happy to look at your watch." I could read his reluctance as he handed me his watch. I remarked to him that I understood his attachment to such a quality timepiece.

"I sent the watch to Rolex," he said and sighed. "It was my father's, and I want to eventually pass it along to my oldest son. Rolex returned the watch without even looking at it. They said that they were no longer servicing watches this old. Dad got it in the early forties, right after he graduated from flight school."

Damn. I was getting so frustrated with these companies that did not understand the intense personal attachment people had to their watches. I'd love to talk to whoever created such a poor customer service policy. They needed to be taught that watches live with and are owned by *people*. A lesson I learned at age ten still guided me now, in 2011.

As I checked out the watch, the customer continued, "I couldn't believe their refusal; it almost broke my heart. I saw your ad in the *Uxbridge Times*. I asked a couple of people, and they said you were the man to see. You would be able to fix a watch this old."

I examined the Rolex model 645. Stupid company...the turning of the oscillating weight visibly turned all the right wheels and everything felt right. I returned to the counter. "The watch can be readily restored. Of course, if I run into a problem where parts are *not* available, I'd just assemble the watch and return it without charge."

"I can't thank you enough, Mr. Marcus. My dad flew Mustangs, the P-51, over Europe. He was an ace. On D-Day he earned a DFC and a purple heart. He was wounded while attacking a column of Tiger tanks trying to get to Omaha Beach. Later he flew escort for B-17s, all the way to Berlin and back. He became a double ace. After Germany was beat he was promoted and flew Mustangs from Okinawa guarding the B-29s going to Japan. Dad stayed in the service. When North Koreans invaded the South, he led a flight of early jets. Dad said he *never* flew without the Rolex."

He smiled. "Once when the Rolex was being serviced, he slipped while getting into his cockpit. He was hurt and out of action for two weeks. By the time he was cleared for flight, he had his watch back. Well, you know how superstitious people can be. He always wore the watch."

As I wrote up the watch, I explained that I would do my best to restore the watch for his family. I'd be in touch if I ran into any trouble. The man left happier than he was when he came in. It is funny how just that fact is so important to me.

Three days later, I needed a heavy watch to set up the balance of a set of six. The only watch heavy enough was the automatic Rolex, so ahead of schedule I had to dive into it. I easily stripped the watch, auto unit, and its many pieces/parts, the ratchet wheel assembly, and the mainspring barrel and...what the hell!? A whole section of the barrel was missing teeth or parts of teeth. Someone facing a ruined barrel had soldered on a strip of hard solder and then by hand had tried to cut teeth into the solid strip. It didn't even come close to working...five teeth were completely gone and more were badly worn. This was the end of this watch, as there weren't parts available.

Time out for a cup of coffee (black, no sugar). I felt terrible. I hated letting a watch owner down. I hated letting the watch itself down. That watch had served its master and thus this country. I had to accept defeat and just put the Rolex back together. I was procrastinating going back to work. I was on my computer looking at headlines, checking e-mails… Wait a second. I couldn't give up that easily. I might as well e-mail Dean, who had saved my bacon several times in the past. I'd learned there was no telling just what he had in older, obsolete, obscure, and precious watch parts buried in his cache. Although I had a hundred-year-old accumulation of parts, I still needed help now and then.

A plaintive e-mail asking about the part's availability and cost (I couldn't even imagine) was sent. I figured that I'd just put the Rolex under glass and set it aside on my bench for a few days while I waited to hear back. I finished my coffee…lo and behold…I had mail.

Dean had a mainspring barrel for the Rolex! Trumpets blared… cymbals clanged…the world smiled. He had one in beautiful shape, and the cost was only… "Holy cats!" And I mean a lot of cats. I'd have to call the customer before I could commit to that much money.

I called and explained the damage I had found. I had located a replacement barrel but the cost would add substantially to the repair price. I offered to split the cost of the barrel fifty-fifty. Frankly, I really wanted to restore the watch to its original glory. His reply: "The watch must be repaired regardless of the price. I believe you can bring the watch back to life."

It was the shortest e-mail I'd ever sent. "Send the barrel." I was surprised to almost instantly receive "On the way" from Dean. Smiling, I went back to the bench and finished stripping the Rolex. I thought about the phrase *bring the watch back to life* and said aloud, "I think I'll watch *Young Frankenstein* tonight."

I once again asked myself, "How can companies not recognize the depth of meaning of their watches for those who wear them?" It was beyond me.

How often have I said, "Now I've seen it all?" It didn't really matter because *now* I really had seen it all. A customer came into the shop, and as I approached, he carefully removed a larger-size modern watch.

"The watch is new and runs fine, but I can't set it for either the time or the date. I don't understand it. Can you please help me?"

"I'd be happy to help," I replied. I reached for the watch, which was a high-grade Movado watertight calendar model. Truly high grade in quality and styling; unfortunately, also high grade on the stupid design scale. On a scale of 1 to 10, this was a solid 26.

The crown, critical for resetting the time and date unit, was deeply recessed in what I called "ears" at the three o'clock position. That was bad enough, but added to that, the crown was absolutely *smooth* as a ball bearing. No wonder he couldn't set the time. It was a common problem but with an uncommon twist. This wasn't a crown worn down from years of use or older fingers that no longer had the dexterity of the past. This was a smooth, hard to grip crown that was *designed* that way. For crying out loud, this didn't just take the cake, it took the entire bakery. My fingers slipped right over the crown. It was like a bald tire during a snowstorm.

I explained the problem…the crown design. I grabbed a pair of pliers off the bench and with a bit of difficulty managed to get the watch set. As I handed the watch back, I suddenly had an "oh no" moment. "Look. This is a thirty-day month; daylight savings time is coming up, and then again in November. Bring the watch back when you need to and I'll get it set."

He was (justifiably) disgusted. "I just received this for Father's Day, so it means a lot to me. Isn't there anything you can do?"

"Movado uses only high-quality Swiss movements, and I have new crowns for them. If, and only if, the case tube is *normal*, I could put on a crown with the proper gripping cuts. It would be like getting a new tire to replace a bald one. The watch is fine for now. Why don't you take it and think about it."

Of course there was no charge for me to set the watch; I knew he'd be back.

He did come back...thirty minutes later. Smiling, he opened a bag and put on the counter a large coffee, sugar, and creamers. "You wouldn't take my money, but I bet you won't refuse coffee. Thanks again."

You know he was right. I never refuse coffee. It was very good and much appreciated.

A sixty-something man came into the shop, a new customer. Faces I usually do remember; it's names that I blank on almost instantly. He had a very "technical" problem with his watch. Would I be willing to set the time and date for him? He couldn't do it. I picked up his watch off the counter; it was a high-grade automatic, day/date stainless steel watch.

I didn't need to look at the watch. I immediately guessed what the problem was (you probably can take a guess at this point). The modern watch industry had struck again. As the man stood in front of the counter, I could see that his hands were afflicted with arthritis. Afflicted not to a serious degree, but enough to prevent the manipulation of the screw-down locking crown.

Gently I asked, "Is the problem that you can't unscrew the crown to pull it out to reset the time and date?"

"How can you tell that without even examining the watch, Mr. Marcus?"

I always hated this moment. How could I kindly say this? "When you put the watch on the counter, I saw your fingers weren't opening easily to release it. Unfortunately, because of the arthritis, you can't get a grip on the crown to unscrew it. Did you buy this recently?"

"I didn't buy it. My children gave it to me this past June for Father's Day. The kids spent a good deal of money on it. My wife's eyes popped open wide when my daughter whispered the price to her. I don't want to tell them the watch is no good. It would upset them terribly. The watch means a lot to me. The kids even had it engraved."

I turned the watch over and exclaimed, "For cryin' out loud, I had the feeling that the watch looked familiar, but how could it? I'm the one who engraved the watch. I had a heck of a time fitting all those names on the case back. I remember thinking about putting a magnifying glass into the box when I returned the watch. The watch is really an excellent watch; it's just the crown that's the problem for you."

"The kids are very proud of their gift. Is there anything you can do, or will I need to come see you every time I need to set it?"

What could I say? The watch was truly a high-quality timepiece. Anything I did would infuriate the watch company, but my concern was only for this gentleman. I took the watch to my bench. Opening the case and removing the movement, I breathed a sigh of relief. The case tube was a good-sized *friction* fit, standard size with a 2.5 mm tube thickness. I had a great diver's crown with double O ring water protection gaskets. Couldn't be better.

"Good news, sir. We can solve the problem without any difficulty. I want you to see what I'd like to do. Here is my watch." I handed him my L. L. Bean Hamilton chronograph. "The crown on my watch is exactly what I'd like to convert your watch to. I'd like you to try and catch your thumbnail under the crown, pull it out, and play with it. I just want to see if it will be a good fit for your hand."

As I expected, he was able to move the crown without any trouble. I explained the "3" position crown and that he'd be able to set the time, day, and date without any problems. The watch was left with me for the conversion and the man left the shop with a smile on his face. Time for a quick cup of coffee (black, no sugar).

Another nice spring day. I was happily working on a middle-aged Bulova while listening to Rush Limbaugh. I listened to Rush daily because he agrees with me. I was interrupted by the chime of the door opening.

I glanced up as I said, "I'll be with you as soon as I can let go of this."

I heard a woman's voice: "When you get up, please turn *him* off."

Oy. I replied, "I'll turn down the volume...it's a bit loud because my hearing is not what it used to be."

The door chime rang and the door was closed rather firmly. There went a potential repair. Not much I could do about that. When I took my next coffee break (black, no sugar), I called Julie to see how life in Maine was going. I told her about the woman leaving because Rush was on. She reminded me of the first time that happened when she and Adam were my L. L. Bean watch shipping and receiving department.

At the time, my shop was located in the old Grants Building a couple of blocks away. A woman came in with a watch in her hand. As Julie got up to help her, the woman demanded that we shut off Rush. She then let us know exactly what she thought about us letting a young child hear such nonsense. I got up from my bench, leaving the radio *on*, and nicely told the woman I would not be looking at her watch. Needless to say, she left in a huff.

Another day, another watch. In my office building, we had the typical gang mailboxes. Quite often our mailman had to come upstairs to the shop. When watches came to me through the US Post Office they were usually sent registered mail and needed a signature or the box was too big to fit into my mailbox downstairs. A couple of the mail carriers were intrigued about where the watches came from.

One morning the door chimed and the announcement was... "This box is from Kansas. They're coming from farther away, all the way to Milford. How do they find you?"

As I signed the receipt, I said, "My daughters tell me people are finding me online. I don't advertise on the Internet, but apparently that doesn't make a difference. I'm just happy when the watches come in."

The package had a single Waltham pocket watch and a short letter. Could I please give an estimate, list the problems, and give the age of the watch; any information about it and what it might be worth. I was happy to see the letter included an e-mail address. It was very convenient to send estimates via e-mail. It cut down on the amount of telephone tag I had to play with customers.

The pocket watch was a 16S seventeen-jewel Waltham Riverside in a twenty-five-year case that was in mint condition. This watch was never abused or even mistreated, which was normal for a watch of this quality. When new, it was a high-end timepiece with a matching high-end cost.

After about ten minutes, I had all the information for him, including the year the movement was made in Waltham, Massachusetts. This watch had come home from Kansas to be made right again. The only information I couldn't supply was the value. As I sold and/or bought *nothing*, I paid no attention to what a watch might be worth. I cared mostly about the watch's value to its owner.

More years in the past than I was happy to admit, I was lectured that often I was really being called upon to repair a person in addition to his or her watch. On many occasions, I'd found the repair of the person was more important.

Today was a day that fit my idea of a good day…mild temperatures, blue sky, and a walk to the Milford Post Office to mail out a nice box of completed watches. Of course even a drizzly day could be good when the errand was to mail out completed work. I had a nice relationship with the mail department. I would leave a box of finished watches for them to deliver, and a few days later one of them would bring me a check. It was a great system… mutual support…plus they were also a nice bunch of people.

I was headed back to the shop at 2:30 p.m., plenty of time to get a few more watches done. As I got off the elevator, a woman was sitting in the lobby. I assumed she was waiting for one of the doctors or the dentist across the hall. I nodded hello and unlocked the shop.

I filed the postal receipt, turned up the radio, and got right back to work. No fooling around…the boss was pretty mean. The door chimed while I had a balance staff in my hand.

"I'll be right with you. Just give me a couple of minutes, please."

"No hurry, *he* will be over in a couple of minutes. I can wait."

What kind of nonsense was this? I changed my glasses and looked up. It was the woman from the lobby. Oy. I think it was the young woman who stalked out of here when I didn't turn Rush off. Why was she back?

There was an awkward silence as I finished up with a Hamilton. Mr. Limbaugh made a point and got a reaction from the would-be customer. "Limbaugh can't really think or believe that," she said indignantly.

I got up from the bench. "Yes, he does. This is a frequent subject and, frankly, a firm belief of both him and *me*. Why do you say he doesn't believe what he says?" Truly, I did not want any kind of argument.

She shrugged and replied hesitantly, "I never listen to him. My friends have told me all about *him*."

Well, I thought, there goes the repair for sure, so I have nothing to lose. "Didn't anyone ever tell you that you can't properly judge anyone or anything from the opinions of others? You've never listened to Rush, so how can you know just what it is he believes or stands for?" I felt as if I was defending a close friend.

The young woman just looked at me and ignored what I had said. She got back to business. "After I left last time, I couldn't find any store that would repair this watch. It was my mother's favorite and doesn't run anymore. The stores all said that they couldn't fix it, but a couple told me that I should bring the watch to you." She took a deep breath. "Despite what I said, will you look at it? Please."

She handed me a long, very thin watch that I knew was 14K gold... both the case and the band. The shape of the back of the watch told me the movement was an FF59. This was a very popular seventeen or twenty-one-jewel movement used in higher-quality ladies' watches.

"I'm sorry to say this watch is totally rusted beyond any hope of repair. When I held your watch and tried to wind and set it, I could feel the stem, levers, and gears that wind the watch were frozen solid rusty."

Her face fell. There was no hope for her mother's watch. I understood her deep sadness.

I quietly continued, "The movement is really beyond hope, but... this is your mother's precious watch and now it should be yours. The case itself is in very good condition. The dial is almost good as new and so are the hands. Many of these watches have been scrapped for gold, and I have a good number of virtually new movements exactly like this one. I would use one to restore your mother's watch. The cost of the restoration would be $XXX."

I was confused when the woman just stared at me. Finally she said, "I came in here once before, insulted you, and walked out. No one else could help. Imagine how I felt when people were telling me…bring the watch to Barry Marcus; he'll take care of it. Today I swallowed my pride and came back as a last resort. No one else would help me, but the man I insulted for having Rush Limbaugh on, despite my rudeness, has been incredibly kind. You understand *why* I want the watch fixed."

"It's not just a watch. This is a direct physical tie to your mother. All I showed you was proper respect as I was taught as an apprentice. I'll be proud when the watch is back on your wrist."

"Thank you." I wrote up the watch, and the young woman astonished me as she left because she turned around and said, "Maybe I should listen to Limbaugh for myself."

I'm happy to report that the watch turned out beautifully without any difficulties. When I put the restored watch on the young woman's wrist, it was quite a moment. The look on her face was a great reward. We talked for a few minutes, and I explained the warranty. I could tell she had something on her mind. Finally she said, "I took your advice and listened to Rush. I haven't changed my opinions much at all, but I was wrong about him. We live and learn. Thank you for everything."

Just as I sat with a fresh cup of coffee (black, no sugar), the door opened and a couple walked in. They looked very somber. I approached the counter with a bit of trepidation.

I was handed a badly broken high-quality watch with a broken band, the crystal missing, and both hands gone. Oy. I knew what this was. "Sir, we've driven down from Amesbury. A couple of years ago you were kind to our friends, and now we've come to you for help. Could you please look at our son's watch? We would like it repaired so we can get it back to him, God willing."

The wording of the request told me all that I had to know and much more than I wanted to know. Did it ever end? Well, back to the bench to check this watch that was another in a long list of casualties of war.

What I had was a ruggedly made stainless steel Swiss watch. Half of the crystal was gone, the rest unreadable with dirt in the dial. I asked for time to pull out the movement, and the couple readily agreed. I wasn't surprised to see the ETA quartz movement. A standard movement, found in quite a few prestige watch brands. It was a wonderfully designed movement; one that I knew could be restored to duty without trouble.

Gently I removed the stem and lifted the movement out of the case. I used a soft bristle brush to clean the dial. Only the hour hand was still attached. It was protected by a sliver of the crystal and possibly the dirt that was forced into the watch. I put the stem back into the movement to quickly check the setting and day/date units. To my amazement, I could see the sweep wheel turning. The watch, with the hand free of the packed dirt, was running. I turned the movement dial to see the brand, and now I was shocked.

The watch was a TAG, a product of one of my less-favored companies. This watch, except for some cosmetic damage, actually survived...possibly in perfect running order. (I have to be honest enough to admit my complaint has always been with TAG, the company, not with TAG, the watch.)

I left the bench and walked back to my customers. What exactly did one say when there was absolutely nothing to say? Except, "I will take care of your son's watch and keep him in my prayers."

The gentleman spoke first. "Mr. Marcus, our friends told us that when you restored their son's watch you refused to take any money for your work. It was your way of giving thanks. I cannot allow you to do that...this is how you make your living."

Talk about being overwhelmed with emotion. I had difficulty wording my reply. "I'm truly sorry, but under those conditions I won't be able to repair the watch. It saddens me to say so. This is a deep-rooted philosophy that I learned in my uncle's store when I was just a kid. My dad had the same policy after World War Two. I have continued on with the family tradition of respecting and being so thankful for our servicemen. I will fix the watch, but there will be no charge…end of discussion. I'll let you know when the watch is ready."

The gentleman said nothing. His wife, in tears, nodded to me. I wrote down their information and bid them good-bye.

Once again I retreated to the office with a cup of coffee (black, no sugar). I just sat and stared over the bank building at the American flag, flying proudly over the Milford Police Station.

The phone rang with another call for help. The man wanted permission to bring his watch in for me to look at. He had sent the watch back to the factory but demanded it returned when told the cost of repair would be what he described as highway robbery.

He was asking me for *permission.* Any time a customer feels it is necessary to ask for permission it is a strong indication that something has gone haywire in a so-called service industry. It was a common complaint…the lack of customer service in many facets of the consumer world.

Chief among the screwed up "service" industries, I swear, was watch repair. It pained me to say so, but something had gone wrong in my industry. Too often companies mistreated the owners of their products or ignored their problems. Sadly, the old heart of watchmaking—the independent jewelry store that sold watches—was now running away from repairing watches. In my opinion, only bench watchmakers understood and respected the meaning a simple watch repair could hold. I had convinced some stores of the value of offering the customer service of watch repair and it had worked out wonderfully for them…and me.

Another realization had surfaced and it (really) pained me to say so, but I might now officially be a crotchety old geezer. Oy. Now I *needed* a cup of coffee (black, no sugar).

Anyhow, a week later, just before the Fourth of July, a man came into the shop identifying himself as the man who called for permission to bring his watch in. He had come to Milford the day before, but he hadn't realized it would take him so long to drive and had arrived after I'd left. I let him know to always call before he came in and I would wait for him. My commute home was all of four blocks, so it wasn't an inconvenience.

As we stood at the counter, he showed me a high-quality Swiss-made watch that looked like it had had better days. The watch had been dropped on a sidewalk and stopped running. Sidewalks and watches do not make a good mix.

"It isn't the fall but the sudden stop that gets you"…an old bad joke that came to mind and I had to bite my tongue.

"I sent the watch back to the factory. The cost was going to be beyond reason, so I had them send the watch back unrepaired."

We might be in trouble. The watch was a TAG automatic…the very company that I didn't like whose watches had been highly complimented in previous adventures. I took the watch to my bench. The dial was actually upside down, a strong indication that the dial legs were broken off. I didn't say this often…I hadn't seen this before. This watch had a unique feature; instead of a normal sweep second hand, there was a small second hand at the six o'clock position. It had broken off when the watch was dropped.

I opened the case to check for further damage and discovered a beautiful variation of the really wonderful ETA 2890 series. This was an exceptionally well-engineered movement that had many different variations built into, onto, and above a single design. Naturally the watch wasn't running with its balance wheel not turning at all. I depressed the detent screw and removed the stem and the case clamp screws and removed the movement, careful to not lose the tiny second hand. I lifted off the broken dial and set it aside. When I turned the movement over and put the stem back in, the watch jumped to life. I realized the hour hand was caught up by the broken second hand, causing the watch to stop.

If I could order the broken second hand wheel and dial, the watch would just need a general overhaul. I explained the damage to the watch and told the man that if I could order the wheel and dial, the watch would be as good as new.

The dial, he said angrily, was the trouble with the factory. A new dial was going to cost $400! That didn't include the repair. $400 for just the dial! "That's why I had the watch sent back, not fixed."

"This is really a beautifully designed dial. The heat needed to re-solder the dial legs would ruin the finish, requiring a costly refinish. I think it's less costly for the factory to go to the parts drawer, take out a new dial, and put the watch back together. I'm afraid the only way I can take care of this is to, honestly, *mickey-mouse* the repair. The watch will be as good as new but would drive the people in the factory center wild. I'll tell you what…I'll explain what I think will work and you make up your mind what you want to do."

"I want the watch to run. You tell me your way and the cost then I'll decide," was his answer.

I tried to keep my explanation to a short Marcus story, but you know how hard that is. Simply put, I described the modern-day problem of the very fragile and soft dial legs. More important to my customer was my *mickey-mouse* solution. Someone had come up with tiny strips of a very thin, double-sided tape and three-milli-meter double-sided "dial dots." A couple or three little strips and dots placed onto a clear portion of the dial side of the movement would hold the dial in place. I explained that I had used "dial tapes and dots" to make repairs on other watches over the past couple of years. When one of those watches came back for normal service, it was a bit difficult to remove the dial from the movement.

He asked with some concern, "How much are these miracle giz-mos going to add to the overhaul?"

With a straight face, I answered, "I guess about forty or fifty *cents*, no more than that." I walked to the cabinet next to the bench and brought back a two-inch by four-inch piece of stiff paper. I showed him the tiny dial strips and round dots. "These will hold the dial securely and you'll never see any difference. I was just joking about the cost. There's no extra charge. It's part of the overhaul; they're just pieces of sticky tape."

His next concern was the missing second hand. I told him I'd or-der the part and was very hopeful I could get the hand. I assured him that the second hand had nothing to do with making the watch run; it was for looks.

The watch would be fixed my way. The customer left happy that his high-quality timekeeper would once again tell him what time it was to do...whatever. It was late in the day, so I would have to wait until tomorrow to try and find a second hand wheel.

At 9:00 a.m. sharp with a cup of coffee (black, no sugar) in hand, I was on the phone to Cas-Ker to see if a mere peasant like me could get the wheel needed for a TAG. When I got off the phone, I was stunned. The nice young woman at Cas-Ker had quickly understood my problem when I explained the unique second hand and that I hadn't run into one like this before. Not only did she know the actual name for the part, the cost quote was so *low* that I didn't think it could be right. I asked her to double check...I don't like surprises. Sure enough, the part was beyond *reasonable.*

I called my customer and told him the good news. Now it was his turn to be stunned as I told him the part would be included in the overhaul as part of the original price quote.

I would like to add a disclaimer to the above story. I have all the love and respect for Mickey Mouse that one should have. I am a long-time fan of Mickey and love his work (and his watches). I'm not sure who first dubbed the term "mickey mouse" to be a negative connotation of a job or a quick fix, but in no way does the term reflect upon Mickey Mouse. That is why when I use the term, I never capitalize mickey or mouse.

There is an old saying, "Give credit when credit is due." Today I had to tip my red boat hat and give a watch company its due. I had a watch in the shop, a Movado that had suffered a broken case/band. A pin of some sort had broken and the band had separated from the "12" end of the case. In the hundreds of varied spring bars and case/band pinning devices I had, there was just *nothing* that would fit this case. I'd never seen a case end so enclosed and so short.

I called the customer and regretfully told her the watch would have to go back to Movado and hopefully they could take care of it. (I didn't want to tell her of the problems so many people seemed to be having with getting their watches fixed by the big companies.) I had her jot down all the numbers on the back of the case and also a number stamped on the hand. Often it was an identifier that might enable the company to tell the owner if parts were still available.

Ten minutes later, an extremely happy customer called back. "Mr. Marcus, I called Movado customer service for a mailing address. When I gave the woman the numbers you gave me, she put me on hold for a minute. The woman came back and let me know they had the really tiny spring bar. She asked if it would be easier if *they* mailed the bar to *me*. I told her the watch was at a watchmaker's shop, and she said they would mail the bar directly to *you*. They are actually going to send an extra one, just in case. I can't believe it."

"Neither can I," I said in disbelief. "Movado is really coming through for you, as they should. This is really great of them. Were the pins costly? They must have been made specifically for this model."

Cheerfully she replied, "The woman said there would be *no charge*. They would even cover the postage, as it won't be more than a couple of stamps. Call me when the watch is done."

Time for a cup of coffee (black, no sugar). I had been very open in criticizing several companies while writing this. I was really happy today to hear that a watch company behaved in a way that met my definition of "customer service." In reality, a couple of free tiny spring bars were not really a big deal, but the way the world seemed to be today, it was an amazing gesture to keep a customer happy.

Apparently sixty-eight years of experience at the bench did not mean anything these days. I had on the bench a virtually new

Hamilton man's watch. Solidly made, stainless steel case, automatic, day and date, plus of course a sweep second hand. The crown, while on the watch, had been broken, but the twenty-something owner had screwed it into place.

"I obtained this in early April, and it's the best watch I've ever owned," the young man explained. "In fact, it ran perfectly until May." Before he said another word, I knew what the problem would be.

He continued, "When April became May, the date was wrong. I read the instructions, carefully unscrewed the crown, and pulled it to the outermost position. I turned the crown, but in the wrong direction, so I advance the *day*, not the date. No big deal, so I kept turning the crown until the correct date was showing, then turned the crown in the other direction, and the date jumped a single day. The day and date were back in sync." After pausing a minute he went on, "I pushed the crown in, but neglected to screw it down. It looked okay and was snug close to the case."

Too bad, but I was right in my diagnosis. I unscrewed the crown and... trouble. The threads of the stem had broken *inside* the crown, where I could not grasp them to free up the crown for a simple stem replacement. This watch, of very good quality, deserved a genuine crown that was of a rugged design and had the Hamilton "H" logo on the outside.

I explained what the watch needed, including the Hamilton crown. He agreed, the watch was written up, and I said I would order the crown from Hamilton the following day.

Of all companies, Hamilton was and still is one of my most respected. The next morning I found Hamilton online, still located in Lancaster, Pennsylvania, and called the parts department. When a voice welcomed me to the Swiss Watch Technical Center, my heart fell. We were in trouble...Hamilton was now part of the SWATCH group. SWATCH did not sell parts to bench watchmakers like me. I tried to place the order and was informed that parts were not sent out except to duly authorized repair centers. In English that meant they wanted a monopoly on everything including tiny parts service. I loudly protested, which did no good at all. Policy was policy. However, I could *possibly* be able to obtain parts if I would come to Lancaster for a couple (two or three) weeks of training.

Need I say it…I blew up over the phone. I explained that I'd been at the bench for over sixty-eight years and needed *no* training in accomplishing the very first actual repair I'd learned all those years ago. By age twelve, after I broke several new stems, I trained my fingers to know how much pressure was just right; I had mastered stems and crowns in 1946!

It appeared that sixty-eight years of experience meant nothing… *policy was policy*. I got off the phone beyond furious. I was brokenheart-ed…to misquote the bard again…Et tu, Hamilton? I needed a cup of coffee (black, no sugar).

The watch was returned to an extremely unhappy owner, who on leaving turned and passed on greetings from his parents, both of whom had watches repaired by me over the years. I was always happy to hear from past customers. (Honestly, the name meant nothing.)

I was busy working on a box of small jobs that I'd been procrastinating. Luckily, the phone rang allowing me to stall a little longer. The call was from a customer in Chicago. James is a watch enthusiast who over the years has sent me watches to restore to their former glory. We kibitzed about what was new; happy that the winter had finally relented. James told me about a ceremony that was happening to present a veteran aviator with a Jardur watch. My heart skipped a beat…bells rang in the far recesses of my brain. I had worked on a Jardur watch many years ago…

An older man walked into the shop as I fought with a stubborn Waltham pocket watch. I asked for a couple of minutes to finish adjusting the balance. "No problem. Take your time," the customer responded. I heard him laughing at his pun…he was giving the watchmaker all the *time* he needed.

The pocket watch was in stable condition so I walked to the front counter. "How can I help you?" I was handed a chronograph that seemed to have too many hands on it. The customer told me that it was very important that I service the watch so that it would once again guide him.

The name on the chronograph was Jardur, a brand name that I'd never seen before. This was an impressive work of engineering. I examined the watch and as I closed the case, I noted the roughly scratched case and initials on the back.

As I got up from the bench, the customer nervously asked, "Can you get the watch to work? The repair charge doesn't matter. The watch must run. A couple of watchmakers wouldn't even look at it." His voice was enough to tell me that this was yet another story of a deep bond between a watch and its owner.

I grabbed the repair tag and jotted down the first two initials and asked for a last name.

"No! That isn't me," he blurted, "the watch was on the wrist of my co-pilot."

This story went beyond the bond between watch and warrior...a painful memory was carried with this watch.

He sighed and smiled, "My co-pilot always kidded me that his watch was more accurate and better than the plane's clock. Even more accurate than when the briefer gave us the *hack* command. I kept making bets with him so I would win the watch but I never seemed to win." He sighed again. "On a long mission near Berlin, our bomber stream was jumped by a defending squadron of ME 109Es and were shot up pretty badly. The starboard outer engine was hit and started to burn but we got the fire out. The starboard inner was hit but kept running. An ME 109E got the starboard waist gunner."

He paused before continuing on, "It was all I could do to keep her in the air. I knew we were in trouble. We fell behind. A couple of Mustangs, with more guts than brains stayed with us and provided us cover. I was so focused on flying and keeping us in the air, I'm ashamed to admit I didn't notice my co-pilot's voice getting softer and softer. He was responding to me so I thought it was a couple of shot out windows letting in engine noise that was drowning out his voice."

Although, the customer stood just feet from me I could see he was fifty-odd years into the past.

"We made the coast and crossed the Channel somehow. We were over England. Just as I was about to tell my co-pilot to start the landing check, he grabbed my hand on the controls. He pulled my hand to him and pressed the watched in it. He said, "It's yours now." Softly he kept repeating, "Time...time...time...time."

I stood perfectly still, holding my breath. His voice trembled and with eyes misted over as he continued, "I screamed for someone to check him, but of course, he was gone. I had to concentrate to keep flying and not dwell on the fact that only three of us were alive."

"My co-pilot always recorded the exact time that the engines were running. He trusted his Jardur more than the fuel gauges. I remembered him repeating *time* over and over. I looked at the watch and saw that we'd been in the air 12 minutes longer than possible. With a prayer, I began to drop altitude. I reached to put the landing gear down and just as I put my hand on the lever, the three engines coughed and quit. The gear stayed up. We started down. Miraculously, a large field was dead ahead. We made the field, and with the gear still up, the crash landing wasn't too bad. Being out of gas, the plane didn't blow up."

With unashamed tears he told me, "I've always believed that the Jardur, telling me we should've already been out of gas, prompted me to drop to a better altitude and glide my flying wreck into a safe crash landing. That's why the Jardur needs to be repaired. This watch enabled me to have a wife, home, children, and now blessedly, grandchildren. Call me when it's done and let me know the cost."

Before I began work on the Jardur, I did some investigating. Having never had a Jardur on my bench before, I was unfamiliar with its proud history in the aviation world. I repaired the Jardur, and it was, to say the least, complicated. However, being well made and logically designed, the chronograph with almost as many hands as an octopus went together smoothly.

A few weeks later, the old aviator returned for his watch. After a little conversation, he asked for the price of the repair. I pointed to the tag and said, "It's paid in full."

"What do you mean? Who the hell paid?" he demanded.

"Your co-pilot."

Unable to speak, he shook my hand and left the shop.

Time for coffee (black, no sugar).

323

Watches wounded during the Civil War, survivors of the Spanish American War and World War I. Watches from the depths of the Pacific, the beaches of Normandy and Pacific Islands, ship sinkings, plane crashes, watches "liberated" at the point of a gun, and a watch received as a gift in a concentration camp, given even as its owner died.

I remember a watch given to a young local man who had unknowingly held his own grandparents at gunpoint in a half-destroyed Italian village. I smiled at the memory of a gent's Longines presented to a young man by his bride in heartfelt thanks for killing her captors and then shooting her.

I mourn a couple of watches, missing in action for fifty years, and those who still wear those watches. I can't forget the watches I adapted to owners coping with serious physical infirmities. My little or not so little watches, whether very old or new, still fulfill their traditional mission. They tell their owners when it is *time* to do whatever must be done. From the daily routine (even mine) to the critical job, people must be told just *when* it is time.

Of course I can never forget *her*, the beautiful young woman who stole a teenage boy's heart, probably years after *she* died. I still wonder if we will ever meet.

I owe immense debts to my father and his brother, Uncle Abe. Both were men of an old school who gave a youngster his life's work, even if I was "born seeming to know how to repair watches, even when my hands were too small." There is also the lonely man who couldn't speak to me, yet helped a young boy learn his beloved trade. In my mind's eye, I can still see the arm with the blue tattoo, helping the youngster who was the same age as his murdered son.

Thinking about things to smile at, I wondered if I coined the expression "will work for food" when I repaired my grandmother's clock to protect my supply of lentil soup.

I even cherish the memory that never was. The grandfather clock that I never worked on, in a house I never visited, on a day I never left my uncle's store, riding to a town whose name I never knew. After all, I was well under the age to drive, so how could I have gotten there?

I began this tale in 2008 at the urging of my daughters, to jot down a few notes on a few of the thousands of watches I've repaired over sixty-eight happy years at the bench. (Sixty-eight years! Oy!) My girls wanted to preserve the *Papa Barry stories* for their children. I wanted to write about the watches I'd gotten to know over all those years and the people who, what was Uncle Abe's expression...*use and abuse their watches.*

There has been no advanced organizing...no advanced planning...and no attempt to put anything in strict chronological order. I put things down in a random order as they popped into my mind.

I surely learned the lessons taught by Uncle Abe and my father: "While we merely repair watches, what we often do is care for the people who cherish and revere them. The monetary value of a watch is not what is important, but its meaning to its user." So very often I was told that "this watch was Granddad's," "this belonged to Mom," or "this watch saw me through a war and we both came home."

I've become quite thoughtful as I typed up my memories of other people's memories. I've realized that often a watch's story was tied into a serious, even tragic event. Over time, emotions have become an important part of a watch repair for me.

I have repaired probably thousands of watches for people who used them just to tell the time. But I have at the same time become part of the deepest memories, hopes, joys, fears, and dreams of hundreds of people as I kept their personal treasures running.

I realize that I have also been very blessed. I've been given the opportunity to help, comfort, or assist the people who happened to come to my shop. All the while sitting at a watchmaker's bench doing work that I love to do.

Thoughtful and blessed…that is not bad for a life's work. Time for a cup of coffee (oh, you know).

O n July 20, 2013, I was typing Dad's story about the mail carrier asking how watches found their way to Milford. Dad answered, "online," so I Binged Barry J. Marcus, Watchmaker. The following are reviews I found. I was so proud to read what strangers wrote.

yelp.com

Review from Linda F. Worcester, MA. 1/3/2011

First to Review

I saw an ad for this business and went to check him out. Mr. Marcus runs a small shop in an office building on Main Street. The building itself is set back from the street so it's easy to miss.

I was looking for someone to repair my Citizen Ecodrive watch— the stem had jammed and I couldn't change the time or date. I've had this watch for 6+ years so I wanted to speak with the person fixing it rather than go to a jewelry store that would send it out to someone else.

He's a very sweet gentleman who ended up fixing my watch for free. It was a simple fix and he was really nice about it. I offered to pay him for his time but he refused. I ended up chatting with him about his work and how long he'd been a watchmaker.

He's a 4th generation watchmaker who's been working with watches since he was 10 years old (he's now in his 70s.) He works on all kinds of watches—expensive, inexpensive, antiques, brand new, etc. I have another watch that needs a major repair and I am definitely bringing it to him.

So if you need a watch repaired, please go see him. He's super nice and really cares about his customers. In today's world of impersonal retailers and zero customer service, Mr. Marcus is a refreshing reminder of how businesses should be run.

Review from Edward R. Boston, MA. 5/18/2011

Brought two watches in for repair. Mr. Marcus is a traditional craftsman watchmaker. 66 years of experience. When I learned that my watch required a battery which is 1) no longer available and 2) $140 when it was, he explained a solution using a different battery which provided less life but at a $10 cost.

I would drive 20 miles out of my way for him to do my work, actually, I did.

Review from Greg B. Newton, MA. 7/19/2011

This guy knows his stuff about watches. He's going to give you one on one service with your watches. You can trust him and he is very fair. He fixed my watch twice and did a great job. He's also got a great personality.

merchantcircle.com

Barry is a GREAT watchmaker, and I would trust him with any fine watch. He absolutely LOVES his work and you can tell. HE has fixed all kinds of watches for me, old and new, pocket watches and wrist watches, and they have all worked out really well. Plus he charges very fairly ($1 to change a pin in my bands—I actually end up giving him more than he asks for). He does have the watch for a while sometimes and may forget to call you, so you should check upon him periodically, BUT believe me, it is WORTH IT!!!!

Superpages.com

Guest564xx
Sep 16, 2008
Marcus Barry J Watchmaker
Milford, MA

Barry is SUCH a great watchmaker!! He has fixed so many watches for me and they've all turned out well. You can tell that he absolutely LOVES his work and he really does care about each and every watch. I would definitely recommend Barry to anyone who needs a watch (old or new, pocket or wrist) fixed or tuned up.

The following is the letter that my dad wrote to the American Watchmakers-Clockmakers Institute.

American Watchmakers-Clockmakers Institute
701 Enterprise Drive
Harrison, Ohio 45030

Note:
In February 2008, I made the sad decision to NOT renew and continue my many year membership in the American Watchmakers Institute. At the time, I wrote a protest letter to you by e-mail, after which you asked me to write back exactly what had provoked my strong rejection. I wrote that letter, which has sat in the hard drive in my computer since. At that time, after the second reread, I decided not to send the letter, thinking that perhaps I would come across as merely a complaining elderly crank.

I gave no thought to sending the letter until this week when I received in the mail a computer generated copy of the article in the latest magazine regarding the disappointment regarding this year's Certification test results. When I read of errors and faults I learned to correct when I was a boy of 13, I knew the letter had to go out.

My feelings are stronger than ever, partially fueled by dealings and conversations with owners of new, very high priced modern watches over their experiences with today's watch COMPANIES. I personally find many of today's Watch Companies sense of business ethics to be totally nonexistent.

I am closing in on 65 years at the bench, and after that time, still rise in the morning with a young man's anticipation of the day's watch challenges. I have come to truly believe that both my father and my uncle, my teachers, were correct when they insisted that I was BORN knowing how to repair watches. I merely had to wait 10 years for my hands to grow enough to hold a tweezer and screwdriver. My uncle said he had to teach me the names of the parts, while I did the rest on my own. Following is my original letter:

In late 1944, when I was 10 years old, a family committee consisting of my father and his two brothers, watchmakers all, determined that my hands had become just large enough to hold basic watchmaking tools. In my hands was placed a 7 jewel, 16S Waltham pocket watch. Twelve minutes later, I knew for the rest of my life I would be repairing watches. Today, 64 years later, I STILL look forward to each and every day at the bench.

Now, with an overwhelming sense of outrage and disgust I write this letter. More than a letter, this is the total belief and observations of a dedicated watchmaker, one who is seeing his beloved trade destroyed from within.

I have come to the belief that there are two types involved in my profession. The two I classify as the "Bench Watchmaker" and the "Horologist." I classify "watchmakers" as those craftsmen who service and repair the watches carried in to their shops wherever they may be. Many of these watches are of little value, and many may be worth hundreds of dollars, but each is the property of our customers, and are thusly to be treated with the respect they deserve.

The others, the "HOROLOGISTS," are a self-promoting group of elitists, who gaze scornfully down on those craftsmen who daily practice their profession. They do this in concert with the so-called prestige watch companies. European factories, meetings with executives, titles, and other perks are truly heady wines, but what do they mean to the man toiling at his bench?

Companies today, far from the practices of training seminars, issuing tech bulletins, and parts manuals, shut off the "bench watchmaker" from his trade. What would have occurred if Bulova, in 1960, decreed that the "bench watchmaker" could NOT repair and adjust the ACCUTRON? I cannot easily count the Accutron sessions that I attended, nor the numbers of Quartz Watch Repair seminars also run by Bulova on a regular basis. Once the skill and dedication of the "bench watchmaker" was a respected and valued thing.

Constantly, in the AWI magazine, I read of the need for "certification." In a recent issue, I read of some of the requirements for the certification process. I proudly did NOT run the magazine through my shredder. What must I know?

I saw the word "TORBULLON" as something important. In 64 years at the bench, I have never even seen one of these, let alone been called upon to service one. Likewise, in 64 years at the bench, behind in the work each and every one of those years, I have NEVER laid eyes on a "REPEATER," nor have I been asked to repair one. Never have I held a "FUZEE" in my hands, out of the hundreds and hundreds of pocket watches I've repaired. Others, of course, have, and I respect their knowledge and skills, but such things do NOT exist in my personal world, nor in the worlds of 90% of the watchmakers in the country.

Does this lessen their skills? Does this lessen their place in the ranks of those who are called watchmakers? I believe not. I believe that only in the world of the "Horologist" does the lack of unneeded knowledge lessen one's value.

Among the ranks of the surgeons, the CARDIAC surgeon is not looked down upon just because he does not operate on the BRAIN. An ORTHOPEDIST is not denigrated because he does not operate on the EYE. Each of us have a particular place in our own world, and we strive to master OUR part of that world. Aircraft engine mechanics may specialize in the monster jet engines for a 747, or may concentrate on the small prop engine of a Cessna, neither crossing into the other's specialty. Both are respected for that which they do know.

The HOROLOGIST may worship the very ground certain watch companies are built on. Companies that daily violate the AWI Code of Ethics. Companies that were encouraged to deny skilled practitioners of our trade the ability to earn their living. I have heard the senseless statement that "XXXXX" Company wants repairs done to THEIR standards.

Only CERTAIN people may be allowed to touch their sacred products. Only GENUINE materials may be used in the repair of their products.

What GENUINE materials do we talk about? Oh, we must use a GENUINE crystal from a company that does NOT own a crystal making facility, but rather crystals made FOR them by a company that specializes in such a thing. There is always the traditional mainspring, made to company specifications needed for a company that does NOT own a mainspring manufacturing facility. How can a company insist on the usage of a GENUINE train wheel when its very movements are GENERIC battery powered movements found in literally dozens of different watch brands? A case back gasket, an 'O' ring in the unusual shape of a CIRCLE must be genuine. I would personally wish to see the address and picture of the PRIVATELY owned GASKET factory of our prestigious watch company.

Does the leadership of the AWI use ONLY the brand of battery specified by the manufacturer of the automobile they own? Would the government permit General Motors to state the installation of a DieHard battery rather than a Delco to negate the guarantee on the car? Not really likely. Or the brands of tires? Or the windshield wipers? What I do see is a betrayal of my fellow watchmakers.

What is supposed to be the AWI Code of Ethics says that I will not lie to a customer as to the needed repairs on his/her watch. Not too long ago, a man came to me with the crown broken from his Rolex. He confessed that when he advanced the date from November 31 to December 1, he neglected to securely screw down the crown, resulting in the crown being broken off within a few days. Despite this, the watch overhauled by me in early summer 2008 still ran perfectly. Because I could not order a new crown from Rolex, and the customer desired a genuine crown with the trade logo, I strongly suggested it be returned to the factory.

Last week, the watch was returned to me, unrepaired and still lacking a crown. The customer was in a state of rage as he told me that Rolex has insisted on the watch needing a complete overhaul and would NOT do just the requested repair. Today, frankly, that Rolex is sporting a very high grade GENERIC crown as it adorns the wrist of an owner who missed NO CHANCE TO TELL THE WORLD WHAT HE THINKS of the Rolex Company. He bitterly criticizes not the watch but the company. He is only one of several Rolex owners I know and service who have had similar dealings with this company "beloved of the HOROLOGISTS."

There are other companies, starting with TAG, who treat watch owners in the same way, and with NO justification got the "leaders" of the AWI to tell me these companies are correct. Watches that contain nothing more than GENERIC Swiss movements, albeit of very high quality, are supposed to be beyond the ability of the "bench watchmaker"? I do NOT take such insults easily.

It is required that I purchase very costly equipment to ascertain that my repairs are up to par. I have owned this type of equipment since the 1950s and stand by MY methods and rely upon my professional reputation that attracts watches for service from across the nation. MY reputation is jealously guarded and maintained as it has been from the onset of my career.

I have been told that I must purchase a multi-thousand-dollar Waterresist Tester. This most modern device will indicate the presence of a leak somewhere. I have a useless pressure tank in a back closet that tells me the fact of a leak. However, it does NOT tell me the location of the leak. It might be the crown; it might be the crystal or even the case back gasket. To correct the condition I must start changing things that may not need changing. No thank you. I will continue to use the current water/air column that shows me EXACTLY the location of any leaks. Both my time and the customer's money are saved.

The extreme majority of watches sold today are, I believe, in the price range between one and two hundred dollars. Many are much less costly, but have owners who wish them serviced. Anyone who believes I should purchase a six and a half thousand dollar water resistance tester for a $124.50 watch is in need of a medication change.

Occasionally I see an extremely high value, deep diving watch that is truly used for deeper water penetration, and in such circumstances I require the owner to return it to the factory for service. These are watches I may indeed successfully service except for the bodily threats by my lawyer.

Being a true professional, I recognize those watches that I should truly NOT repair. Part of my professional obligation to a customer is to give proper advice, even if that good advice means the watch is sent out for specialized servicing.

The "industry" that I was raised in, the world of the family jewelry store, is in the final stages of its demise. Today, it is replaced with "store 185" of such and such chain company. Management is geared merely to the selling of the new, ignoring and scorn for the old. Watch repairing and the watchmaker are regarded as a nuisance to be avoided.

A man's Hamilton is brought to me with a story. The watch was returned to the family, with personal effects, after his father was killed in Korea. The baby boy, never to see his father, grew up and eventually received his dad's watch. Worn daily, it eventually required service and was taken to a "national jeweler" in a prestigious mall. In our "brave new world" it was pointed out rather bluntly that it be a waste of money to repair such an outdated and outmoded watch. It was strongly suggested that a new up-to-date battery powered watch with all the modern features be considered. An angry man left the store with his watch, and then found his way to Milford, where he left his "treasured watch" for complete repair. Cleaned, oiled, polished case, and retimed, the Hamilton was returned looking and running as though it was six months old. Four months ago, the watch was brought to me once again for complete servicing.

The old, outdated, outmoded, obsolete watch was now to be presented to the GRANDSON of the original owner. A simple man's Hamilton, manual wind, not shock-resistant, not water-resistant, no calendar, day, or date—just a timepiece that has been treasured for three generations, with hopefully more to come. This is MY WORLD!!

What has my trade descended to? Long after beloved family members have gone, Grandma or Grandpa, Aunt Betty or Uncle Ed have left behind few possessions save the watches that children have grown to cherish. I have two ladies Pendant/Pocket watches that come in for service as needed, each for about forty years now. Both watches are in beautiful condition save for twin parallel dents in both front and back covers. When I first suggested removing the dents and smoothing the case, the words of outrage were never to be forgotten. The "dents" were sacred memories of "baby teeth" chewing too hard on Grandma's chain watch.

The BENCH WATCHMAKER remains at work, as he has for so many decades. Tending to 150 year old pocket watches and 6 month old quartz models at the same time. We struggle with the modern watches that flood our benches with engineering faults that cause them to fall apart. People come to my shop, having driven many miles through many towns to reach a "real watchmaker." Again and again, I'm told of Mr. So and So who "retired and moved" or died last year, leaving NO watchmaker in a town that once had three or four, all of whom made their living as respected members of the community.

I see, in issue after issue of AWCI times, stories and reports of watch innovations that will NEVER be seen on a watchmaker's bench. I scan reports of technical brainstorms that will not be seen by more than 3% of the watchmakers of the world. I read of an organization that actually applauds the shutting out of its members from their world.

This story began in 1944, as a 10 year old boy was handed his very first watch movement, the entry gate into a happy productive life. It continued in 1994 when THAT boy held his 3 year old grandson on my lap as I gently wrapped his tiny hands around a Hamilton 992B, running in all its art-like glory. A small face turned to me, his eyes alight with a joy that I truly believe mirrored mine oh-so-long-ago. The story ends two years ago, when a teenager asked his grandfather the wisdom of "learning the family trade."

Tragically, I had to advise my grandson to not consider watch repair as his life's work. At that moment I had broken a chain that reached back four generations.

I can NO longer remain a member of an organization that, in my mind, no longer exists.

BARRY J. MARCUS, WATCHMAKER
Milford, MA

ACKNOWLEDGEMENTS

This book has been a family project. I'd like to thank my dad for first for putting his 'Papa Barry" stories to paper and then for his patience as we went back through time, again and again. The process of publishing *Watches I Have Known* took far more time than I had envisioned.

I'd like to thank my kids, Adam, Katie and Sarah Beth, for their encouragement, support and for not rolling their eyes every time I said, "How does this sound?" The cover graphic is the work of Katie's talent.

I can't express the gratitude I have for my husband, Michael, who throughout this project has been incredibly supportive. Michael can spot a typo a mile away.

I'd like to thank Mary Petit and Martha Dumont who were brave enough to tackle our first effort with pink pens and Post-It notes. I appreciate all the enthusiasm and encouragement from so many; you helped grow a group of stories into a book.

Thank you to C. C. Shermer, president of Jardur Watches for his interest in our project and the wonderful quote for the back cover.

~ Julie Campisi

I would like to thank my daughters for insisting that I write down my stories to save for all time (pun intended). I would like to thank everyone who has encouraged Julie and me to publish *Watches I Have Known*. I would like to give special thanks to Julie for turning "Papa Barry" stories into a book.

Thank you to all the people who have trusted me with their precious timepieces and family histories. It has been an honor to help preserve their memories for their next generation.

~ Barry J. Marcus

ABOUT THE AUTHOR

Barry J. Marcus worked as a watchmaker for over sixty-five years. The only time he spent away from his workbench was the two years he spent in active duty for the US Navy.

Marcus currently lives in Milford, Massachusetts. He has three daughters and five grandchildren.

Julie Campisi graduated from New Hampshire College (now SNHU) and is proud of her father's long and storied career as a watchmaker.

Campisi currently lives with her husband and three children in Saco, Maine.

Made in the USA
Middletown, DE
02 June 2017